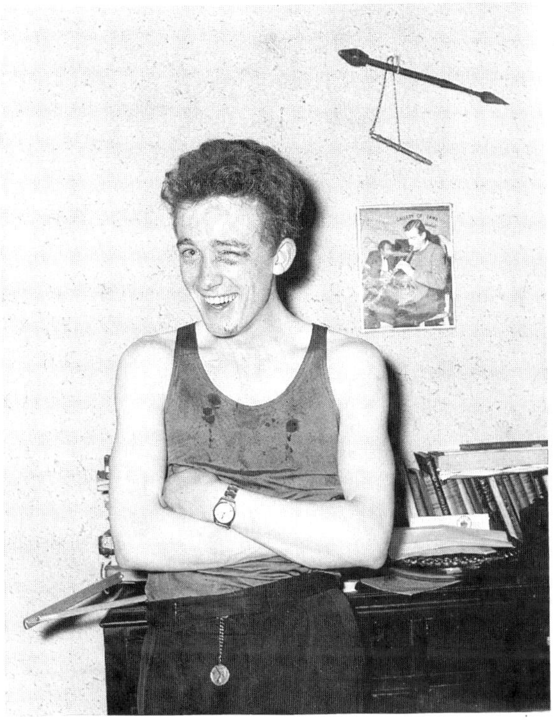

ONE IN THE EYE

Terry Cryer

Yorkshire Art Circus
1992

Published by

Yorkshire Art Circus, School Lane, Glass Houghton, Castleford,

West Yorkshire WF10 4QH Telephone (0977) 550401

Editor: Ian Clayton

Design: Kevin Reynolds and Anna Turner

Support team: Rachel Adam, Ralph Bannister, Olive Fowler, Brian Lewis, Tony Lumb, Linda McGillivray, Andrea Richardson, Reini Schühle, Richard Staszynski, Rachel Van Riel, Pauline Wigglesworth.

ISBN 0 947780 86 6

Classification: Photography

Typesetting and photographic screening by Lasergraphics,

Stuart House, St Andrews Court, Leeds LS3 1JY

Printed by Thornton and Pearson Ltd,

Rosse Street, Thornton Road, Bradford BD8 9AS

Yorkshire Art Circus is a unique book publisher. We work to increase access to writing and publishing and to develop new models of practice for arts in the community.

For details of our full programme of workshops and our current book lists please write to the address above.

Yorkshire Art Circus is a registered charity (no. 1007443)

We would like to thank the following organisations for their support towards this project:

Yorkshire & Humberside ARTS

West Yorkshire Grants

POULTER COMMUNICATIONS PLC

ONE IN THE EYE

I would like to dedicate this book to Ma Thompson who provided a home. Billy Bowskill who opened the doors to jazz and photography. And an unknown woman who once told me to stand on an ice cream and made me laugh.

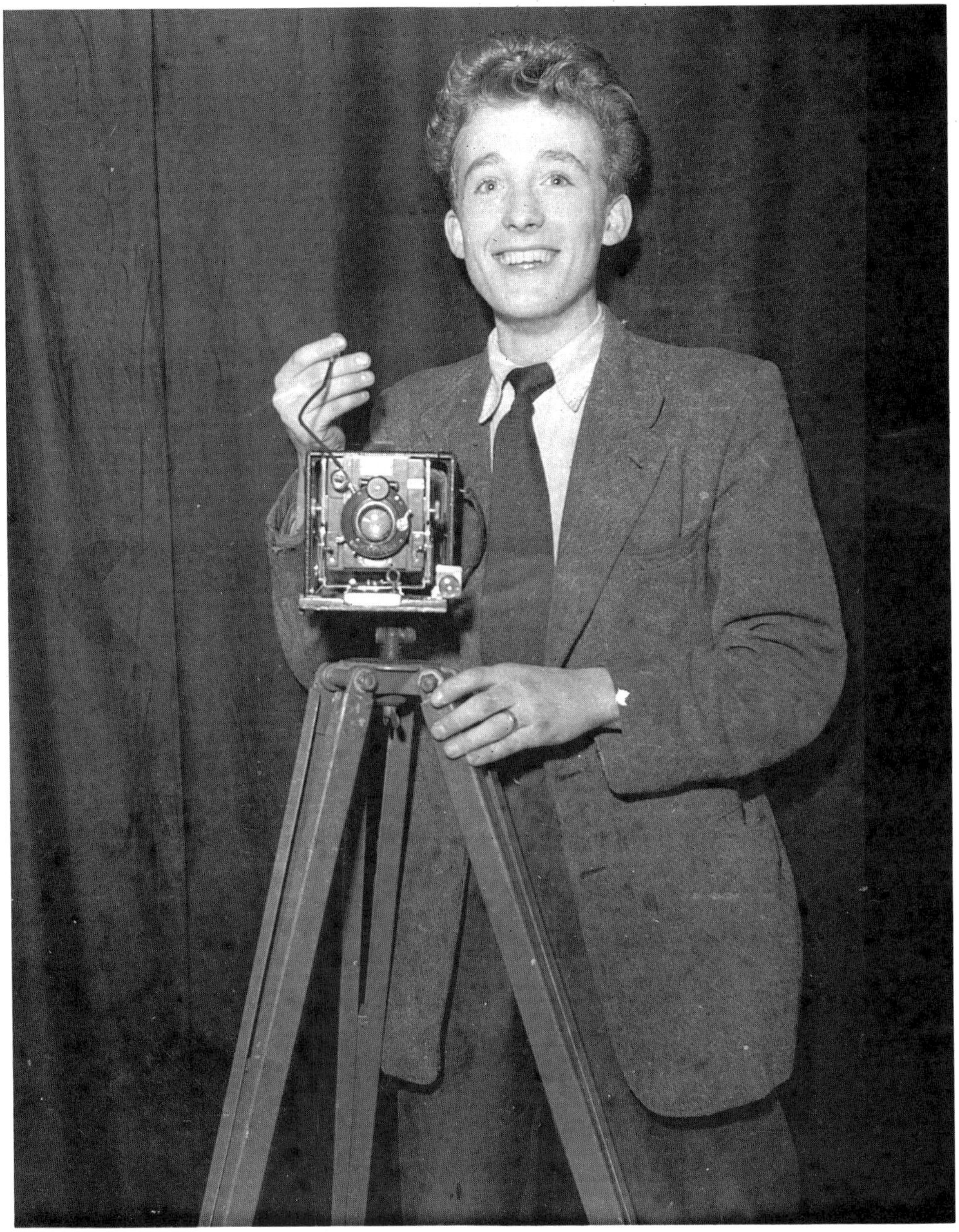

A friend once asked me if I took up photography because of an inability to draw. At the time I thought, 'What a prat! What a bloody silly question! What has drawing got to do with photography?' I didn't know at the time about Fox Talbot who invented modern photography for just such a reason.

Some time ago, before toning black-and-white photographic prints became fashionable, Terry Cryer began racking his brains to determine how the Victorian masters of the toned image had achieved their superb effects. Painstakingly he experimented with various chemical combinations. The results were impressive, but achieving the perfect green eluded him. When he heard of an elderly technician who had worked with the process, he wasted no time in seeking him out. He found the man near to breathing his last, and sat down beside him, notebook in hand, anxious to glean whatever knowledge he could.

It took him some time before he was able to bring up the subject of green-toning, but finally the opportunity arrived. The old man recalled the procedure, finishing with a description of how he threw in a particular chemical at the end. Terry leaned forward, expectantly: 'Right then. Now, what was the stuff that you used?'

'Oh I don't know what it was called,' came the reply. 'It was just some green stuff!'

It's the kind of story that will be greeted with a chuckle of recognition by others who have travelled a similar path. It takes someone from a background of on-the-job learning to appreciate how satisfying it can be to work things out for yourself even when it is not always the easiest way. I can think of few other photographers who would spend hours analysing Victorian chemistry only to discover that all the formulae are readily available in books. But then, at the time Terry was learning how to become a skilled photographer, the idea of toning prints was passé.

It seems to me that a refusal to take the easy way out, the need to arrive at your own procedures, have something to do with developing your own texture of life. By confronting the process itself, the lesson stays more completely learned. Today, Terry Cryer the photographer is widely acknowledged for his superb printing and mastery of toning techniques. But it was no overnight journey as this, his own story, tells.

When I began to take snapshots of visiting American jazz musicians in London at the end of the 1950s, Terry's byline was seldom out of the music press. Long before he had any idea of my existence, I knew who he was. Brash and relaxed, he was the fair-haired guy in the gabardine raincoat who always seemed to be emerging from the stage door around which I was hovering in the hope of gaining entry. Sometimes he would be sharing a laugh with one of the famous jazz 'names'. Always he had a smile on his cocky young Yorkshire face. Had I known then that he was still finding his feet in Civvy Street and had only lately discovered the glamour of showbusiness, my reaction might have been somewhat different. But I was too young then to make such distinctions. Hanging out on the sidelines, and still a fan, I was awed by his suavity and professionalism. Terry was the kind of photographer I wanted to be.

Years would pass before we got to know each other and become friends. Just as well, for back then, the possibility of a relationship based on mutual respect would have been impossible. The social mores of the day permitted few women to enter the hallowed world of the male professional and press photography circles were among the worst. The scorn reserved for women drivers automatically greeted the arrival of anyone of us who appeared with a camera. And to be honest, my credibility was not helped by the fact that I made my debut while still using a fixed-focus Agfa Isola I.

But I wanted to learn and to take the kind of pictures for which Terry was known. His solid portraits and action shots of the American greats appeared in Jazz News every week and that was good enough for me. I watched how he and his colleagues operated, absorbing what I could at a distance before trying it on my own.

Reportage style which used available light had yet to make much impact in jazz photography here. The environment was generally too dark and films, apart from Kodak's Royal-X Pan which had grain the size of coarse sand, were far too slow. Terry's striking close-ups were nearly all taken with electronic flash. He held his flashgun at arms length, high above and to one side of his subject. This created deep modelling on the face while throwing the background into shadow, a useful dodge that helped to eliminate dingy conditions backstage. It was a method that worked extremely well with black faces. Back then people of colour presented a technical challenge which even many jazz photographers were unable to handle. I was not surprised to learn later that Terry had developed this technique in an attempt at replicating his earliest photographs. These, taken during his army service in Egypt, where the midday sun created stark shadows beneath people's features, were taken under conditions most photographers shun. But in Egypt, he had little option. With the skill of the ever-adaptable, he turned the situation into an advantage. His first jazz portraits, notably one of Count Basie's guitarist, Freddie Greene, with its remarkable skin texture, reveal what can be done with this simple overhead lighting. Once I realised how such results were achieved, I was well away. I ditched my one-off sizzling flashbulbs, acquiring an electronic flashgun and the all-important extension lead, not long after buying my first 'serious' camera, a Rolleicord.

By the time my own photographs began to appear in the music papers, Terry had vanished. I heard that he had joined The Associated Press. But his jazz photographs continued to crop up and I often wondered whether he saw any money. From time to time I attempted to trace him; one of his former employers informed me baldly they thought he was dead. I suppose this was their way of ignoring the fact that they owed him money, but the statement remains in my mind, sadly reflective of Britain's North/South divide. For Terry had committed the social crime of turning his back on Southern opportunity and going back to his Yorkshire roots.

I was pleased when I eventually ran him to earth. First, because it gave me the chance to thank him for being my early inspiration, but secondly, because it gave me an opportunity to spend time with a like-minded person in Leeds, not too far from where I first saw the light of day. It was only an accident of wartime that caused me to be born in the county, and I wouldn't pretend to be anything other than a Londoner. Nevertheless, I've always relished the notion that – well, gender aside – I could have played cricket for Yorkshire.

Walking into Terry's house, named after the place where Julia Margaret Cameron lived, was like seeing myself reflected. It's something impossible to explain: we come from opposing cultural backgrounds, our experiences are vastly different. He's a pictorialist while I'm a documentary photographer through and through. And yet I recognised a sense of sharing similar values at the end of a long, hard, grafting road. He has given me a sense of pride in my printing and shown me how to tone prints with a wild chemical recklessness that puts formal teachers to shame. I love watching him carelessly sling salts and acids about in his funky old darkroom. Only his intimates know he has two: one for his award winning print making, an older one out the back where he does his toning experiments – including green. His casual manner reminds me of my learning days spent in the box room under the roof with an old Gnome enlarger and no running water. And when the fumes get out of hand, it takes me back to when I nearly choked myself in childhood, manufacturing chlorine in my mother's kitchen. It's dangerous, sure, but it's fun. And it's a welcome antidote to and temporary escape from the unhealthy sanitised and packaged world in which we are forced increasingly to live.

Val Wilmer 1992

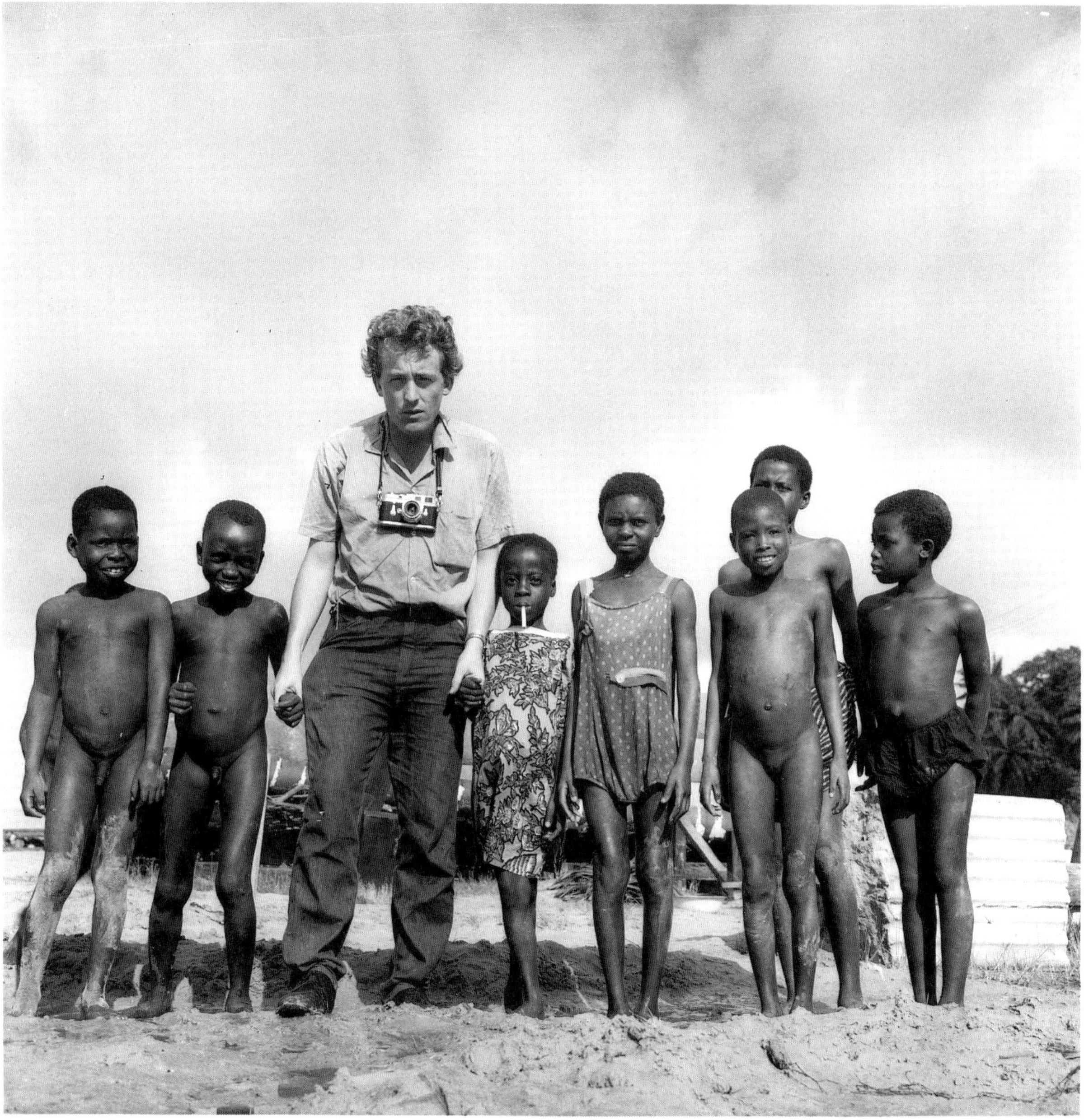

Experience as a professional photographer has taught me that there is a lot more to photography than the Kodak slogan, 'You just press the button and we do the rest.'

Some assignments are difficult, like trying to get a splinter out of your arse with boxing gloves on. My trip to Uganda was one of these. The client, an American Catholic educational publisher, wanted a series of pictures showing life in Uganda with a strong Catholic flavour. The requirements were all listed quite specifically.

1 Native women reading rosary beads round the village well.

2 A native making clothes from the bark of a tree.

3 An African bull elephant with ears extended.

4 Crocodiles on the banks of the White Nile.

5 A seaplane landing on Lake Victoria.

There were another ten pictures which were quite straightforward but these five were just short of ridiculous. The last seaplane to land on Lake Victoria was in 1930, the natives last wore bark cloth in Dr Livingstone's time and, as I was using a Rolleiflex with a standard 75 mm lens, the crocodile picture and the bull elephant didn't bear thinking about.

I knocked off the ten easy shots without too much difficulty and air freighted the films back to the UK then sent a telex about the difficulties with the remaining five. The Associated Press reply came quickly; 'Complete assignment soonest, every confidence, stop.' I contemplated a suitably worded message, 'Up stick job, stop Rude letter to follow, stop.'

I went through two days feeling more and more helpless. Then it clicked, if the publishers wanted pictures of bark cloth and rosary beads then I'd give them some. There was a shop in Kampala selling curios. I bought a couple of square yards of terracotta bark cloth and took it out into the bush where I found a thatched hut. I found an old woman, took off her sunglasses, sat her down in the doorway, gave her a stick and said, 'Hit this piece of cloth, love, and I'll take your picture.' This she did in total bewilderment, accepted the ten shillings, muttered something and walked off smoking one of my cigarettes.

To get the next picture I took a flight to Nairobi in Kenya and bought ten sets of rosary beads. Mary Nambrienbi, the wife of Smitty the Ugandan Associated Press stringer, helped me. She rounded up half a dozen of her friends sat them round a water hole and gave them some beads to play with. When we had finished they accepted money and gave me the beads back. Mary was the only Catholic in the picture.

The easier ones were in the bag. I had a word with the head game warden of the district and he advised me to go to look for elephants and crocodiles at the Murchison Falls, the spot where the Albert Nile plunges 120 metres through a cleft in the rocks a few metres wide. Murchison Falls meant hiring a Land Rover so a driver and I set off in the early morning. When I explained my requirements, the driver was not happy. Most people go photographing wildlife with lenses half a yard long; I had what looked like a box camera.

We drove for a couple of hours through the bush; there were no roads. When we approached a rocky outcrop he stopped dead. Standing all over a dried up stream bed were about eight adult elephants and one or two calves. We were just a few feet away from three of them.

'Sit still, Bwana!'

Bwana! I'd only ever heard that in a Bob Hope film.

'Sit very still, please.'

'Which one's the bull?' I said, taking out my camera.

I don't think he wanted to know because by now there was one closing in behind us. I slid open a side window and pointed to a Behemoth about thirty feet away. 'Michael, how do you tell a bull from a cow?'

'Don't know, Bwana, they all look the same to me.'

That was it, if he didn't know, who did? The amazing beast was standing head on and since I didn't know what an elephant's balls looked like I guessed many Americans didn't either. 'What about that bugger?'

'Yes, Bwana, that's him.'

Setting the Rolleiflex at 30 feet I poked it out of the window and waited, hoping the beast would flap its ears. It didn't. The animals at the front of the vehicle had started to move away and my driver was about to gun the engine and risk a mad dash to safety. There wouldn't be another chance like this so I banged my hand hard against the side of the door. The elephant took a menacing step forward and obligingly extended his ears; people told me later this is a very bad sign. I snapped a quick shot as the driver, on the point of nervous collapse, dumped the clutch, shot the car forward and didn't stop in the next hour except at the falls where, in similar dangerous circumstances, I made the crocodile picture.

The Associated Press were pleased. The only picture I didn't take was the seaplane but I did manage a print with a couple of stock pictures and a scalpel. It was a pretty effective montage.

The end of my assignment coincided with the Belgians pulling out of the Congo leaving the Africans to fend for themselves. Naturally, all hell broke loose as refugees scattered across Zaire and as far as Uganda seeking flights. I was lucky, I grabbed a seat on an old Dakota, made a hair raising flight to Khartoum and so reached home.

◆

My mother left my father around the same time as I fell downstairs and fractured my skull. Dad suffered with rheumatic fever and had a weak heart.

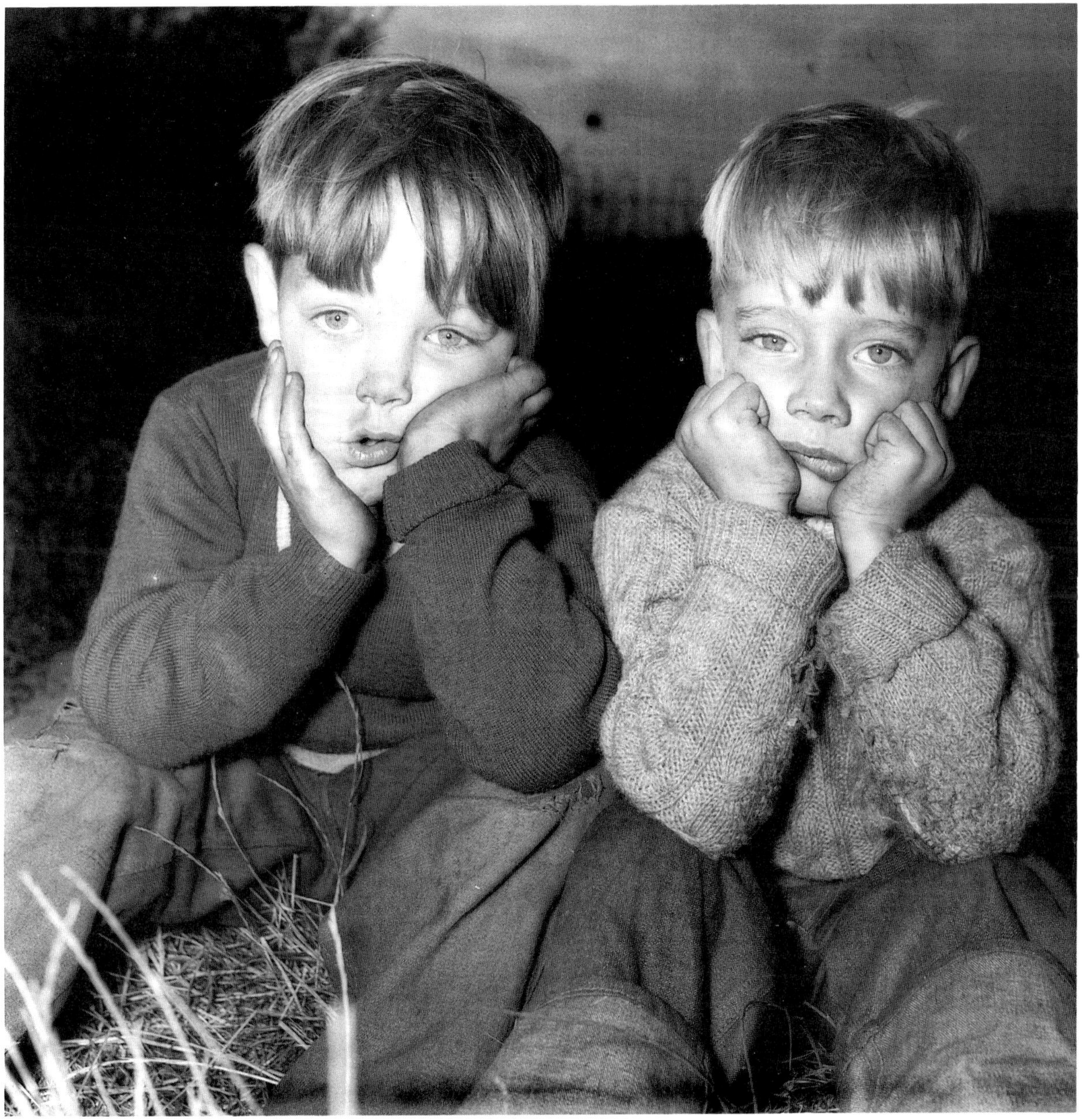

Two street urchins in York Road, Leeds, 1956. When I was a year old I fell down the stairs and fractured my skull. A few weeks later spinal meningitis set in. I was lucky to survive as the ambulance crashed on the way to the hospital. The year was 1935. Antibiotics were just being introduced but in my case they were either not suitable or not obtainable. Lumbar punctures were tried unsuccessfully so finally my back was laid open with the knife and the poisonous fluids drained. My survival was considered miraculous by relatives and neighbours who from that day on looked upon me with special regard and fondness. This in a nutshell could be the story of my life.

Our income was seven shillings a week; sixpence of this was collected every Friday by the Catholic priest as a contribution to the parish poor.

What a dad. He was a spinner of wonderfully bizarre stories, a good improviser, a conjurer, trick snooker player, marbles champion, pub singer, fighter and cook. Liked by everyone he appeared to us kids as a hero. Young children don't know what poor is, they are either happy and fed or unhappy and unfed. My brother Peter and me were happy most of the time and fed some of the time.

Our house stood at the terrace end of the corner of Bickerdyke Road and Ironstone Street; one room downstairs, two up. The primitive gas lighting system was supplied from a penny-in-the-slot meter. When the penny ran out the mean yellow light faded to a tiny blue glow then disappeared with a soft plop. That was the sign for the cockroaches to come out, hundreds of the little sods. They crunched underfoot as my father groped around the room in search of a penny. Like everyone else we had bugs. Every house in the street was infested. The blue distempered bedroom walls crawled, the squashed bodies forming random patterns around a chromotype print of the Immaculate Virgin.

Adjacent to our house was a large open patch of waste ground called The Oller. Overnight once a year this site was used to accommodate the feast. The Oller became a bedlam area for stomach-churning pleasures. Steam calliopes, chair-o-planes, carousels, waltzers, bumper cars, boxing booths and ghost trains changed everything. The star attraction was the Steam Shamrock, a pair of single-decked tram cars each hanging from two arms in which about thirty people sat on wooden benches without seat belts. To prevent folk from falling out a rope scramble net was stretched from the roof to the side walls. As hundreds watched, these carriages started to swing slowly in opposite directions, gradually increasing momentum until each reached a vertical position. Women screamed, men threw up and those daft enough to let go of the bench were thrown about like peas in a whistle.

At the feast my father always found work. Without a mother to anchor us down we eventually joined forces with the feast and spent some time touring all over Yorkshire. It was a wonderful interlude but the burden of rearing two small boys started to get Dad down. With the prospect of war making it easier to earn a dishonest living, it wasn't long before Dad jumped at the Government's offer to have us evacuated.

◆

Aged five and six we assembled with several hundred children at the Central Bus Station in Leeds. Ladies from a voluntary organisation attached luggage labels to our coats, gave us each a large tin of biscuits and loaded us onto buses, school by school. At the time this method of placing children in new homes appeared a simple and straightforward matter. Over the years, however, I've come to reflect on it as a portrayal of the British ability to muddle through by compromise.

After a journey of a couple of hours our bus ended up in a small village in South Yorkshire. We lined up in twos and crocodiled off down the village main street stopping at every cottage. One or two of the teachers then brayed on the door and asked the startled occupant if they would kindly take in a child or two for the duration of the war. The sight of thirty-two scruffs, half of whom had violent purple dye decorating their impetigo scabs, proved too much for a few and doors were slammed. But on the whole these kindly people reacted generously and the crocodile got smaller and smaller.

My brother Peter and I were the last to go. By now it was dark and we were very hungry. We called at a farm which had a lovely stained glass window over the front door and a stone lion couchant in the garden. The farmer's wife answered the door carrying an oil lamp. The two teachers, quite plainly wanting rid of their bewildered responsibility, were told she could take one not two. I liked the look of the oil lamp and the coloured glass and seriously considered abandoning my brother but he refused to be separated. On we trudged.

Eventually we were taken in by a family called Whitely. We were just in time for supper, bread dipped in hot bacon fat. It was Saturday and bath night. Wonderful! A tin bath was placed in front of a warm fire and, being the youngest, I was first in. Sheer luxury. Outside a stay in hospital I'd not had a hot bath before.

For reasons I never found out we did not stay long at the Whitelys, but we moved on to live with Mrs and Mr Fisher. Albert Fisher, a kind man, was an ARP warden and a railway worker at the local pit. His wife was beautiful and sang all day as she busily dusted and polished the house. There were plaster ducks flying up the wall and souvenir ash trays from Cleethorpes on the window sills. The back garden had a stream flowing through it and at the top of the field behind the house was a large stand of trees which provided great sport for climbing and ransacking birds' nests. Back home in Ironstone Street there were no trees.

We both attended the infant school down in the village. Our teacher took us once a week on rambles around the countryside. For the first time we saw chickens with their clothes on; apples growing on trees; milk coming out of cows; black-faced miners walking home from the pits; farmers hunting in bright red coats; threshing machines; sail binders; balers. We soaked all this up with eyes like organ stops.

The headmistress, Miss Nelson, made allowances for our different cultural background and was constantly rescuing us from the village toughies. On one occasion in the school lavs, Peter and I ganged up on an older kid called Freddie Trueman and escaped unscathed. We were born lucky.

Mrs Fisher became pregnant and couldn't cope with us any longer so once more the WRVS lady arrived and we moved on. She took us in a car to the next village, Braithwell, where we were found a home with a ploughman called Spooner and his wife. Mrs Spooner was a mean woman who knocked us about a fair deal. We lived on scraps and boiled potatoes. Every morning Mrs Spooner sat in front of the fire dipping a broken comb in a pot of tea and then running it through her hair. We were very unhappy.

Then in 1940 when we were in the village pantomime, Mrs Spooner became ill. After the last performance on Christmas Eve the WRVS lady gathered us up yet again. We walked through two feet of snow up to a cottage at the top of the High Street, went through the front door and entered a place of sanctuary. There were seven or eight people sitting in front of a kitchen range in which blazed a huge fire; they were roasting chestnuts and listening to Harry Lauder on a wind up gramophone. On every wall hung gilt-framed watercolours. There was a settee, four chairs, a large kitchen table, a sewing machine, a side-board with blue plates and a flag stone floor covered with peg rugs. Stability, for the time being anyway. The walls were two-and-a-half feet thick; you could sit in one of the windows.

The couple who took us in were called Mary and John Thompson and both were well into their sixties. Christmas in the country is a very special time of year but for Peter and me it was extra special. Behind the kitchen door hung a huge cock bird with a deep green tail. Around its neck it had a fringe of beautiful orange feathers and its comb was so big that it flopped over on one side. I helped to draw it. Ma Thompson explained all the bits and pieces as she drew them from inside the body; gall bladder, gizzard, livers. The gizzard was full of little stones which were used to grind the corn as it passed through the bird's system.

Mary Thompson was a small industrious woman who had been in service as a maid in London at the turn of the century. I stuck to her like a day old chick to a broody hen. She showed me how to pluck pigeons, skin rabbits, draw fowls, bottle fruit; make jam, wine, sloe gin, rosehip syrup, Yorkshire pudding, dumplings and, my favourite, suet pudding with treacle.

Pa Thompson stood over six feet tall, a slender slightly stooping figure with lovely silver hair and a wonderful patrician nose. He was a road sweeper and mender who trimmed hedges, mowed verges and was responsible for keeping a neighbouring village tidy. Because it was a country job it carried with it dignity and respect. He and Peter got on well.

All the cooking in the home was done on an open range set in one wall of the living room. Almost all the food we ate was produced by our own efforts; the only things bought were milk, sugar, tea, cocoa, flour and condensed milk. Fruit was picked either wild or from our small orchard. Any illness had to be treated according to Mrs Beaton's *Book of Household Management*. In winter I always suffered from croup which turned to pleurisy but these ailments were put right with a diet of stewed apple rings, spoonfuls of goose grease and potions made from various plants and lichens.

Peter and I slept together upstairs in a terrifying bedroom. Hidden behind one wall was a secret room without windows which had a tiny concealed door. Every night a death watch beetle clicked away in the old beams behind that door while we cowered away under the patchwork quilt. The house stood right on the main road so every car that passed threw its headlights on to the bedroom wall and the light travelled round the room from one wall to the next before disappearing abruptly. Quite often convoys of army tanks and lorries droned through the village at the dead of night.

There were only six electric lights in the house. We took no newspapers and had no radio. The only books permanently around were 1910 Liberty Catalogues and a few magazines filled with pictures of Queen Victoria but Ma Thompson read to us every night from library books while the old man quietly snored away in his chair with Nell, our old wire haired mongrel, wrapped round his feet.

Nell was a demon for rats and yellowhammer nests. On the long family walks we took each Sunday she always managed to find one or two because yellowhammers foolishly build their nests on the ground under hedges, easy prey for a dog with a good nose. Nell had a good nose and always telegraphed her find with a wagging tail. By the time we got to her and pulled her off, the nest and contents would be sticking out of the sides of her mouth. She ate the lot, eggs, babies and nest. I followed her once on my hands and knees along a track straight through a field of Dutch clover; at the end, in a warm depression, were 16 olive green eggs. Not knowing what they were other than food I gathered them up and shot off home. Ma Thompson said they were partridge eggs and fried them up that night, four each with some fried bread and a pot of cocoa; luxury for us, a little less for the gentry.

In the end Nell went blind, poor bitch, and as we lived on a main road the old man decided it would be safer to have her put down. One Saturday morning, the local butcher came round with his captive bolt pistol and, whilst I held her collar and her milky opaque eyes stared blankly into my face, he shot her in the forehead. We buried her at the bottom of the garden. Later we planted Jerusalem artichokes over the grave. The old man cried every night for weeks.

◆

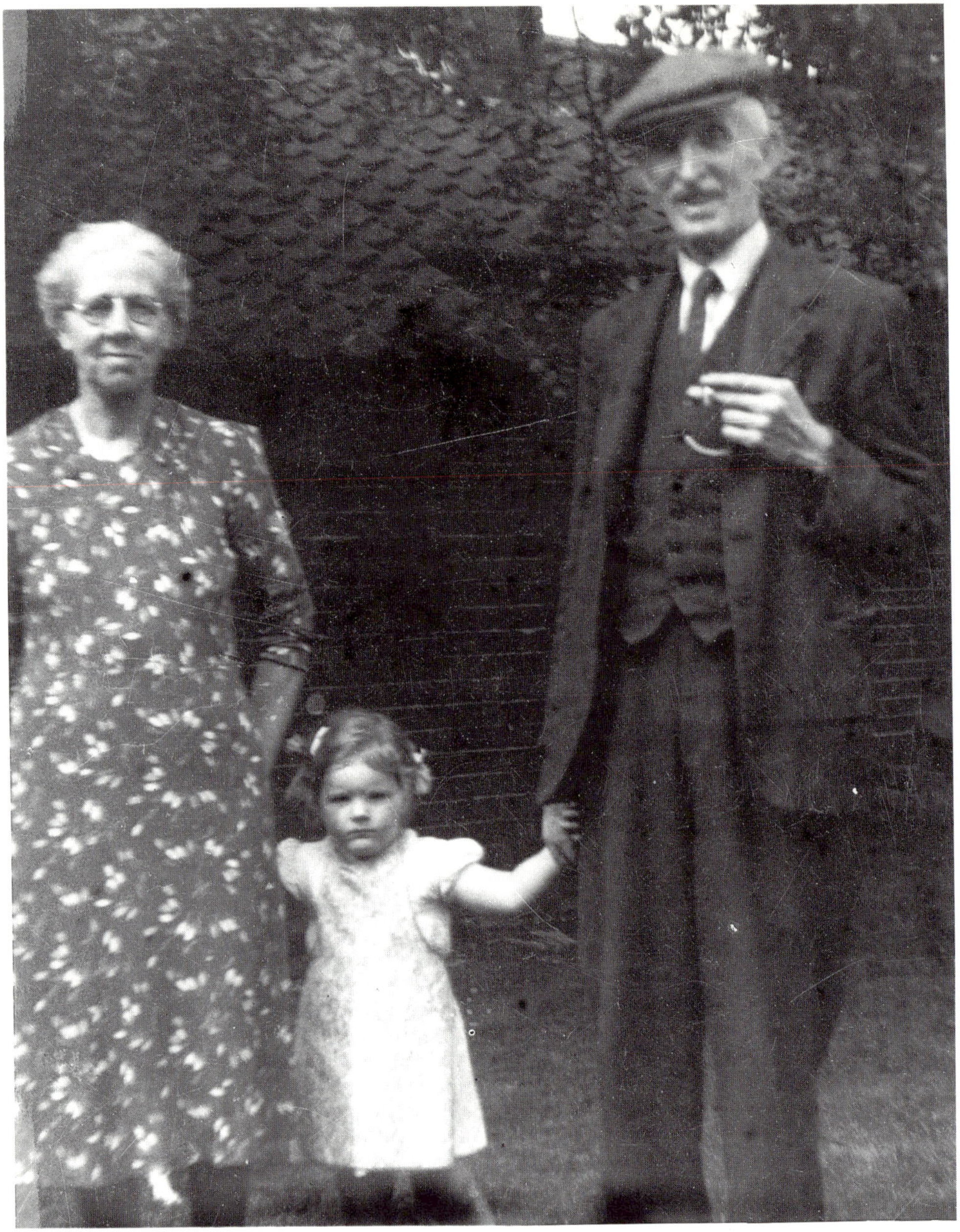

Ma and Pa Thompson. The first photograph I ever took. I used a Box Brownie that I'd swapped for a Boys' Own book given to me by the Women's Voluntary Service when I left Braithwell.

Jimmy Burton's dad was a winder at the pit in Edlington. His was a job that paid better than average, which was reflected in the quality of presents Jimmy got at Christmas. My brother Peter and I got a bar of chocolate, a red apple, some pencils and a brand new shiny penny. We were as happy as Larry so there was no jealousy on my part. One Christmas morning Jimmy came down to our cottage with his goodies. It never fails to amaze me that a trivial incident can affect the pattern of lives and how chance favours the prepared mind. Peter and I were drawing with our new pencils. He could draw like Michelangelo; I couldn't.

Jimmy's star present was a small hand-cranked projector with a spool of film. It didn't work from the mains, a good job as we had no electric sockets anywhere in the house, but worked from a torch. We took it into the coal house at the back of the kitchen and on the whitewashed wall we watched amazed at 60 seconds of a Mickey Mouse jazz band. I was gobsmacked. Then a brilliant idea occurred. If we stopped winding the handle the picture was frozen on the wall and with my Christmas present pencils I drew around the figures. Shades of Fox Talbot.

Shortly after Christmas Mrs Thompson took Peter and me on a shopping trip to Doncaster and as a special treat bought us both a little toy, Peter got a kaleidoscope and I got a periscope. This magic device opened up new worlds. It made me a foot taller. I could see over walls, into birds' nests and round corners. It also enabled me to see without being seen. Jules Verne is credited with the invention and like Fox Talbot was canonised and placed in my list of heroes.

My first attempt at photography came about when I was eight. I borrowed a book from school which showed me how to make a pinhole camera. I got a shoe box with the back end cut away and covered this with a sheet of greaseproof paper from the butcher's. I liberally smeared the paper with bacon fat. I then put a small pinhole in the front and jammed the contraption into the fork of a plum tree. Covering my head I stared at the screen and saw nothing. Normally this would have put me off but I felt a bit special standing by a plum tree with my head in a bag. Was there anyone else in the world doing just that at that moment? Exclusive! In the distance I heard the school bell; dinner break was over. It was time to get off but quite suddenly on the screen I could make out a door and a figure. Upside down, it was Ma Thompson waving to me. It was the most exciting thing I'd ever seen.

'Terry, you'll be late for school.'

'Just come and look at this Ma,' I shouted, completely ignoring her waving. She came over. 'Put your head under this bag.' She did. 'What can you see?'

'Nowt,' she said, and went back in.

I had missed the start of the first lesson and Johnny J Fox, the headmaster, was never a man to overlook a transgression. He was an ex-Indian army officer and also a bully. He tried to instill in us that all Asians were little brown so-and-sos. From him I learned to be intimidated by authority. If a particular piece of work didn't suit him he kicked it up into the school rafters. One day he dragged a little kid from class to class because he put some chalk marks on his face like a Red Indian. We were all encouraged to jeer.

I stood outside the classroom door frightened to go in. J J's face was black as thunder. He looked at me and pointed and said, 'See me at my room tomorrow, nine o'clock.'

This could only mean the stick. I was terrified and next day I refused point-blank to go to school. Eventually I was led there by Ma Thompson. She tried to get me out of it but J J wasn't having any. Years previously he had been a Sergeant Major in India and in a mood of nostalgia had kept his lead filled drill stick which he used to keep order amongst eight and nine year olds. I managed to survive the caning. It was worth it considering the magical experience by the plum tree.

◆

The village boasted a Home Guard unit and JJ was the Sergeant Major. Although he had a violent and explosive temper he was thought to be a good teacher and as a stalwart of the church was well liked. Manoeuvres were held regularly. The women of the village were expected to operate the stirrup pumps and provide cups of tea during mock battles. The Home Guard at this point had not been issued with rifles but paraded with pitch forks and broom handles. Farmers had shotguns and there was the odd posh middle class chappie with a shooting stick or an old military sabre. As the phoney war ended and the proper one hotted up bombs started dropping on nearby towns; bits of shrapnel could be picked up in the village street. In December, Sheffield twelve miles away, took a terrible pounding; the glow from the burning city lit up the sky night after night. An air raid shelter was built next to the school and once a week we had air raid drill. Gas was the thing everybody feared and every citizen was issued with a gas mask. In order to gain familiarity we wore them once a week during a lesson, a practice abandoned because the perspex window steamed up and schoolwork ground to a halt. Never stuck for an alternative the powers that be sent round a gas wagon; children filed in ten at a time, the doors were closed and the interior filled with tear gas. We were told that if we liked we could lift the edge of our mask to see what it was like. I did. It was awful, my eyes were bloodshot for days.

Occasional aeroplanes which couldn't make it to the RAF base at Dinnington a few miles away came down in our fields, a big event for the village life. They usually just missed the church and flew lower and lower until belly-flopping in a suitable open space. Once we were playing in some fields when we saw a plane gliding low over the hedges, smoke pouring from its tail. It had failed to get its undercarriage down and pancaked in the centre of the grass field, slithered for two or three hundred yards and struck an oak tree with one of its wings. Surprisingly the wing didn't break off. The plane just spun round the tree and skidded off in almost the same direction from which it had come. By the time it came to rest we had almost reached it. The pilot slid back the canopy, quite casually climbed out, sauntered over and asked if we could lend him a bike to cycle back to Peterborough, at least 80 miles away.

Peter and I were gradually absorbed into village life. I spent my time hanging round the slaughter-house attached to the farm and watched the whole cycle of animal life; birth, death, dissection, Sunday dinner.

One day playing in a field of spring wheat four of us set up a rabbit. It was a large field with no cover. We pursued the animal, hurling stones and screaming. In panic the poor creature took cover in a Cambridge roller but with our terrier standing guard at one end and Spike Seymour at the other it didn't stand much chance. Tony Franklin, me and Jimmy Burton went in search of long sticks to poke the little sod out. The sticks were found but proved only marginally useful. The terrified rodent was pushed and prodded nearer and nearer the far opening but we couldn't get to him. Excitement had by now reached delirium. Jimmy Burton was pounding on the cast iron casing with a rock, Spike Seymour demanded the right to kill it and Tony Franklin was wetting himself. I was busy poking with my stick. The rabbit edged slowly towards the only avenue of escape.

We took it in turns to peer down the roller and give opinions on what effect the assault was having. The creature was so close I could see bits of loose fur sticking to its black eyeballs. One of its ears had a small tear and its little brown body was quivering. We each had a go at reaching in to try and grab it but the spokes in the various segments of the roller frustrated our efforts. In the end Spike suggested a fire and produced matches. The fire took a bit of lighting as most of the kindling and tinder was damp but eventually it got going and smoke drifted slowly down the roller, escaping at intervals through the articulated sections. The rabbit edged nearer the exit. Spike, who had the longest reach, could just about touch it. He pulled out tufts of hair and held them aloft jubilantly. My hands were smallest. I reached in and clasped a leg.

Captured, the animal lay in my arms rigid. Even though we poked and prodded it there were no signs of life. An argument about possession began with my claim of priority by right of capture. Spike wanted to gut it and roast it there and then but by now I was feeling sorry for the poor thing. My hand and clothes were getting wet from the pee leaking from its body so I placed it gently on the ground. As I was wiping my hands on Spike's jacket there was a sudden scuffle and the rabbit was off like a shot. It passed between three pairs of stamping feet and disappeared through a distant hedge. I had felt compassion for the animal, paroled it, spared it from Spike's penknife and I was pleased about the escape.

Once Mr Thompson had killed one of our tame rabbits for Sunday dinner. While I held the body he had started to gut it with a penknife but it wasn't dead and started to scream. I was horrified and hurt. That Sunday I had jam and bread while the family tucked into the roasted body.

The escape of the rabbit was blamed on me and my three pals danced around poking fun and hurling insults, laughing at my naivete. The fight that developed flattened about forty square yards of wheat. A truce was declared when an outraged farm worker appeared in the distance.

◆

Two or three times a year a man wearing a long white coat paraded a huge Shire stallion through the village and called at farms where there was a mare to be covered. The stallion was the biggest creature I had ever seen; 19 hands, with feet like dinner plates. Its tail and mane were plaited with coloured ribbon. On either side of its head, pinned to the halter, were blue and red rosettes won at show grounds all over the county. The steel shoes on the massive feet struck sparks from the pebbles set in the road. If we were lucky and found a suitable vantage point we could witness the mating of this wonderful beast.

Corn thrashing was a magical yearly event. The humming of the thresher could be heard in all corners of the village and attracted kids like flies to a jam pot. The thresher was driven by a steam engine with a huge fly wheel and a long leather belt. Sheaves were tossed up to a man who stood on top of the thresher to cut string. The corn went down a hole, chaff poured out of one chute and grain from another. The attraction for us kids was the mice. When the stack reached ground level we could rush in and grab the ones which scattered in panic from every sheaf. We stuffed them by the dozen into a cloth flour bag which got thrown open into the village pond at the end of the day. If they could make it to the other side they were safe, that is unless a terrier pounced on them.

As I got older I was able to supplement the family budget in spring with rook eggs, forty or fifty at a time, from nests in the village rookery. The trees must have been eighty feet high but I could climb most of them by the time I was nine. The trouble with rooks eggs was the whites; when fried they remain transparent and look most unappetising, consequently they were mostly used in Yorkshire puddings and cakes. One of my favourite bits of poaching was to find a wood pigeon's nest with eggs newly hatched and tie the squabs' legs to the nest. A month later I would return to collect them fat.

Every year the farmers fell into an orgy of killing during the annual rook shoot. In the centre of the village stood six acres of sycamore trees, each with ten to fifteen nests, containing four or five young. When the squabs were feathered and able to hop around the branches, the farmers attacked. Dozens of guns blazed and mangled bodies and feathers fell like black snow. We collected the cartridge cases as if they were precious stones and the smell of the cordite was almost habit forming. But I always thought it was a pointless massacre. Every year there were just as many rooks; the numbers never diminished. They were harmless birds and ate a lot of wire worms and leather jackets, the farmers' real enemy.

In spite of the war village life was stable and safe. Our lives had settled into a comfortable routine. We picked snowdrops in February, primroses on Good Friday, bluebells in May, violets in June, blackberries in September, hazelnuts in October. We had Advent, Christmas, Epiphany, Lent, Easter, Whitsun, Pentecost and Trinity. The churches had been forbidden to ring bells throughout the war and this was the only thing lacking in our perfect rural setting.

◆

The mills of God grind slowly but those of the Catholic church grind even slower. It took them two years to find us. Catholic priests were a rare sight in Braithwell so the day when Father Mullane phut-phutted up the high street on his two stroke, the hens stopped laying. He thundered on the door and I answered it. He was a big man, slightly soiled. He'd learned his craft at the hard end in the Belfast docks and he had more edge than a cut glass sword. Peter and I watched the confrontation between this blustering giant and the diminutive Ma Thompson with trepidation.

He wanted to know why we weren't attending church. Of course we were going to church and Sunday School as well. When he learned it was a Protestant church he became apoplectic. He told the old lady that we belonged to the Catholic church and he would have us taken out of her care if we didn't attend Sunday Mass every week in Maltby, four miles away. Ma Thompson, a spiritualist, had a healthy disrespect for papist priests so showed him the door. My brother and I were beside ourselves with excitement. The battle continued in the front garden with the good Father losing on all fronts. He eventually settled for a compromise. Because of the war there were no buses between villages on Sundays, so a weekly attendance at the Catholic church was out of the question. Father Mullane asked if we could get over the following week and make our first confession. Mrs Thompson, being a fair-minded woman, agreed. Peter and I were perplexed; what was confession? We hadn't done anything and what's more we were not going to admit to anything even if we had. Eventually though we footed it to Maltby, a big mining village over an hour's walk away.

The church was a corrugated tin hut, a big let down after our lovely Norman building at Braithwell, but inside the place was amply furnished with pleading bleeding statues and twelve bas reliefs showing Christ's agony in various stages leading up to the Crucifixion. In one corner stood a plaster model of a monk. On his outstretched arms were perched doves and robins; at his feet sat Peter Rabbit and Bambi. This miraculous icon instantly appealed to me. I was stroking the rabbit when Father Mullane came in. His manner had undergone a change, as manners do when intimidated by being on hallowed ground and he was almost affectionate. We sat for half an hour while the ritual and meaning of confession was explained. Mortal sin, venial sin, sins of omission, sins of commission, heaven, hell, purgatory, penance. Peter and I had no background of Catholic doctrine, other than Dad's weekly sixpence, so we had no idea what he was talking about. Why was religion so complicated? Back in Braithwell, church was easy to understand. We sang nice hymns, *Rock of Ages*, *From Greenland's Icy Mountains*, *Abide With Me*, *All Things Bright And Beautiful*, although the Vicar was a bit unchristian in not letting us take conkers from the tree in his field, especially as it was the only one in the district.

The interesting part of Father Mullane's instruction was forgiveness. It appeared that if we were truly sorry for our transgressions then they were wiped from the slate. By now there were a few things hovering at the back of my mind that I would have been pleased to get rid of, even if until now they had not appeared to be of any great significance. The priest's explanation of the true nature of sin had put them into a new perspective. I entered the confessional trembling.

My first admission was the taking of a sugar beet from a field. We had tried and failed to make sugar. This was followed by raiding orchards, taking a tin of condensed milk secretly from the larder, writing 'J J Fox is a silly old sod' in green chalk on the school wall; killing a blackbird; drinking some of the beer we were fetching for the harvesters then topping up the jug by peeing in it; chasing sheep; not eating the pastry crust from Mrs Thompson's rhubarb pie; tearing a page out of a school book; kicking a goose. Ten or twenty venial sins later the Father Confessor's yeses got more abrupt. His fingertips were pressed to his temple as if he had an aching head and now and again his scalp moved forwards then back. He absolved me and gave me a penance of two Hail Marys and one Our Father. Peter got three and two. Neither of us knew what a Hail

Mary was so on the way back we sang *Jerusalem* and, feeling shriven of all past misdeeds, we chased some sheep.

◆

I remember when they first mentioned our return home to Leeds there was some talk about me staying in Braithwell and Peter returning alone, but nothing came of it. We were both reaching school leaving age and could bring in a wage. Dad couldn't miss a chance like that.

Ma Thompson took us to the railway station at Doncaster and put us on a train. The memory is still painful. We were met by our dad at Leeds and taken by tram to our new home. The route up York Road took us past our old slum. Leeds was an awful shock; clanging trams, lorries, cars, skies yellow with sulphur, old men hacking and spitting, gloomy gas lights, cobbled streets fouled with dog shit.

While we were evacuated Dad had taken up with a widow called Mary Cosgrove, mother of two boys and a girl. The girl, Maureen, was my age, the two boys three or four years older. Peter and I shared a bed that night with our new stepbrothers sleeping head to tail. A few yards down the road the British Oxygen Company on night shift maintained an orchestration of clanging gas cylinders. The dawn chorus in Leeds was a knocker-up, factory hooters and barking dogs. Trains a mile away at East End Park shunted and whistled until early morning. The pain of those first few months has haunted me ever since. I cried myself to sleep every night. I dreamt about my mother. But it wasn't my mother. I'd forgotten what she looked like. It was an image of a blonde woman who was beautiful and loving.

◆

I staggered rat-arsed out of a working men's club in Poznan one night in 1961. My partner on the trip had disappeared with a whore and the car. I had no idea of my whereabouts and couldn't even remember the name of the hotel. The area was badly lit, 25 watt bulbs hanging from telegraph poles 100 yards apart. The place itself was an industrial shitheap. I lurched across a bridge, over a marshalling yard and then I paused to spit or was it to honk. A train passed, clattering across the points, hauling what looked like cattle cars. I started to think about how these had been used twenty years previously, in my lifetime, for Christ's sake. The thought of all those poor souls, kids, old women, young girls, rabbis, cantors, chazzonim; hungry, terrified, people with no food or water for days, came to me. I broke down and sobbed.

◆

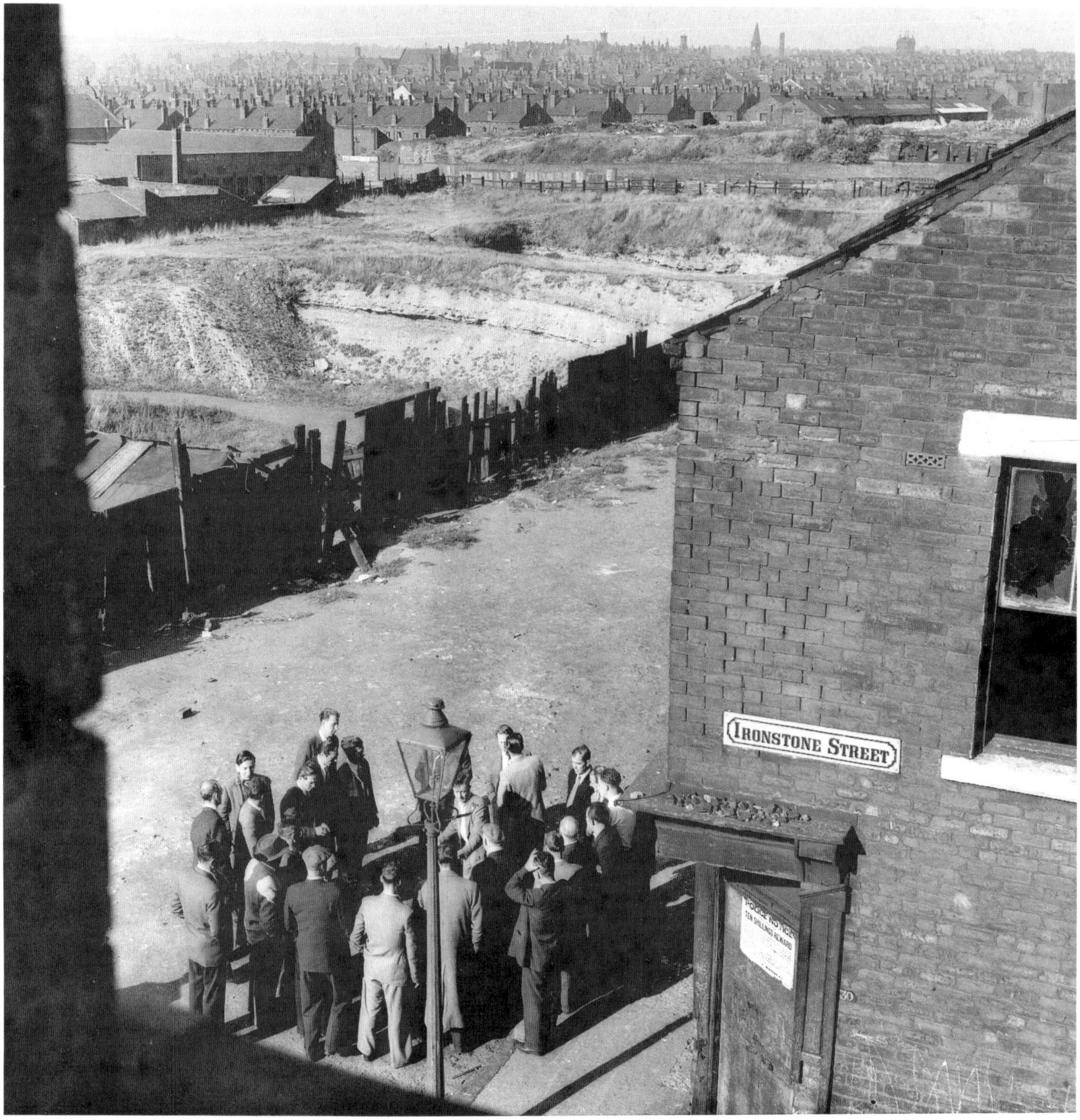

The first picture I took when I got back to Leeds. This is the view from my back bedroom. My father is the one with his back to the camera scratching his head.

Being the youngest boy I got stuck with all the household chores. Every Saturday I queued at the grocer's for the week's rations, I took the laundry, shook the peg rugs and walked two miles to the market in town to collect the meat from a relative who would sell us his ration. The tram fare was a penny each way but my father wouldn't give me the money. A change had taken place in the years we had been away. He had made his home with a new family; Peter and me weren't part of it. Both Peter and me felt rejected. We'd been dragged from pillar to post for five years and when we finally got home it seemed as though we didn't belong. I wanted to go back to Braithwell. Dad went out boozing every night and left us. I think he only took us to the pictures once, that was to see *The Quiet Man*. We still respected him but the image was becoming tarnished.

When Peter and I had gone away at the start of the war our dad was unemployed; when we returned he was still unemployed, officially that is, but in fact he made a very good living standing with all the other chancers at the back of Leeds market buying and selling bits of gold and silver, anything he could turn round for a profit.

On one occasion two likely lads brought him a gold chain with inlaid stones. It was in fact the Lord Mayor of Bradford's chain of office which the lads had nicked from the glove compartment of the council Roller which was foolishly parked unlocked in a very seamy side street in North Leeds. It weighed in at 30oz troy. Dad gave £80 for it and knocked it out to a North Street Fagin for a not inconsiderable mark up.

◆

We were enrolled in the local school, St Charles', which was Catholic. Seeing as we had been brought up as Anglicans this presented a dilemma for the teachers and the parish priest, so it was decided to give us special indoctrination at the priest's house every Wednesday evening. One evening we were told to wait in a small anteroom as the priest we were to see had not come in from a sick call. About twenty minutes passed and there was no sign of the missing man so I decided to have a look round. I crossed the hall and creaked open a door. The room was long with a refectory table running down the middle. It was set with about twelve places. Apart from the masses of cutlery surrounding each plate there were Waterford crystal decanters, wine glasses, flowers and finger bowls. From the ceiling hung a chandelier. Were these the people who collected money from the parish poor? Did the meek really inherit the earth? Doubts crept into my mind. I was only ten. By the time I was fourteen the doubts had blossomed into a complete distrust of the clergy.

Dad's bronchitis was getting worse. There were

times he couldn't get down to the market and would sit hunched up in an easy chair coughing and spitting onto the fire, the hot coals distilling his life up the chimney. Mary, my stepmother, was in full-time employment working in a sweat shop in Mushroom Street. She was a good grafter and every night after school I'd call at the shop and bring home a dozen sports coats for her to underbaste before she and Dad went to the pub.

◆

In my later life I often photographed weddings at the Synagogue in Chapeltown Road. It's now the Northern School of Contemporary Dance and I'm taking pictures there again. Nadine Senior, the principal, introduced me to the Phoenix Dance Company and I started taking pictures of them; five blokes built like Greek gods. The sessions lasted ten years. Strangely enough, Phoenix are based in a converted old clothing factory no more than three hundred yards from my old school and in the very sweatshop where my stepmother slaved, under-basting sports coats at sixpence each.

◆

Once a week we spent an afternoon at woodwork. The class was run by two sadists of late middle age, remnants of a scandalously unfair education system. These two bullies had failed as carpenters, failed the IQ test to get into the police and, as a last resort, had ended up in education as unqualified teachers.

We didn't like these two men and responded to their bluster with sullen hostility but there were lighter moments. At roll call we would all line up behind the work benches and number off one to fifteen. Then one master would stand forward and count the line to check that the numbers called coincided with bodies present. When he started to count, a boy at the end would duck under the bench so the tally would be fourteen. The silly old sod thought he had made a mistake and would start again. This time, when he reached five, number one had ducked down, sneaked up to the end and stood up to be counted number sixteen. The permutations of this little game were endless. One day when numbering up, one, two, three, four, five, six, seven, eight, nine, ten, the last five shouted, Jack, Queen, King, Running Flush, Full House and got whacked across the arse with a three foot steel rule.

◆

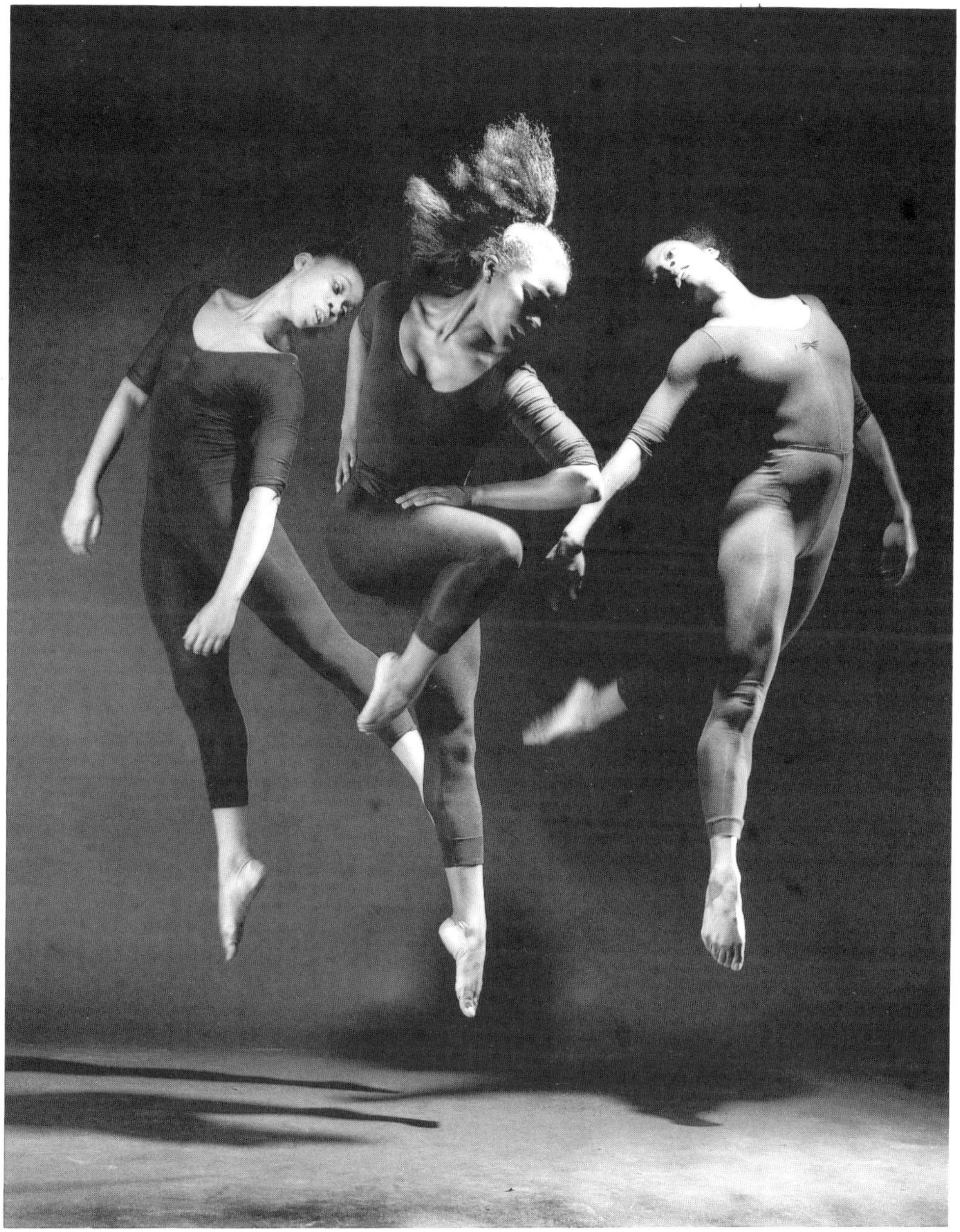

These three women joined Phoenix round about the same time. I like this image; it took me just three shots to get it right. I used to borrow a studio in Hunslet from a friend. I knew nothing about studio work and I still don't really. Tim Green a mate of mine would set up an overhead light and I'd press the button.

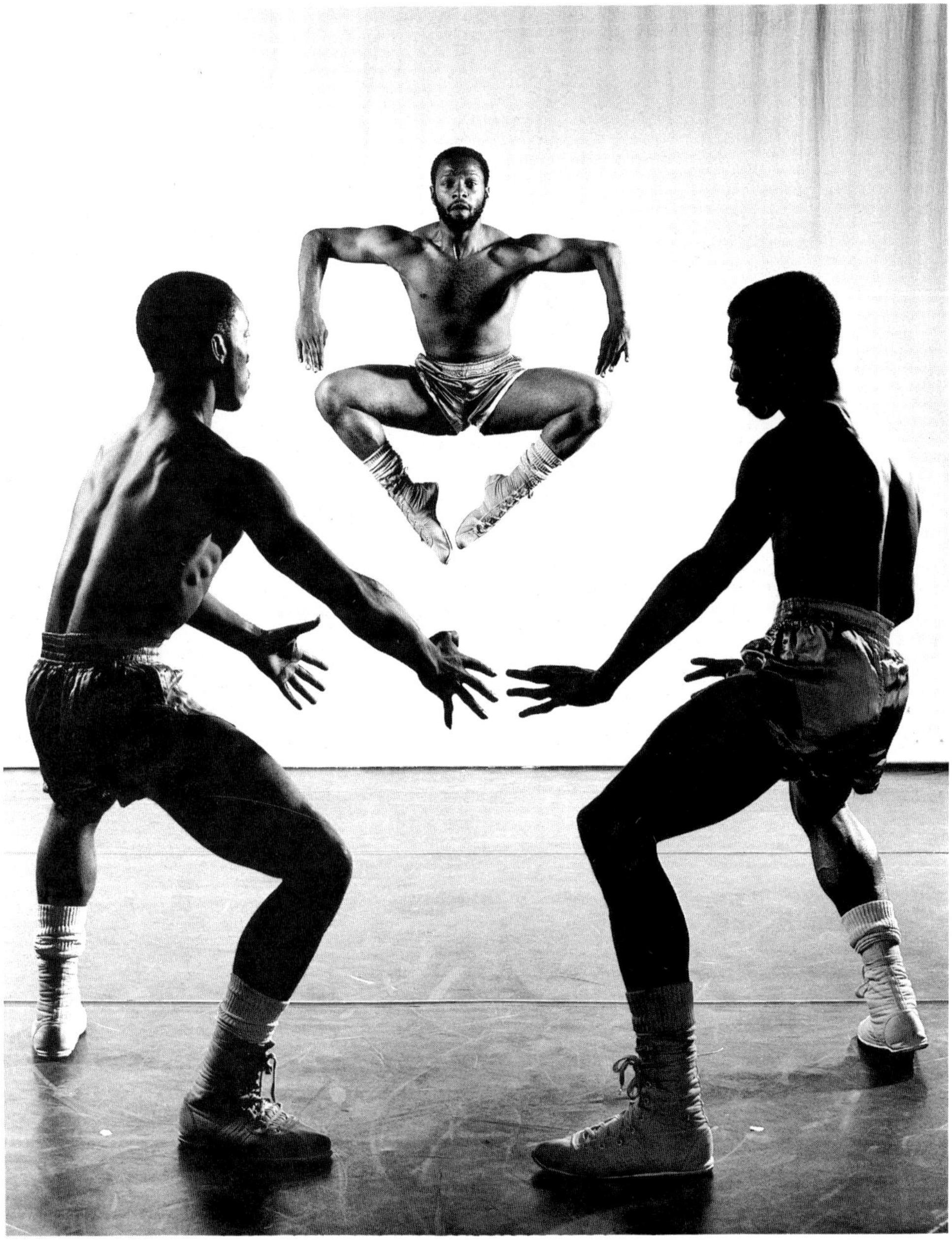

This shot was taken for Phoenix's Australian tour. I staged this picture at the Theatre Royal and Opera House in Wakefield during rehearsals.

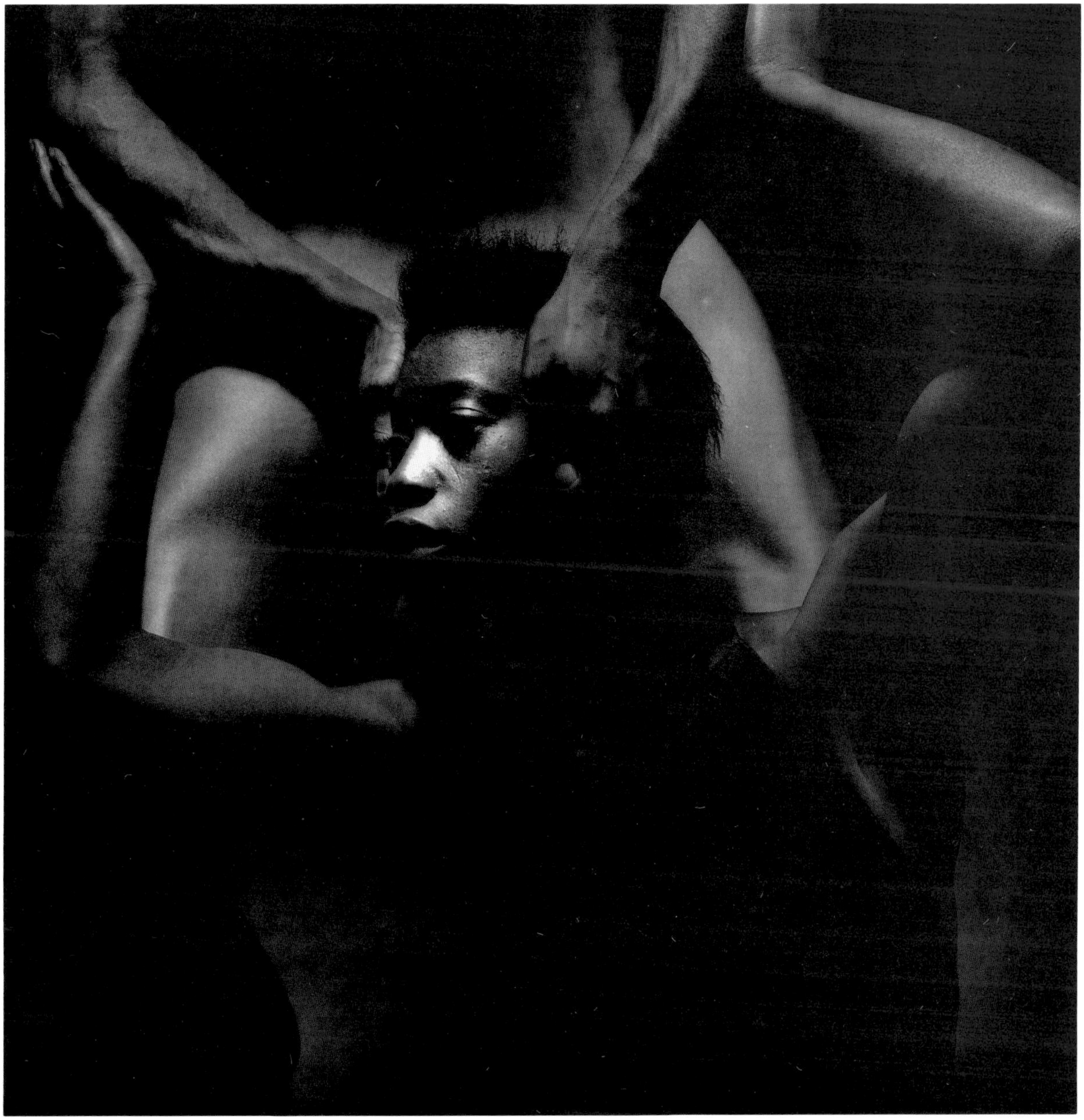

Paul Liburd and Seline Thomas of Chapeltown, Leeds. Chapeltown gets a lot of bad publicity in the newspapers. It's as though the remarkable talent that exists there never happened.

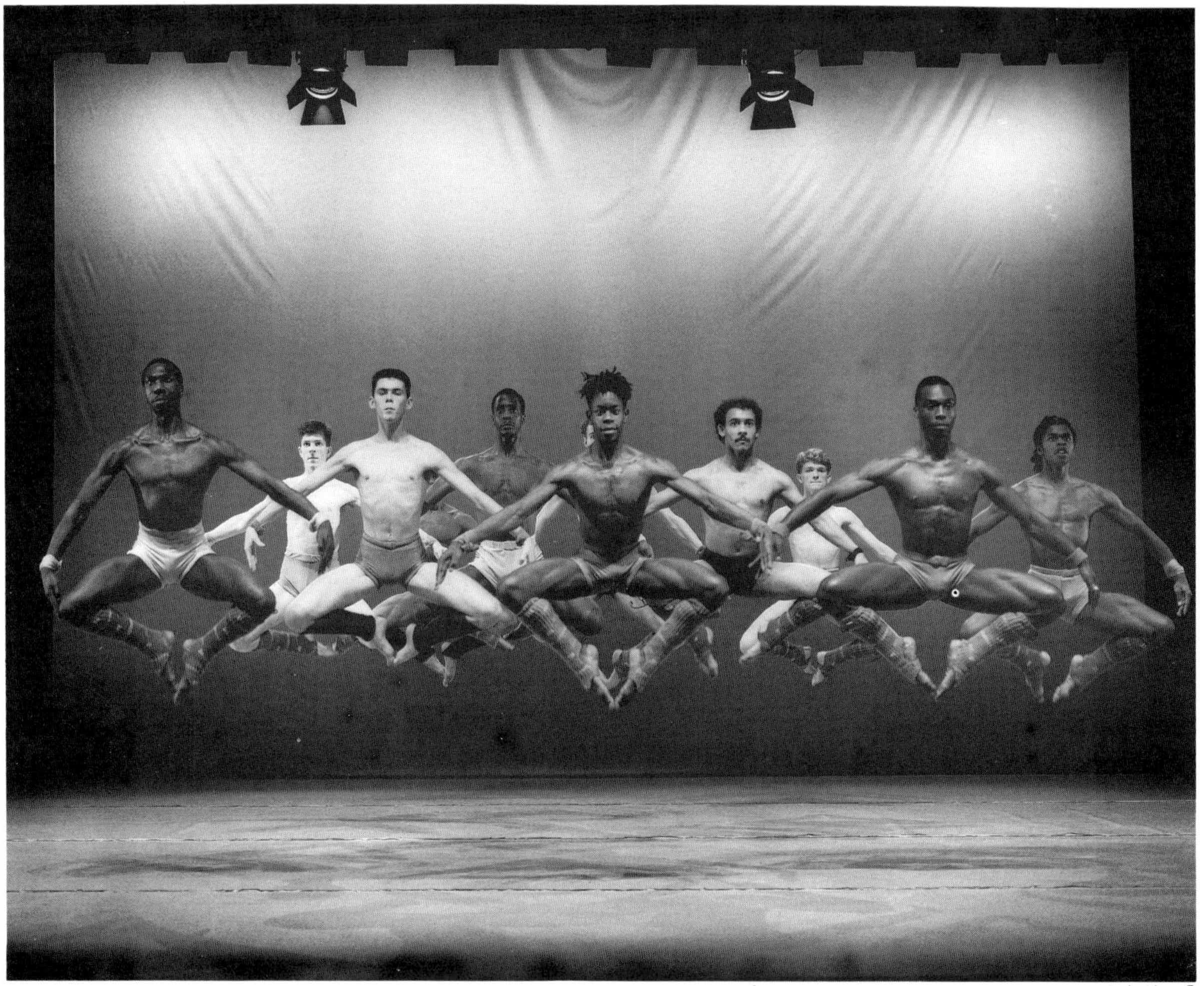

Troy Games. Third year students at the Northern School of Contemporary Dance. I took ten pictures in fifteen seconds as they constantly jumped up and down. This is number 8, the only one that worked. It's done with available light only.

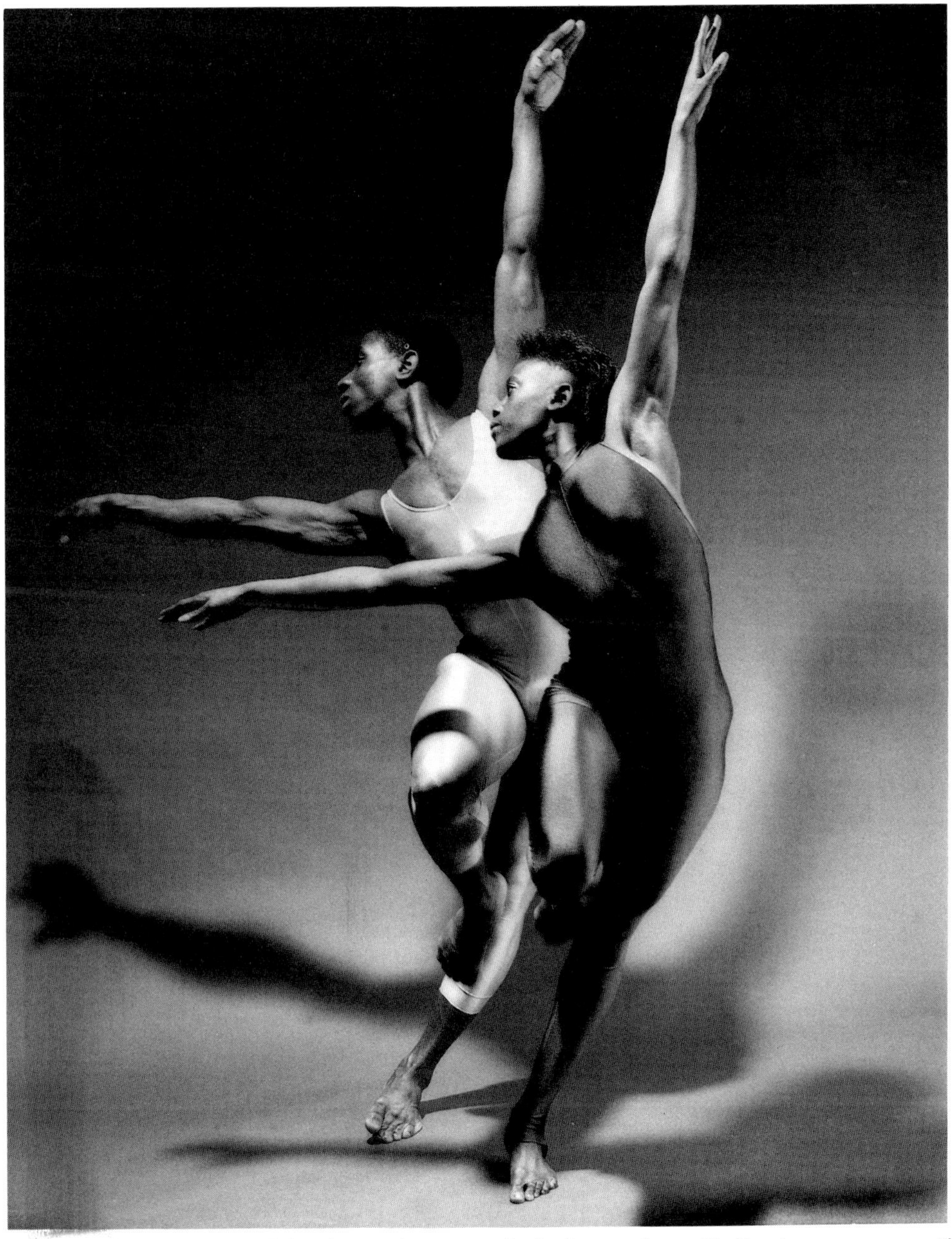

Paul and Seline again. This picture is not particularly popular with the dance cognoscenti because Paul's big toe is off the floor.

In 1948 we got changed to another woodwork centre where the teacher was young, qualified, firm and fair. There we were given a test to make a dovetail joint. Three of us came top and were transferred to metal work; there's logic for you.

By this time we were in Mr Kirwin's class. He was a staunch Conservative, well educated and feared by all. It was obvious to us he was used to better things. He took snuff constantly and frequently left the room for ten minutes or more. When he did one kid dashed to the door to dog out and two of us would lean into the fireplace, light a Woodbine and blow smoke up the chimney. The kid keeping watch at the keyhole would warn us when he was about to return.

Although he was not particularly liked we had a certain respect for him, the main reason being he could read us like a book. Nothing got past Kirwin except the smoking. We figured out that all the years of shovelling Top Mill up his schonk had burned out the lining so he could smell bugger all.

Mr O'Neil, the singing teacher, was a short, stout man with a beefy face and lacework of red veins in his nose and cheeks. He was not a qualified teacher either and told us sod all about music. We spent every lesson singing American Civil War songs and rousing propaganda bullshit; *Hearts of Oak*, *Land of Hope and Glory*, *Faith of Our Fathers Living Still*. Like Kirwin he knew us to the bone. His prediction for us was two or three to the gallows and the rest barrow boys in Leeds Market. He was wrong on the first count but fifty per cent right on the second.

◆

My mate Duce lived in a grotty rat-infested, back-to-back in Freehold Street, next door to a woman who for some strange reason was nicknamed Orange Box Face. Every Monday she went to the pawn shop across York Road to hock her husband's shirts. This gave her about 7/6 to see her through till Friday when she would redeem them to enable her husband to go out on the piss with some semblance of respectability. She had been doing this every week all through the 1940s. On this occasion when she pushed what was left of the shirts across the counter Uncle pushed them back and said, 'Nay, Mary love, we've stopped taking dish clouts.'

Duce's father had a regular visitor who we called Blind Pugh. He was an ex-boxer, about seventy years old, six foot six inches tall and sightless. One night walking home a wall collapsed and dropped on top of him. He was taken to hospital where he lay in a coma for a week or more. When he recovered consciousness all he kept muttering was, 'Me dogs, me dogs.' The RSPCA was called and it was realized his five dogs hadn't been fed during the past week. An inspector was dispatched with a key and a basket of sheep's lights. When he opened the door a howling pack of slavering large dogs fell on him and caused him severe injuries. We found this funnier than the Marx Brothers. Blind Pugh recovered.

◆

Time passed and by a process of elimination I became cock of St Charles' and, because of my better education at Braithwell, I soon became the teachers' favourite. St Charles' had been a good rugby school but had gone over to football and was doing very badly. I was asked to go to the staffroom.

'Come in, Terence.' Everyone in the school only had surnames except me. 'Mr Sommerville wants a word with you.' My mind was working overtime, thinking of all recent breaches of the penal code, cataloguing defensive rebuffs.

'We've been thinking, Terence, that as you are the strongest boy in the school you will be pleased, very pleased, that we are appointing you Captain of the football team.'

'No, thank you, sir.'

'Do you mean that you are turning it down?'

'Don't like football, sir.'

'It's for the school, Terence.'

'Don't like any sport, sir.'

Mr Moran butted in, 'What do you like, Terence?'

'Fighting, sir, reading, keeping pigeons.'

Mr O'Neil chimed in, 'Let's put him in the City's Schoolboy Boxing Championships.'

They did and I got thrashed, but that was the only time I was ever beaten in a fight.

Most of the lessons were childish. English was always 'write a composition' so we never covered grammar or punctuation. Maths, 'add this sum of money to that sum of money,' 'take this figure from that figure'; it gave us sufficient nous to fill out a betting slip and tot up the winnings.

For most of my time at St Charles', I was in Mr Moran's class. He was a decent teacher fighting an uphill battle in a slum school. He had a particular regard for me and, as a result, caned me every day. The performance was a ritual. Picking up the cane which was about two foot long, he paraded around the room doing practice strokes in mid air.

'Come out here, Terence. I'm sorry about this but I expect you to set an example. Hold out your hand.'

He then leant slightly back, slowly bent his knees, his right leg would rise about two feet, his arm went up beyond his head and he crashed down with his whole body weight behind the stroke, before repeating the performance on the other hand. The choreography was wonderful. 'I like caning Terence because he always smiles,' he would say.

The school had no monitors or prefects but the staff never failed to co-opt me into relieving their more tedious duties. Every day I had to march the whole school down the road to St Patrick's Boys'

Club for school dinners. Then I had to stand up in the boxing ring and make sure there was no talking or fighting. This was bad news as it meant I got my dinner late while my mates shot off to pick up dog ends or do a little larceny in the market. If Mr Moran couldn't finish his dinner he sent for me and asked me to finish it for him. He thought I looked half starved; I was.

The standard of teaching was primary school level. Lessons and exams presented no difficulty so eventually Mr Moran allowed me to drop out of most lessons. One of my jobs was duplicating exam papers. This really gave me no advantage as I could have answered any of the questions when I was eight years old. Education after all is the one thing they can't take away from you; that's why they didn't give us any.

◆

In 1947 the wonderful Phyllis Dixie came to Leeds City Varieties. Phyllis was a stripper of great charm, she spoke and looked like Anna Neagle and had the deportment of a duchess. She was also a bit of a fake, wearing behind her ostrich feather fan a full length, pink silk body stocking. We paid a tanner to sit up in the gods just beyond the front of the stage, which enabled us to see behind the fan. She did a season of five weeks. Leonardy and I went every week and every Friday we told the priest at confession. On her last appearance she smiled up at us. She looked just how I imagined my mother to be, blonde, beautiful and desirable.

Friday night I called on Leonardy, we were going to confession together and, on the way, would look for dog ends in the gutter. Cigarettes were still hard to get and the only smoke available to us came from that rarity, the discarded stub. Most people in our area saved the ends in a tin then rolled them up midweek when they were skint. If we saw a middle class gent smoking in the street we would follow until he'd finished and threw the tab end down. Then we would pounce on it and hold it with a hair grip to our lips. We walked down York Road without any luck, then outside the Hope Inn we simultaneously spied half an orange in the road. Apart from in photographs I'd never seen an orange, neither had Leonardy. He was off like a greased pig but I was a very close second. We wrestled in the road, Leonardy screaming, 'Mine, mine, I saw it first.'

'Shares Leno, equal shares!'

With me being considerably tougher, he saw sense and prepared to tear it in half. That's when I noticed that it was only skin, the flesh had been removed.

'It's okay Leno, fair's fair; you got it first, you can have it all.' He did; the greedy little bugger scoffed the peel.

In the church Len went into the confessional first and I strained at the door to hear what he was confessing. Suddenly the door crashed open and Len lurched out, honking a rainbow of half chewed orange peel. The priest rushed out of his hole and gave us both a severe bollocking.

'You're Terence Cryer aren't you?'

'Yes, Father.'

'Are you here to confess?'

'Yes, Father.'

'Get in the box.'

I did; through the grille that separated us I could see him scowling and thought, 'Oh my God this is going to be three decades of the bloody rosary.'

'Bless me, Father, for I have sinned and it's one week since my last confession and I accuse myself of...' Where do I start. Len was still retching somewhere in the church. I ran through a litany of minor misdeeds worth one Our Father, two Hail Marys at the most, but then I came to the biggy.

'We,' get Leonardy to share the guilt I thought, 'went to see Phyllis Dixie at the Varieties.'

This was the fifth Friday he'd heard this from me.

'Are you truly sorry, my son?'

'Yes, Father.' This was a cinch, I was going to get away with it.

'Well, I don't think you are and I'm not giving you absolution.' He shut his little door.

Christ, this meant I was a lost soul; no confession, no Holy Communion, no Easter duties, automatic excommunication. Leno was waiting for me still looking green.

'What happened Terry?'

'He wouldn't give me absolution.'

'Me neither.' I looked at the mess on the tiles.

'Have you been eating bacon rind?'

'Yes, I think that's what made me sick.'

Hardly surprising, some of the pieces were three inches long.

'What we going to do about school?'

'Look he's not allowed to squeal on us, so we can say what we like.'

Confession, Mass and Holy Communion were compulsory and listed ritually in a big book every Monday morning.

'Okay Leno, tell nobody about this and I mean nobody.'

'What about the priest?'

'Fuck him.'

'Yeah, fuck him.'

And we shot off down town to find some more fag ends.

◆

Eight hundred years after the Exodus, the Assyrians invaded Judea with the intention of crushing the rebellious Judah. A blast fell upon the Assyrians' camp and annihilated it. The Rabbinical sources ascribe this occurance to the two Archangels

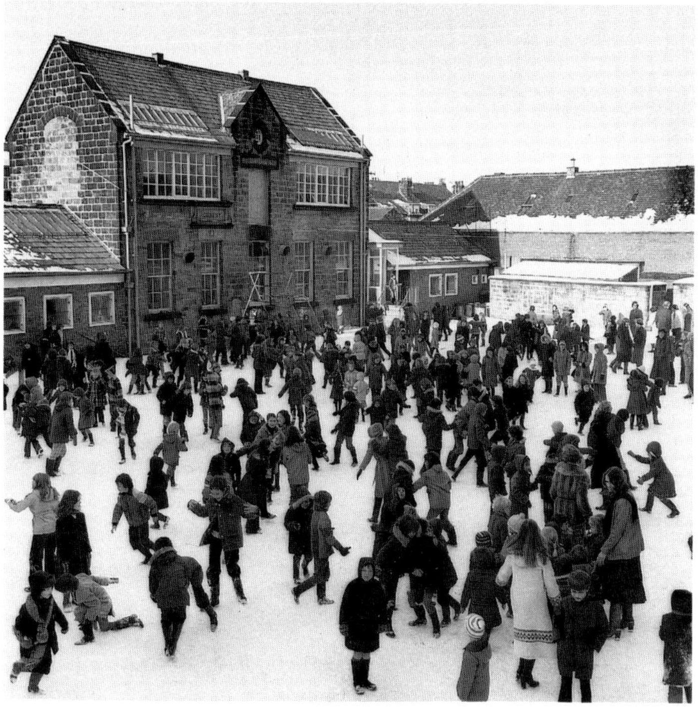

I took this picture for a headmaster in Harrogate in 1979. He wanted to show that there wasn't enough room in the playground. Things don't seem to have changed much since I was at school.

The top of Freehold Street very close to where I gave Mike Howley, the wrestler, a punch on the jaw. It was a lucky punch.

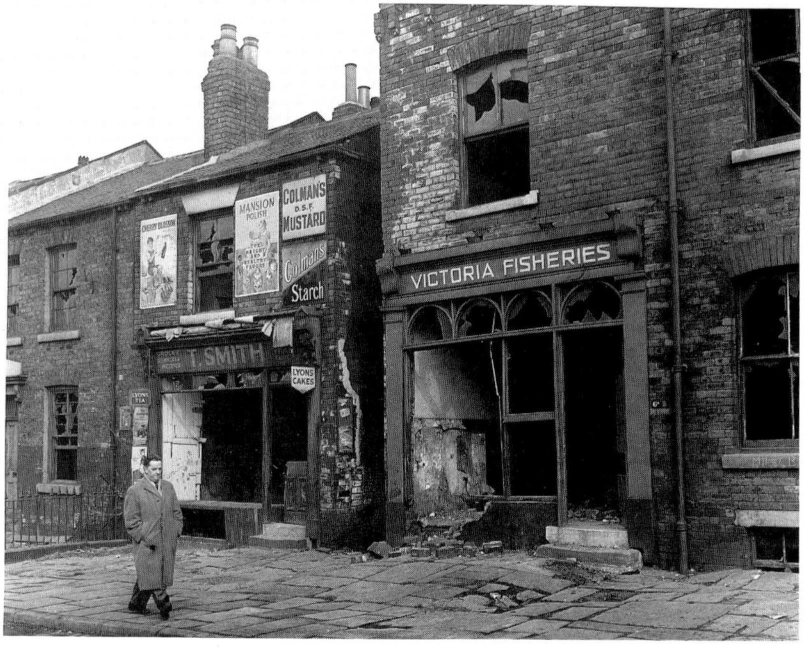

Gabriel and Michael. The Catholic Church depict St Michael with a flaming sword and the motto 'Quis ut Deus' 'Who is like unto God.' Actually the angel appointed over fire was Gabriel not Micheal so the Catholics got it wrong but then we were children of the church and swallowed distortion blinfold.

One lunchtime I ducked school dinner with two friends and went into town. Outside the Town Hall Bert Ramelson, the full time industrial organiser of the Communist Party, was lecturing a crowd on the benefits of communism and the stranglehold that Christianity had on people's minds. When he saw us three lads and recognized our school caps he began slagging off Catholic idolatry and the Virgin Mary. We started a slanging match. Bert was a past master at handling insults and soon had us looking foolish but before we retreated we decided to tip him off his soap box. An old man standing near overheard our plan and approached.

'Can I have a word lads?'

We took him to be a fellow traveller and expected a further argument, but instead he handed me a piece of paper on which he had been writing.

'Get these books out of the library and read them.' With that he turned and walked away without another word.

On the paper were written the titles of three books, Madame Blavatski's *Secret of the ISIS Unveiled*, Thomas Paine's *The Age of Reason* and Frazer's *The Golden Bough*. I took them out of the public library and read them. The doubts which first crossed my mind in the priest's house when I was having instruction on Wednesday evenings were reinforced and a year and a half later I stopped going to church altogether.

Faith is nice but doubt gets you an education.

◆

The industrial appetite of Leeds in 1948 demanded a steady supply of foundry fodder. Schools like St Charles' supplied the necessary quota. I thought 'Stuff that.' Leonardy had gone labouring in a brush factory, Duce was unemployable but the powers that be had put me down for an apprenticeship as a lithographic artist. Dad wasn't having any of that.

'What the bloody hell! Seven years at 15 shillings a week – you expect me to keep you!'

'It's a skilled job, Dad,' I whined.

'Well, what the hell is it anyway?'

'Don't know, it's something to do with pictures.'

'What do you mean you don't know? How can you do a job you don't know?'

'I'll be learning, Dad.'

'Seven bloody years! Not sodding likely, you can go get a job!'

His reaction annoyed me. He wanted a quick financial return while I had been pleased as I looked upon it as a step up.

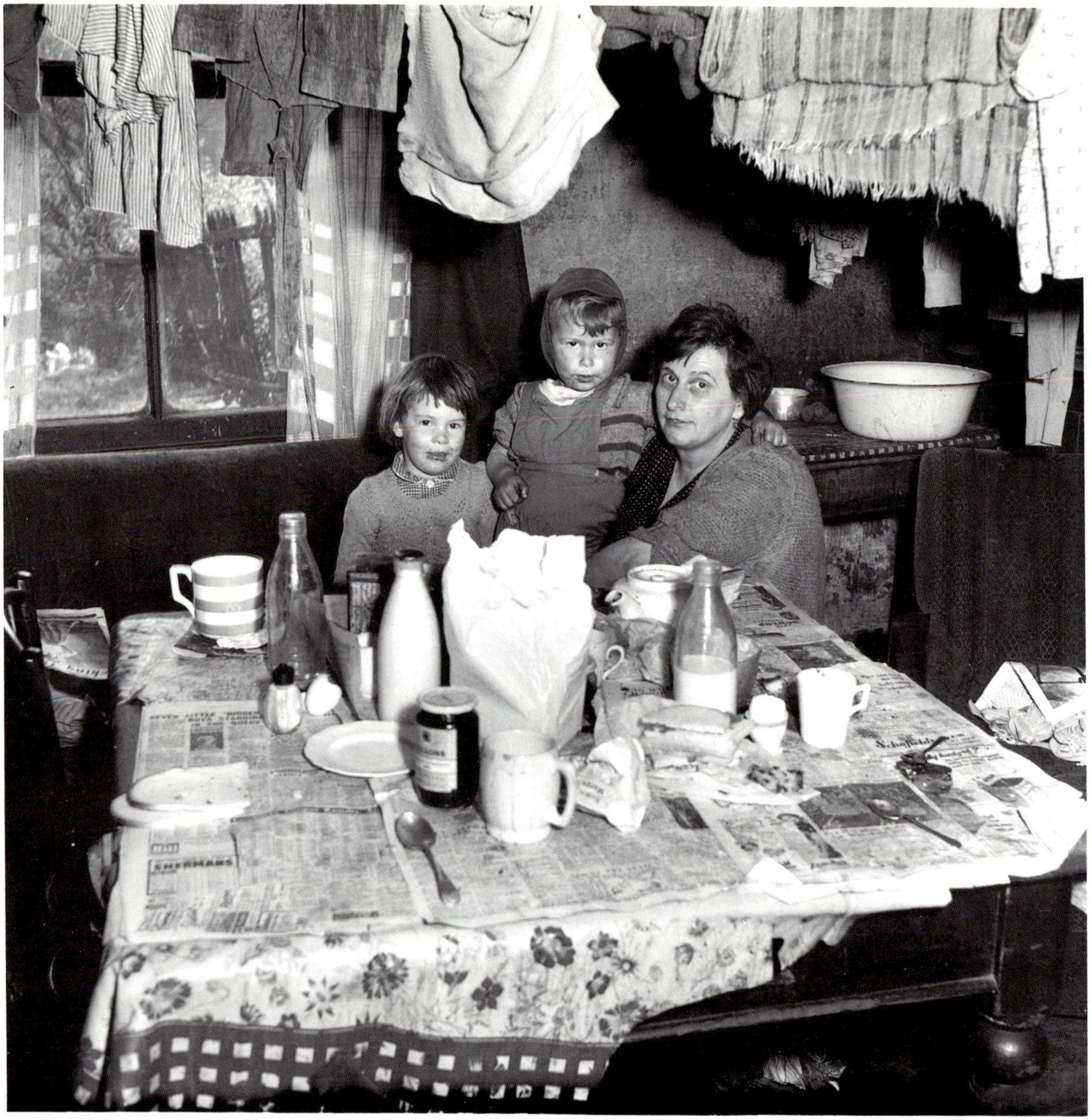

Reggie Marks was the headmaster of a school for children with learning difficulties. He wanted me to help him to get some families rehoused from Camp Road. I went to this woman's house, pointed the camera, clicked and this is the result. Camp Road was pulled down some time later. Reggie was a man who gave me good advice. He once walked into a party where I was out of my head on purple hearts and benzedrine. He said, 'Terry you're a special photographer and you're just dissipating your psyche, whoring and boozing – you ought to pack it in.' And I did.

My mate Billy Bowskill was working at a developing and printing firm and got me in at 29 shillings a week. My jobs were glazing contact prints on a rotary and helping to mix bulk formulas in one hundred gallon lots. This involved weighing out chemicals in exact quantities and mixing in a special order. The names were magical; pyrogol, bromide, eikonogen, gold chloride. I felt like the sorcerer's apprentice. The job seemed to come naturally and the boss, well-pleased, gave me a shilling a week rise. A few months later a man offered me a job as a messenger boy delivering photostats and blue prints round Leeds' engineering works. This appealed to me as it involved a form of photography and paid 2 shillings a week more which hopefully could be supplemented with a little fiddling of the postage money.

I was like Dad, a real chancer. He would bend the law but in his dealings with friends he was straight as a die. Although politically he bent to the left, in business sound capitalist principles were employed; maximum profit, minimum outlay.

A photographer is the ultimate chancer. Photography is a purely contemporary experience. You snap up a moment in time and hope that you get it right. If there's one thing that Dad taught me it was to seize an opportunity. An old Jewish gentleman would meet him at the market once a month to buy small silver charms to attach to bracelets. Dad sold them to him at 2 shillings each and the old lad would buy as many as he could get. Over the months Dad became friendly with him and in a rare moment of charity told him he could get them from Woolworths, like he did, at a tanner each.

◆

On November 5th 1949 the Saville Green slum was still standing although sporadic demolition was taking place. A huge crowd had gathered on The Oller round a large bonfire. They were celebrating the cruel burning of a Catholic. I was wearing a pair of suede shoes borrowed without the permission of my stepbrother. In the crowd were some of the Green Road gang, keeping a low profile. They were after something. A few weeks before I had had a ruck with the youngest of three Collinsons who were the putative hard case family in that crowd. The odds were they were looking for me so there was going to be a confrontation. The drill was that they would put forward one of their lieutenants who they felt could give me a good kicking and so redeem some of their lost prestige.

I kept close to the few people I knew, aware unfortunately that none of them were hard cases but kids who would be gone like a turd off a stick at the first sign of aggravation. Nowhere in the crowd could I see a reliable face. Pete Simpson, Tommy Duffy and the like, really hard men and family friends, were absent. This could cost and I felt that to slip away would be the best plan.

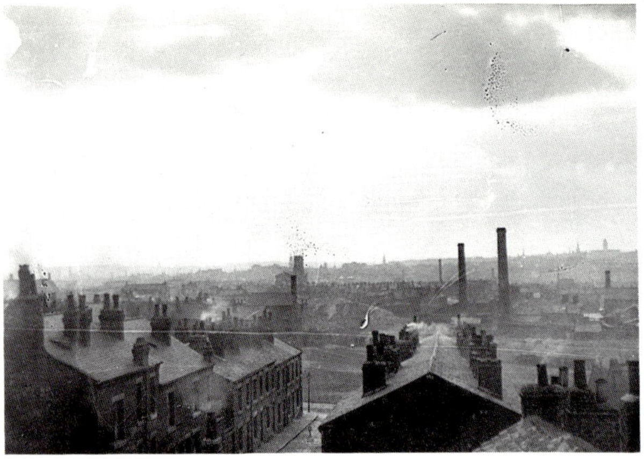

A photo I took with my box camera from the roofs while we were chasing pigeons. This was taken at nearly 11 o'clock at night. In the late 1940s the clocks went back and forward two hours instead of one. They called it double summer time.

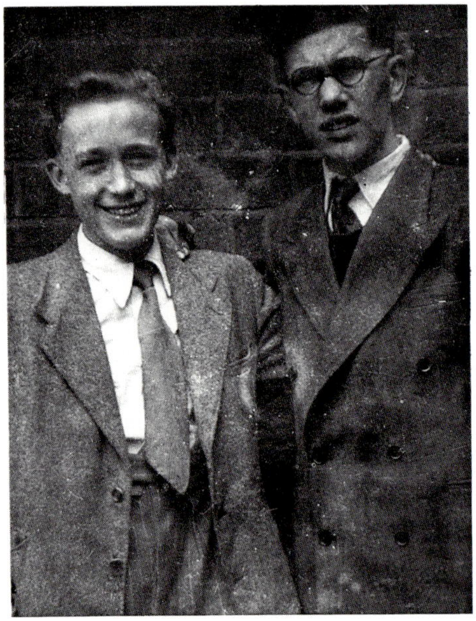

Duce and Me. Duce ended up in Caracas Venezuela and as far as I know he's still there. I was once in Caracas, for just twenty minutes. I stepped off the plane to see the tarmac being raked with machine gun fire. I ran over to the booking office and got the next flight out.

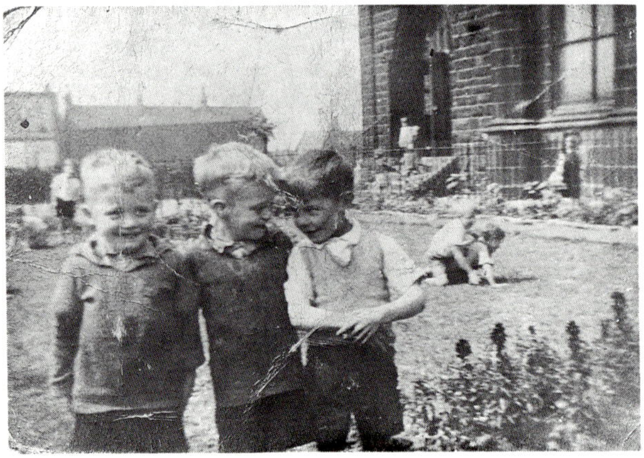

Me, brother Peter and cousin Brian at school in York Road, Leeds.

As I was debating my tactical withdrawal an old enemy Nicker Thompson approached. I had had a slight altercation with him at the Star Cinema some months before but it came to nothing as the staff intervened before I could kill him. He was a third rate thing in the Green Road Gang but tonight he was going to settle matters. 'Hey Cryer,' he called, 'I hear you're looking for me.' He was medium height, unintelligent and very loutish, with a loose mouth and a head that swaggered. My borrowed suede crashed into his groin, he doubled forward and I grabbed his hair and kicked him two or three times in the face. After that he was done for but I wasn't. Taking him by the hair and one arm I swung him round and round, each time sending him closer to the fire. The crowd were shouting, they were going to get a real Guy Fawkes. With every turn the light caught his face. Blood was streaking out from his nose splashing the spectators who got too close. The Collinsons were trying to get at me but were held back by the few who wanted to see foul play. One to one dirty fighting is seen as fair, but five to one is not on when playing away from home and the Green Road mob had picked the wrong arena.

In a street fight a tremendous amount of energy is used in a very brief space of time, adrenalin floods the system then fades, weariness rapidly overtakes, there's no victory in delay. My anger had subsided; I couldn't throw him in the fire in cold blood. The Collinsons had lost face, the crowd although on my side were a bit unhappy at the obvious lack of sportsmanship and the way I had beaten him.

That's the style of survival in mean streets. You have to be good at something or end up in the shit. The fact that I was good at fighting allowed me to remain myself in an awful place.

◆

The year after the war was a good time for slum proles. There was no shortage of work; things buzzed around road repairs, dustbins, factories, sweat shops, labouring. The pubs were filled seven nights a week. There were, however, very few opportunities for kids to grab a share, few that were legal anyway. Paper boys could make five shillings a week, but had to get up at six o'clock. Stuff that! We had to be prized out of bed ten minutes before school started.

Good stewardship around the district could earn a little coin. The very youngest of us could rive up floor boards from derelict houses, chop them up into small chips and sell them for firewood at sixpence a bundle. As you got older and wiser, lead became the prize, kitchen pipes, outside lavs and flashings from roofs.

The possession of lead without valid proof of ownership was a criminal offence; its very nature also made it difficult to conceal and transport. In order to change its shape and thereby disguise its origin we melted it down in Boyle's Quarry and poured it into the frog of a house brick, making it into nice, shiny little ingots. We carried these to a bent scrap dealer where they fetched seven pounds a hundredweight. It took several trips to make it worthwhile. On one such trip Duce got his collar felt and spent two days on the long bench in the town hall nick. After that we decided to move out of lead and into protein.

All major cities have in common a large natural resource, pigeons, and we were going to harvest them. The method used was simple. We got several yards of cobblers' thread with a noose at the end and placed a few bits of bread in the noose. Down came a pigeon, a flick of the arm and the bird was caught. On a good Saturday morning two of us could take six or seven birds and sell them in Leeds market. Prices varied according to the markings. A plain chequered or blue barred fetched 1/9d; white tips to the wings 2/- and white tips and a white head 2/6d or even 3/-. On a bad day when sales were poor we took them to MacFisheries on Boar Lane. There the manager gave us 1/6d each with the feathers and feet off. Who knows from wood pigeons?

Eventually our activities started to attract attention and on several occasions one or the other of us got threatened or chased by outraged citizens. Most were women. Although what we were doing was in no way illegal, the law did get involved when the birds we had caught had racing pigeon rings on their legs. I had noticed that when the MacFisheries manager was paying us off, his pencil had about twelve such rings decorating it.

'They're nice,' I said, hoping he would give them to me. 'Where did they come from?'

'These? Oh, we bought a batch of game from one of the stately homes in North Yorkshire.'

It's nice to know the peasants and aristocracy have something else in common besides pissing in the sink.

Eventually inclement weather and an outraged public made us rethink. For a year we had done quite well but we were now a year older we needed more money. It was Leonardy who came up with an ingenious idea.

'Look at that house on the end of Freehold Street.'

'I'm not doing any house, besides what are they going to have worth a toss?' I was already in a spot of bother over a football.

'No, look at the roof up at the point, near the chimney. Pigeons have been coming in and out for a bloody year. We'd get fifteen or twenty in one haul.'

'Sod that, Len, at this end of the street the bloody houses are three stories high, that chimney is sixty feet up. What if we get seen?'

'We won't get seen if we go up at night.'

'Sod that.'

In the end he convinced me that it was a good risk if the logistics were worked out. Leonardy and me did a recce. The only house at the back with a safe fallpipe was eight houses up. As there was a yard gap between each pair, that meant that a good fifty or sixty feet up there was a yard gap to jump; three times there and three times back in the dark.

At night there was little or no chance of us being seen once we were up. The street lights were gas lamps about nine feet tall and no one could see the sky above unless there was a full moon. We decided to have a crack at it.

The pubs were full by 9 o'clock. It was only two years after the war and most people were still celebrating the rich pickings war provided; black market, fiddles, factory work, overtime. The pubs called time at 10 o'clock, then twenty minutes supping up time and queue at the chip shop. The drunks wouldn't be home till 11 o'clock. We'd got two hours. It was a perfect night, cloudy and no moon. Leonardy was the first up and he went like a greased rat. I followed and Duce after me. Getting over the lip of the roof was the hardest, then came the forty degree crawl up to the ridge where we sat elated, feeling like gods. We were in a new world. Trains hooted and shunted over at East End Park; lit up trams glided down York Road. We could see down into the street but we were confident that they couldn't see us.

We ran along the ridge, one stockinged foot either side of the coping. The yard gaps we jumped were terrifying and the thought of having to do them on the return was a bit disturbing. Leonardy coped amazingly. In all other respects he was next to useless but on a roof he was like a monkey.

The hole in the slates wasn't quite big enough to allow easy access so we enlarged it and piled the slates up on the chimney stack. Getting from the hole up in the peak down onto the beams below was a problem we hadn't foreseen. The drop was about nine to ten feet so jumping down was out. However, the original builders had left the odd brick jutting proud in various places. These, combined with decaying lime cement, afforded fingerholds so me and Len climbed down leaving Duce sitting on the hole to prevent any escapes. Panic stricken birds were flapping all over the place. To catch them meant leaping about on the beams a foot apart. We surveyed the situation, holding a stub of candle nicked from St Pat's church, and decided to go for the squeakers, the baby pigeons. That night we got seven and three adults, two of which were Tipper Pabs, one with a racing ring; it was a good haul. We stuffed the birds in our windjammers and climbed out.

Getting back wasn't as bad as we had anticipated, but getting off the roof onto the drain pipe was a nightmare. Going up you can see where things are but coming down you're blind. I'll never forget that first time and throughout I never liked that part of the operation.

These loftings became frequent events and we

spread our activity all over the Leeds 9 area, including churches and factories. Our worst time was in winter when the rain gutter was filled with ice and the roofs became a foot deep in snow. We still did it though and sometimes on our way to school we would look up and see our footprints on the roofs. Nobody else seemed to notice. I suppose most people in that area tended to walk with heads down hoping to find a tanner in the road.

We kept up lofting for about eighteen months but then Leonardy fell off a couple of roofs. He got away with it once when he fell into a privet hedge, but the second time he ended up in hospital. Although he wasn't badly hurt we decided to quit.

◆

Mick Howley was a professional wrestler. A communist and a hard case, he had a reputation for hitting people, women as well as men and small boys. One afternoon I was on my way to a back street bookie to place a bet for my stepmother. The bookie's house faced Howley's across a small back yard. As I entered the yard my dog, Laddy, who had followed me, started a fight with a mean little Jack Russell. The Russell was getting the worst of it, a door flew open and out shot Mick Howley. He planted a kick in Laddy's side and followed up with a broom handle. I was outraged and grabbed at the broom, he swung round and slapped me violently round the face, dropped the broom and pinned me to a wall. I was shitting myself as the awful truth of my situation dawned, then he made his mistake. He stepped back and in blind panic I crashed my right hand to the side of his jaw. He dropped spark out. Christ my lucky day! I was on him in a flash and pounded his head on the stone steps. By now his wife had appeared and seeing the perilous state of her husband she grabbed me by the hair and hauled me backwards. Mick was coming round, blood pouring from the back of his head. He was a professional fighter and used to ignoring injuries so I decided for my own well-being to sod off. Breaking the wife's grip on my hair and leaving her with a good handful, I shot off across the yard through the crowd of punters who were enjoying the spectacle of Howley getting a thrashing from a fourteen year old. A small wall barred my way. I cleared it with two feet to spare. Old man Dunkley told me later he wished he could back horses over the sticks the way I cleared that wall.

◆

On Saturday nights we all went to the 101 Rhythm Club, a dance hall at the back of Leeds market. In the late 1940s this was a favourite hangout for the black population. We idolized them. They wore the most incredible zoot suits and wonderful wide brimmed trilbies. After one session and a half of bitter I jumped down a flight of stairs and ripped the tendon in my ankle. At the hospital my leg was plastered up to the knee and on Monday morning, with stout encouragement from my dad, I reported for work. In two days of wet weather I walked the bottom out of the cast. I spent half a day at the hospital having it re-done and lost half a day's pay, a percentage of which was stopped out of my half a crown spending money.

◆

Halfway through my seventeenth year I enlisted in the Army. I had had a succession of jobs, all to do with photography; reproducing legal documents, engineers' plans, that sort of thing. For a while I worked for Geoffrey's Studios on Boar Lane, a cheap studio but very profitable. On a Saturday they could get through 150 to 200 sittings with set lighting, 15 x 12 paper negatives, 12 quarter plates to each sheet printed by reflection in an epidiascope. I was shown how to use it one morning and told to get on with it. By the end of the second day I was quite competent. I also had to develop all the films brought in by customers,which amounted to about 50 a day. I liked this as it meant locking myself in a dark room, sometimes with one of the girls who did the bookings. We only kissed and cuddled and often the films were grossly over-developed. I suppose I'm a good printer today because I've had so much practice with bad negs.

Things at home were deteriorating. By this time my father had remarried and he and my stepmother were constantly rowing; there were slanging matches every night. In the end Peter ran away and found our mother in Halifax. Round about the same time I got chickenpox. Dad shut me in my room and said, 'If you can't go to work you're not going out at all.' I climbed out of the window, took my stepbrother's bike and set off to my mother's. I lost my way on Gelderd Road on the outskirts of Leeds and came back home. In retrospect I'm glad I didn't make it. I didn't really want to go to my mother's. It was more of a protest against my father.

Two of my stepbrothers were doing National Service. Money was short. Most of my mates were getting themselves ready for National Service, and almost everybody appeared to be in uniform. Let's face it, people in uniform had just saved the world. I enlisted at seventeen-and-a-half in the Royal Engineers. I told them I was a photographer and they believed me.

After my square-bashing, watermanship course, mines, explosives, booby traps, field manoeuvres, knots and lashings, bailey bridging and so on, I was sent down from Scotland to the Royal Engineers, 32nd Assault Squadron on Salisbury Plain. In my tests during training I had gained 100% in explosives and booby traps. That wasn't good news; the last occupation in my list of no-no jobs was prodding for mines with a knitting needle. But before I left Scotland a Company Clerk told me that orders had come through for a trainee photographer who was also a regular. This had got to be me. My records were filled with job descriptions and all were to do with photography. The fact that the only cameras I had ever owned were a shoe box and an Ensign Full Vue was no great problem. Who knew that? In my CV I'd also included archaeology, crystallography and bird watching and nobody had questioned so far. I always reckoned it's better to travel hopefully, than to arrive. I suppose I was full of myself at this point in my life. The authorities soon tried to knock it out of me.

On my arrival at the Salisbury camp gate a guard told me to ask for Sergeant Major Pongo and, as I didn't realise this was a send up, I did just that and was marched straight in front of the CO by the outraged NCO.

'Right, Cryer, you are off to a bloody bad start.'

'Sorry sir, but...'

'Silence when the officer's speaking!' screamed Pongo.

The CO opened my orders and read through them. 'It says here you were a photographer in civilian life, Cryer. What kind of photographer?'

'Babies, sir.'

'Well, we've no babies here so forget it. You can work in the cookhouse until we find a spot for you. March him out, Sergeant Major.'

On the way I slipped on the polished floor and put my boot through a door panel. He was right. I had got off to a bad start.

My cookhouse duties were quite simple. First thing in the morning thirty loaves to be cut up into three hundred slices. Then I was company runner till lunchtime. After that there were one-and-a-half hours in the black hole washing up all the cooking pans in cold water.

'Sergeant, can I have hot water? The grease won't shift.'

'No.'

He was articulate, the Sergeant, and sometimes used words with two syllables. What is it about army cooks? In Egypt all they ever did was lie in bed in kitchen whites scratching their balls. The only time I ever ate a decent meal out there was with the dhobi wallahs in Tel El Kabir.

As the company runner I had to dash between camps with bits of paper. One day I was late getting back and there was no time to slice the bread for tea. My excuse was the distances between camps. This was accepted and to prevent further cock ups the CO allowed me the use of his bike. This did wonders for my skiving and enabled me to spend more time at a cafe in the nearest village.

'Part 2 Orders, 1756 Sapper Cryer, report to Company Office, 0900 hrs.' I was wetting myself. The squadron had several flail tanks to explode, mines, not my thing at all. Or was it bailey bridging?

Sod that, the bloody panels weighed a quarter of a ton each and were a six man load, that's about 186 pounds each. My total weight dressed was only 110 pounds and it was a hell of a job lifting myself out of bed on a morning without building triple triples over imaginary ravines.

Pongo marched me in to the CO's office.'Left, right, left, right, mark time, halt! Salute, you dozy little man!'

Me, little? The odious little prat.

'Sapper Cryer.'

'Yes, sir.' The CO was looking at me as if I'd disgraced the regiment.

'Your orders have arrived. Report Monday next to the Home Postal Department in Knightsbridge.'

'Yes, sir.'

'Pick up a travel warrant and a day's ration at 07.30 hours Monday morning. March him out, Sergeant Major.'

Left, right, left, right, all that toy soldier bullshit again. Where the hell was Knightsbridge? At mess call an old soldier put me right.

'You lucky bastard, you're going to London, right in the bloody middle! Picture houses across the road, whores...'

'What's the Home Postal Department?'

'Oh, you'll be sorting Army mail; it's the Post Office.'

That Sunday afternoon I took the CO's bike to Tidworth and sold it for three pounds. Monday morning, fully booted and spurred, I left for London.

On the train to London I used some of the CO's bike money to have a lunch, finishing the meal with Danish Blue cheese. I thought this was very exotic. It was in fact the first cheese I had eaten since I was seven years old.

I was put off cheese one summer's day in 1941 when Jimmy Burton, who could run like Wilson the Wonder Athlete, Spike, Ting and me had pinched an old clay pipe from a cottage behind the church. We had a little black shag in it but not enough so Spike Seymour suggested dried clover knobs. We looked around and found one but not enough to fill the pipe.

'I know, what about dried hoss tods?'

'Tony, you get some dried hoss tods.'

'I'm not going to pick up hoss shit.'

'I'm not going,' I said, 'I've got the pipe.'

In the end somebody fetched a handful from the road and we mixed the whole melange together and stuffed the pipe. Using half a box of stolen Swan Vestas we got it going and saw it crackle and stink like a garden bonfire. That done we sat in a row on the church wall and took it in turn to suck on the stem. Spike could blow smoke down his nose but then he was two years older. We tried with varying success.

'My uncle can make smoke rings.'

'That's nowt, my uncle can make smoke come out of his ears.'

'Gerron!'

'Honest, my dad says so.'

I believed him for years. Afterwards when the pipe finally went out, we put it back on the cottage windowsill and wobbled home at about 2,000 feet. God knows what the horse had been eating. Ma Thompson was putting tea on the table, war time cheese on toast. The smell of it turned me green and I collapsed on the sofa with violent pains in my stomach.

I was put off cheese but it didn't put me off smoking. Nearly fifty years on I still do twenty a day.

◆

Having spent the CO's bike money on the train I had no money for a bus and had to walk in full kit to the Home Postal depot in Knightsbridge.

'You're Sapper Cryer, right?'

'Yes, Corp.'

'What do you mean Corp! What the bloody hell do you think these are?' pointing at his stripes, 'Bloody Scotch mist?'

'Sorry, Corporal.'

'You're one of these bloody photo wallahs for the War Office.' He was waving a list of names in my face when the Sergeant Major came in. I dropped my kit and shot to attention.

'What's your name, laddie?'

'Cryer, sir.'

'How old are you laddie?'

'Nearly eighteen, sir.'

'Have you started shaving, laddie?'

'Yes, sir.'

'Well stand closer to the bloody razor next time.' He turned to the Corporal. 'Send Cryer to 15 Belgrave Square.'

With that I joined two other lads and we stomped off to Belgravia.

The houses in that part of London were unbelievable, great white mansions set all round beautiful squares. We took the basement; four beds, a huge kitchen and pantry. After transit camp and training this was cloud cuckoo land. Hyde Park was just across the road, the West End a five minute bus ride. There were cinemas, museums, no parades or guard duties and with almost everybody in uniform I could get lost in the crowd and wear my blue suede shoes with the white stitching.

Next day we reported to the War Office and were directed to the C3 department, a minor branch of Intelligence. Their offices were situated on a top floor in Greencoat Place, Westminster, over the Army & Navy Stores' warehouse. Inside we were sworn in and made to sign the Official Secrets Act. None of the people in the department were military and most of them worked on photographs snatched from the Eastern Bloc. The photographs were usually of appalling quality. Most were made from 16mm negatives, enlarged, air brushed and so retouched, that in the end they bore no resemblance to the original object. The darkrooms were superb with all the latest and most expensive equipment. We hardly got to use the equipment because most of our time was taken up in classes doing theory. We did go out one day with the head man to photograph Sir John Harding, Chief of the Imperial General Staff, at the War Office. Apart from our practical exams that was the only experience we got with actually taking pictures.

For the exam I was assigned to photograph in St Paul's Cathedral. I was given a half plate Kodak, five double dark slides with glass plates and a Gandolfi tripod but no exposure meter. In those days you either knew the light values or you didn't. I didn't but as the plates were dish developed by inspection in a green light, compensation could be allowed for under or over exposure. The results were quite good and I gained a little confidence.

At night we made for the Nuffield Centre, a refuge for soldiers just off Trafalgar Square. Free tickets for all the London shows were available midweek and when I wasn't washing up at Lyons Corner House, for 2/6 an hour, I went to the theatre. I saw Donald Wolfit in a season of Shakespeare at the Old Vic. Some of the plays I saw twice.

One morning out of the blue we assembled in a room adjacent to the C3 photographic darkroom; sixteen sprogs in a dead straight line down the centre of the room. We had been there 20 minutes when the door opened and in walked the fat CO from the Home Postal Department with an entourage. He hated our guts and mine in particular but as we were under the protection of the War Office we were fireproof to a certain extent. That served to make him even more venomous.

Why were we here but, more important, why was he here? The fat swine walked slowly down the line followed by the Beast, the dreaded Sergeant Major of the HPD. His hatred of me exceeded that of the CO, mainly because of my habit of wearing blue suedes whilst in uniform. He had caught me a couple of times, once while I was sitting on the wing of Field Marshall Montgomery's black Rolls Royce, having my picture taken. It was parked outside our billet so why not?

The CO walked back up the line, the Beast followed. Every now and then he nodded and the Beast wrote something in a little notebook. I stared straight ahead, and had almost reached a state of trance, when they came to a halt in front of me. My eyes were focused through the CO's head on a wall some distance away. That's the secret of being inspected on parade, you must focus your eyes on infinity. The officer can easily get a line on you if you look at him instead of through him; he can tell by the distance between the pupils. If you look at him he presumes you are thinking and thinking on parade is forbidden because it is taken as evidence of an over-developed sense of one's own being. It is dumb insolence and therefore a criminal offence.

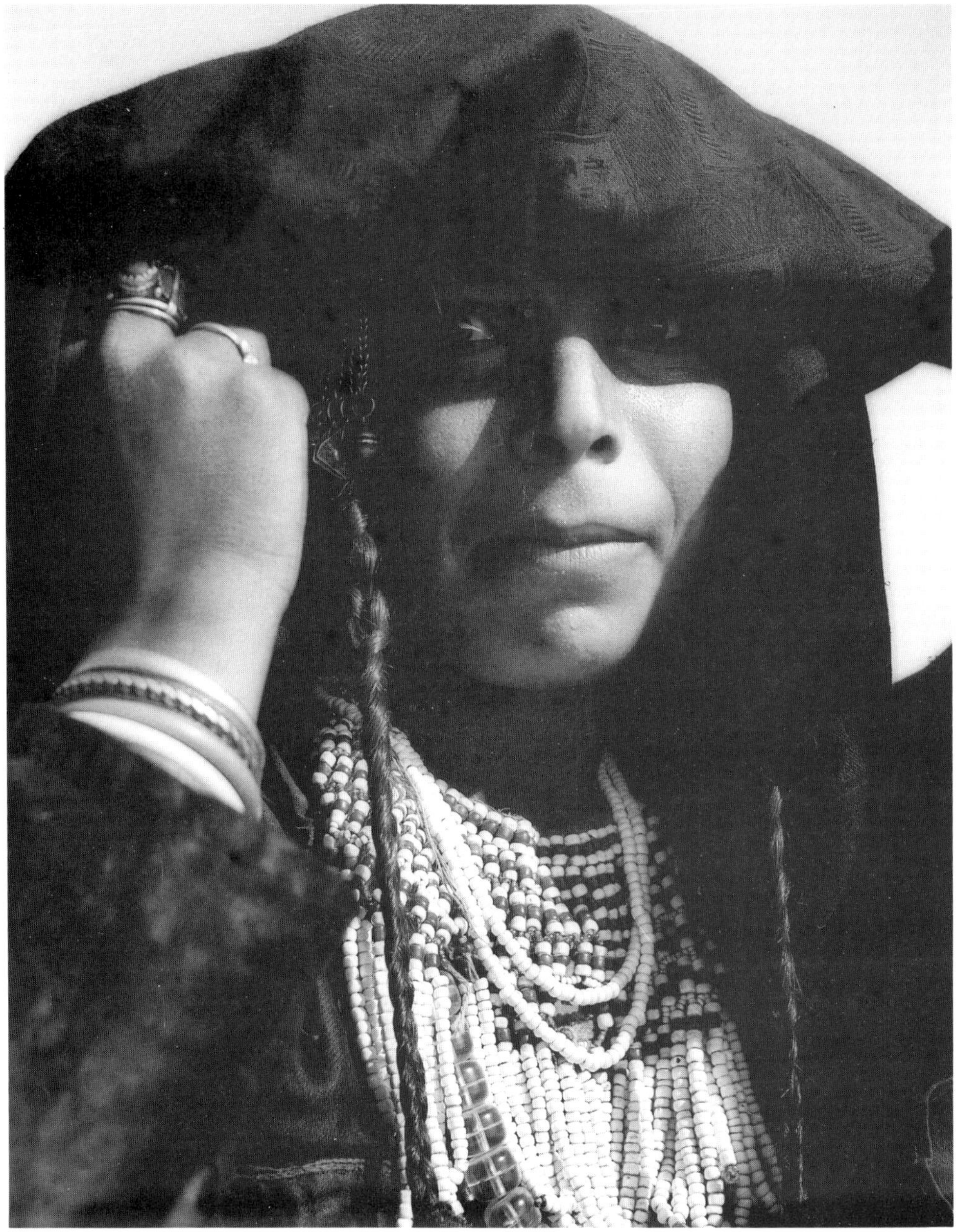

I bought a Rolleiflex at the Hole in the Wall camera shop in Fayed, the same shop where I sold knocked-off army photographic materials. This is the first photograph I took with that camera. This picture opened the door for me; it showed me what the photographic image is all about. I still consider it to be my best ever shot.

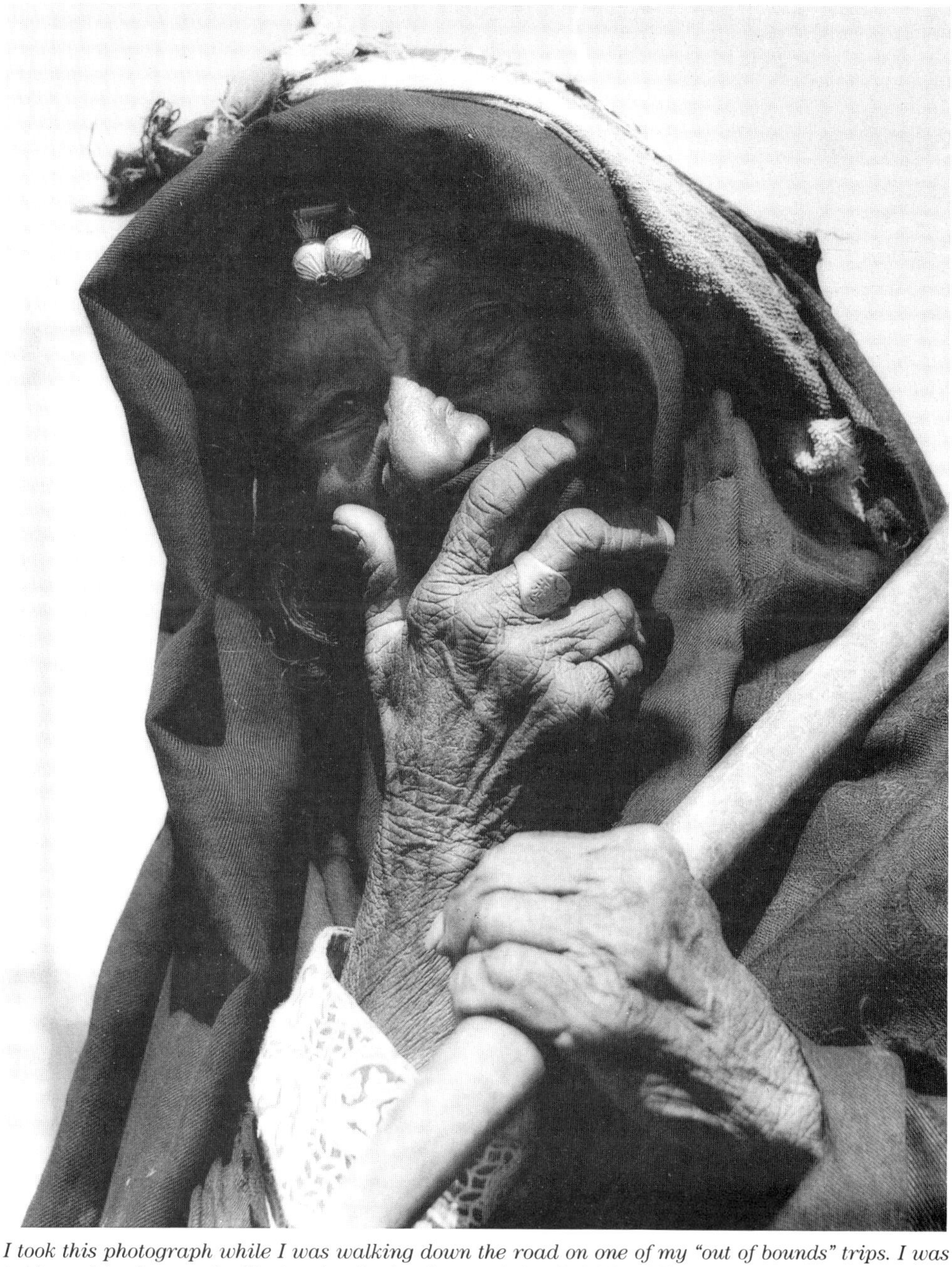

I took this photograph while I was walking down the road on one of my "out of bounds" trips. I was taking a big chance, the Moslem brotherhood were doing British soldiers in, but I tried not to think about the risks.

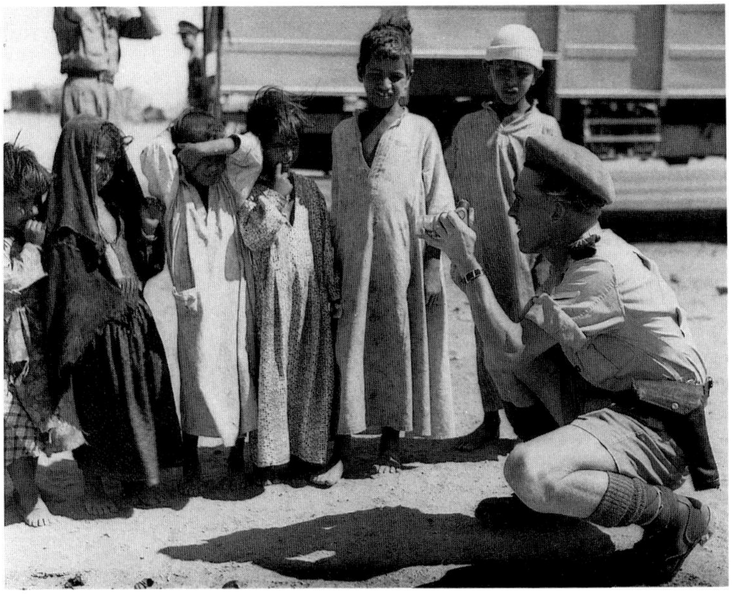

On the Moses route to Mount Sinai I got drawn again to photographing kids. Everybody likes pictures of kids. In that respect it's the easiest type of job. For many years I tramped the streets photographing babies.

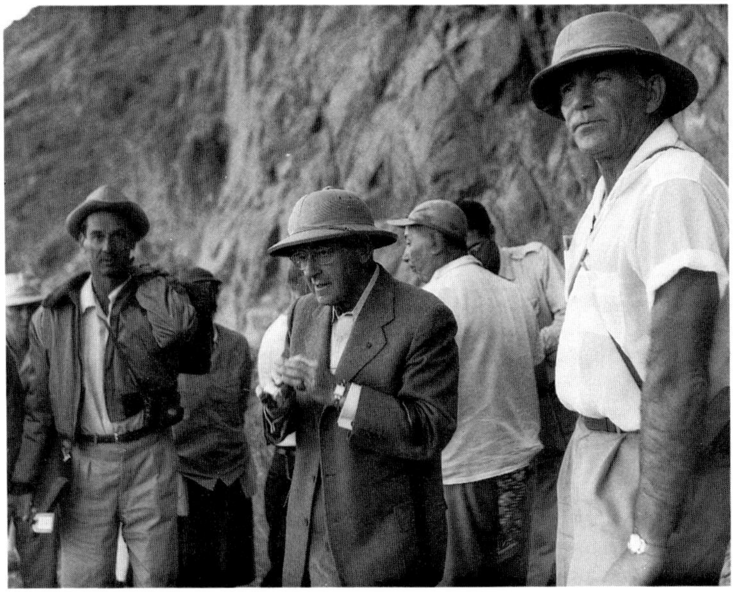

Cecil B. De Mille during the shooting of the Ten Commandments on Mount Sinai. I went up Mount Sinai with Charlton Heston. Cecil B De Mille got me back down with the words, 'Get that boy a camel'.

The fat CO left the room and the Beast read out eight names including mine.

'Go down to the stores at Knightsbridge and draw chevrons at 0800 tomorrow.'

'Chevrons?' I said to Butch.

'That's something to do with goat's cheese.'

It wasn't. They were stripes and I had been promoted to full corporal.

A few days later the beast pulled me up outside the billet.

'Cryer, we've had complaints about you from residents, whistling late at night. You're not fit to live in Belgrave Square, pack your things and move them to Eaton Place, number 42. And watch it.' When I lived at number 15 Belgrave Square, the Chief of the Imperial Staff lived at number 14 and Field Marshall Montgomery at number 16. I often wonder which one shopped me.

◆

My mate Butch and me were working a skive at a lovely little camp on the edge of Lake Timsa in Egypt. It was a cushy posting, proper huts, palm trees, hot showers. Unfortunately, there was a grain of sand in the oyster so it didn't produce a pearl. The irritant was a corporal cook, an odious man, physically dirty, with boils. His cooking was worse than his appearance. This swine even served hot watered milk on cornflakes. One day I saw him drop a whole dixie of hot cooked mince on the kitchen floor. He left it there like a monstrous cow flop while it cooled, then he scooped it up with his hands, put it in a container, covered it with mashed potato, warmed it up and served it at lunch.

The CO selected this man for a special job. Being a bit of a box wallah, somebody who lived by the rules, he had decided that there were too many dogs on camp. These were not wild pariahs but pets of the soldiers, creatures which brought a little comfort and caring into a miserable tour of duty.

National service and regulars had a rotten time in Egypt but Butch and me had it cushy. Whatever camp we were in it took weeks for the War Office to connect so we had days on end to swim and lark about. We did no parades, no inspections and in three years I only did one guard command and that was a favour for a mate.

Lance Corporal Harry Stapleton came into the billet. 'Come outside and just look at this silly pillock.'

'Who?'

'The fat little arsehole from the cook house. He's gone bloody mad.'

We shot out hoping he had so that we had an excuse to restrain him with the maximum amount of violence. No such luck. Still in his kitchen whites, he was waddling up the camp lines with a shotgun; a side lock, if you please. We watched dumbfounded as he raised the gun and blew the bottom jaw off a

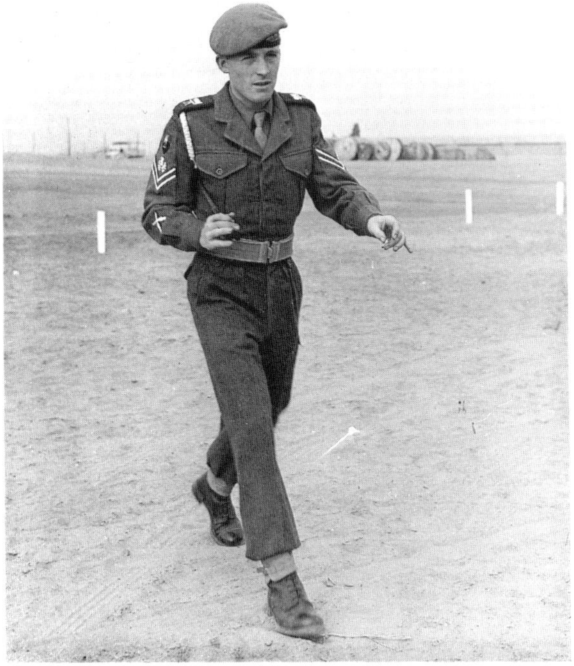

Tel El Kabir. In full dress with swagger stick. One of the few times in Egypt when I bothered to wear a uniform. The beret is khaki, not many soldiers in the British army in Egypt wore a khaki beret.

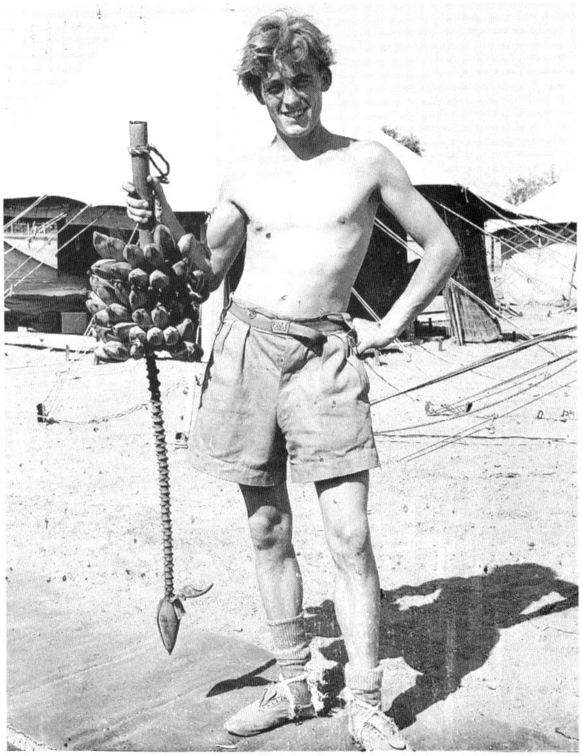

Tel El Kabir. In shorts with bananas. This is more typical of me in Egypt. With nobody in charge of me I was able to run about much the same as I had done in my early days in Leeds ... untamed.

small puppy from about four feet. The dog ran off blood spurting from severed veins. At Ma Thompson's the butcher's lad put old Nell down, clean, fast and with a little dignity.

'That bastard's in deep shit,' Butch said. 'You know whose pup that is?'

Harry Stapleton knew. 'It belongs to that lad convalescing from 9th Para.'

'Jesus, he's going to kill the bastard.'

'They'll hang him if he does, there's a portable gallows at 10 BOD.'

'Then he will die happy knowing he's done for that bastard.'

When the lad heard the news about his dog he broke down and wept but never killed the bastard cook.

That night we sat around in the billet talking mutiny.' The CO's a bastard. He ordered it.'

'Can't see that, must have been the Sergeant Major.'

'No, it was the CO. It was his shotgun.'

Harry Stapleton was right. He'd seen the gun at the Company Office.

'That Para was crying when he found his dog, it was still alive.'

'Crying. A Para. I thought they were hard cases.'

'Don't be a twat, he loved that pup. Hard men do cry.'

I thought of the nights I'd cried myself to sleep in Leeds when I was ten years old.

Death itself didn't particularly worry me. When you are 19 years old you feel immortal. Death is always a possibility when you are a soldier in a foreign land and if it came I hoped it would be quick and clean, no less than that for an animal.

Then I thought why mutiny when we can go and play fuck with the CO's garden? So we jumped up and down all over his water melons.

The army in Egypt was vicious, pointless and boring, unless like me, you could get out of bounds. Egypt was one of the birthplaces of civilisation but the British Army brutalised it.

I served a month over my time in Egypt and so did Butch. We were demobbed together on 27 April 1955, flown back to the UK in a York, kitted out with appalling Burton's demob suits and turned loose.

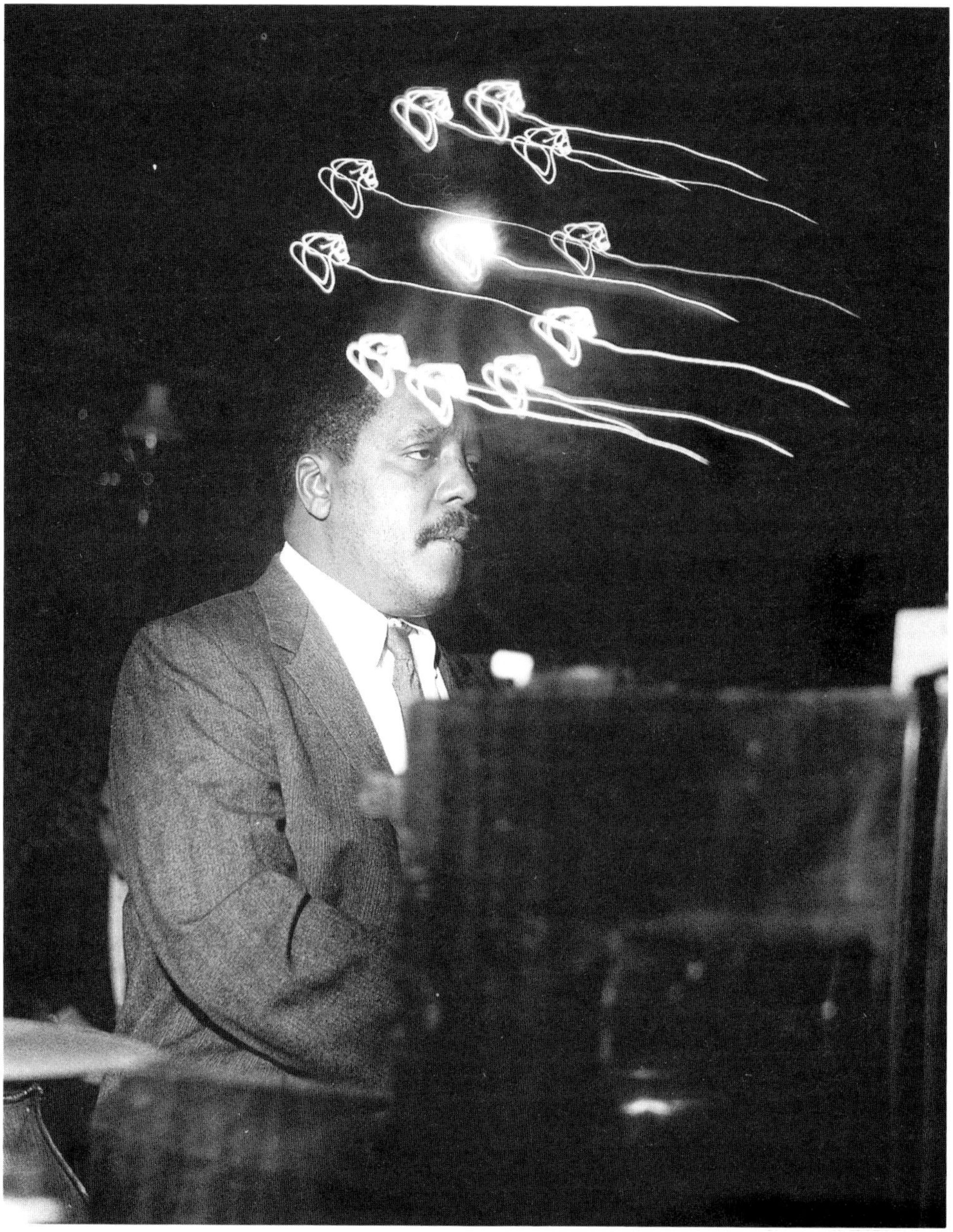

Bud Powell at the Blue Note, Paris. I got a job as a freelance for the Jazz News. I faked myself credentials by cutting out photographs from obscure local newspapers that couldn't be checked on and I got myself a press card. Was this honest? Who cares. I broke the rules because it was a lot more exciting than following them. The establishment move the goal posts to suit themselves. Why shouldn't I?

When I got back to Leeds the first thing I noticed was that things hadn't changed much, a few more slums demolished, Armley Nick still overcrowded. Jobs were a buyer's market, menial and underpaid. It wasn't so bad for National Service men, most of them had guaranteed places, but regulars were regarded with suspicion. I signed on at the dole centre but by the second week they said, 'Get a job or no dole,' and offered me an interview at British Rail.

'Have you got a pencil, Mr Cryer?' Had I got a pencil? I had a bloody Schaeffer with a gold nib and was wearing a Rolex Oyster.

'Yes,' I said, biting my lip.

'Right. Go down that corridor to Exam Room Number Two and sit at one of the desks.'

The room was half full of men all at desks. By the look of their haircuts they had all recently been demobbed. A man came in and gave us all a handful of papers.

'This is a small exam. Will you try to answer all the questions as best you can?' Looking at the paper I almost laughed, this was going to be a doddle. In the Army we were always sitting exams and tests so after a bit of practice, exams presented no difficulty. This one was no different and with my glowing Army CV attached, a job was in the bag. Sure enough a few days on, a letter arrived, 'Please report Monday morning 8.30.'

I pressed my demob suit, washed a shirt, bulled my shoes and reported prompt. An inspector took me up Leeds Railway Station to a small hut in the middle of the concourse. Inside he handed me a dog tag with a number on it and a large sweeping brush with a head about a yard across.

'Take this brush and sweep the pavement in front of the Queen's Hotel. After that, do the main concourse which should take you to about 11.30, then come and find me.'

I was gobsmacked, a bloody street sweeper and me in my best suit! My mind was groping for insults sufficiently offensive to tell him what to do with his sodding brush. I stopped to think, 'Was I too proud to sweep a street?' The answer to that was obvious, 'Yes, I bloody well was.' But then I had to live with myself; I couldn't chicken out at the first obstacle.

The pavement in front of the Queen's Hotel was about twelve feet wide, hence the big brush. There wasn't much litter about as junk food outlets hadn't been thought of. Most of the rubbish was dog ends and tram tickets. I pushed these into a neat straight line across the pavement, then I moved forward each alternate yard to make a kind of military formation. From there I pushed on into a redoubt and then a spearhead, slowly advancing, glaring occasionally at clumsy pedestrians walking across the pattern. By now it was nearing 9 o'clock and trains were spewing out hundreds of office workers. Looking up I saw coming straight towards me five girls; two of them were old flames. This and me in my best suit and highly bulled shoes.

The inspector was having a pot of tea in his hut.

'You can stick your frigging job and the bleeding brush,' and I threw it across the floor.

'I'll have to report this.'

'Report what the bloody hell you like, mate. I didn't do three years as an NCO in the Royal Engineers to end up sweeping streets.' He muttered something, I stormed off and was back in bed by 9.45.

Next day the dole clerk handing me my cards said, 'Mr Cryer, you're struck off' and smiled. This wasn't the first time a Jack-in-Office had tried his best to make my life uncomfortable. When I flew back from Egypt the customs at Stansted Airport charged me £90 on my two year old Rolleiflex camera. The English have a charming way of rewarding 25 months of dysentery, sunburn and rotten food.

◆

After the debacle at British Rail things got very tight. I was sharing a flat with Billy Bowskill and Brian Goldsborough in Chapeltown and they kindly supported me with the rent. Billy was a photographic printer at the Yorkshire Post and Brian was a banjo player of immense talent with the Yorkshire Jazz Band. It was through Billy six years earlier I had been introduced to the mysteries of printing photos, and now he opened another door, jazz. We had been mates since childhood. Billy had done national service in the RAF where he had got his taste for the music. He is a full time jazz musician now, a double bass player, but at that time he was messing about with a trumpet. He started off traditional. It was him who took me to Studio 20, the only jazz club in the North of England at the time.

He was always a sharp dresser while I was a scruff, never fashionable. It was the way I was brought up. Billy was very fashionable. Influenced by what he saw on newsreels, he had a strong leaning towards Teddy Boy stuff; full drape, blue suede crepes and a duck's arse hair style.

They had a radio in the house and we didn't. Billy used to listen to a lot of music. Radio Luxembourg and Voice of America always played a lot of jazz. There was a Musicians' Union ban on in the fifties which meant that American musicians couldn't come over to Britain unless British musicians went into the USA on a reciprocal agreement. The first band to come over and the first band I photographed was Louis Armstrong's Allstars. They were followed by Eddie Condon, Duke Ellington, Woody Herman and Jazz at the Philharmonic. I photographed them all.

For a while Bill did the printing as I didn't have a darkroom but eventually I took a flat on my own and used a kitchen which had no exterior windows. For a safe light I used my red nylon army vest wrapped around the bare bulb. After a while the heat of the bulb melted parts of the vest so I gave that idea a miss and for a while worked in the dark, gauging development of the prints by guesswork and instinct.

◆

In the summer of 1955 I took a job at Butlin's Holiday Camp, Filey, as a press printer for Len Chetwyn, an ex-army photographer. Len taught me a lot. He used a Kodak Medallist and produced perfect negatives. Ten films a day for sixteen weeks, that is about 11,000 frames. I printed every one including print orders. By the end of the season, with bonuses, my bank account showed only £200 but I was a red hot speed printer.

My experience at Butlin's stood me in good stead because when I got back to Leeds, a firm of photographers in Chapeltown offered me a job. It wasn't much but at least it was photography. Two or three days a week I developed films coming in from chemists' shops. Two days a week I went knocking on doors in mining districts and on council estates photographing babies.

◆

One lunchtime Billy took me to a club called Studio 20 which had just opened in the town centre. Studio 20 was underneath the Odeon cinema in Upper Briggate. It's a Chinese restaurant now. You went down the stairs into a tiny basement about 35 feet by about 25 feet. The lighting wasn't all that low; it wasn't lit for effect. There was a small stage at one end. Steak and chips were served and the sauce was on the counter. Mural silhouettes of musicians playing painted by a student from Leeds Art College were on the walls under a slogan which read 'Gallery Of Fame For Uninhibited Idealists.'

What a lot of bullshit! I can say that now but at the time I thought it was cool and so did a lot of others. People used to come from all over after the word got round. Visiting musicians signed the wall. It's hard to imagine such a club now. There were no bouncers and people wore duffel coats and beards.

I was in at the start when the club had only been going a few weeks. The owner was Bob Barclay, the leader of the Yorkshire Jazz Band, one of the earliest trad bands to be formed in the United Kingdom. Bob looked like a Brazilian, he was thick set with crinkly hair. His real name was Tony Rea.

I went once with Bob and Dave to Manchester to a Louis Armstrong concert. Bob was an important musician and as a consequence got us in anywhere. He was also much older than us and was teaching us the ropes. Half way up Piccadilly on the way home he stopped the car and got out. He crossed to two whores at the side of the road and asked 'How much, love?' One said, 'You can slap me for saying it darling but I don't go with niggers.'

We drove along in silence. The word nigger in 1956 was not recognised for the offensive word that it is. After a few minutes Dave Levine turned to Bob and said, 'Hey Bob, I didn't know you were a nigger.' It came as a surprise to us you see, because we knew him just as Bob. We'd never thought about him being coloured.

Bob brought Big Bill Broonzy to Leeds and Big Bill stayed with him in Brunswick Terrace. Bill Broonzy was a Mississippi feet-in-the-mud-of-the-Delta musician, whose mother lived to be 102. She could remember the slavery days. Him and Muddy Waters were the principal blues musicians of the period. In later years they had a massive influence on British music but in the fifties they didn't have a following in this country apart from being popular amongst the cognoscenti. To bring Bill to Leeds was an important event in musical terms, even though he only played in an upstairs room in Boar Lane. He was refused a drink in The Griffin. When he asked why he was told 'We don't serve Blackies!'

Bill also appeared in a cinema at Castleford. Bob told Bill he was going to go see somebody and he could come for a ride. He took him to a Saturday matinee and during the interval in between Flash Gordon and the Lone Ranger, Bob pushed Big Bill onto the stage and he had to play to a house full of children. Bob pocketed the money and told Bill the appearance had been done as a favour.

Student bands appeared every night of the week at Studio 20 but there was no bar. Bob did steak and chips and chicken and chips. In the fifties this was the only place in Leeds where you could get a meal at midnight. It was so popular that stars at local theatres from all over Yorkshire came back there after their shows. We went every night. Jimmy Rushing came there, as did Basie and the British stars, Ronnie Ross, Joe Harriot, Tubby Hayes and Ronnie Scott. It was natural that I should start taking pictures there.

The first photographs I took of a musician were of Ed O'Donnell. He has just retired but still plays a trombone and has been a big influence on music in Leeds. Sunday lunchtime, Wednesday night and Thursday and Saturday night, he never stops playing. The biggest problem in a little basement jazz dive is smoke because the flash bounces back at you. I realised that I had to put the flash to one side, so that it cuts across the smoke. As time went on I used to give enlarged print copies to Bob in return for free nosh and he put them on the walls. Eventually the walls were covered with my photographs. Although I never thought of it that way it was my first public exhibition. After a time the musicians' agents became interested and I started taking pictures further afield.

It was at Bob's that I met both Humphrey Lyttleton and Chris Barber. Lyttleton was at the club quite often. He said it was the best club he'd played in, other than a similar one in Zurich, Switzerland. He liked clubs where they could play what they liked. He would just turn up and start playing. Chris Barber also came down regularly. Like Humphrey he was a very sharp dresser, they all wore suits on stage with collars and ties.

I spent my Saturdays photographing weddings; some Jewish, some West Indian and the odd Polish one. I got more expert as time passed because there are a few technical considerations when you photograph black faces, especially that of a black bride in a white wedding dress.

◆

The first time I had to consider the technicalities of photographing black faces was once in Egypt. We were booked for the day into Number Ten Battalion Ordnance Depot to photograph four hundred Askaries of the East African Pioneer Corps. At 0900 hours when we arrived the sun was well up and all the Askaries were on parade, kitted out with small pack and bullet pouches.

It took twenty minutes to set up the gear. Everything was standard: two lights, one on either side at 45 degrees, 3ft 6 inch up 4 feet out; two number two photofloods; HP3 film 100th at f8. From then it was standard; each man came in with an eight digit number on a plastic disc across the chest, click, out; next, man in and out in thirty seconds. There were some delays. Most had stretched ear lobes hanging down in a loop about six inches long. On army instructions we had to get them to wrap these up; it looked as if they had a giant Walnut Whip stuck on each side of their face. Only one man had a wrist watch and this was passed down the line for each one to wear, a bit of a futile gesture seeing as we were only doing head and shoulders.

By midday the temperature was well over 100 degrees and there were still 200 men on parade. We took a short lunch and were through by 4.30 and got back to camp just in time to miss tea.

Next day we developed the films; thirteen rolls, one at a time. The developer was 90 degrees and, as there was no ice or fridge, we had to dilute fifteen to one to get the time down to two minutes. We knew by the first film we were up the creek.

The War Office had established a set technique for these pictures but had tested it out on white faces. We had made no allowance for black ones so all the frames were two stops underexposed; all that showed were eyeballs and teeth.

During our time spent in Egypt, Butch and I had made quite a few enemies. We spent most of our day swimming or lying in bed and we dressed pretty fancy. This created envy amongst other ranks and suspicion with the officers but since we were War Office we were fairly fireproof. This disaster, however, could have nasty repercussions. So, like photographers the world over, we blamed the camera.

Two months of skiving passed while our chiefs at Greencoat Place found us another camera. In that time we had a drunken week in Cyprus, spent time swimming in the bitter lakes, and volunteering for a little work at JIBME - Joint Intelligence Bureau Middle East.

When the new camera arrived it was a Reid, the British Leica copy but a load of rubbish. Our first job was to re-photograph the four hundred askaries. The routine was exactly the same but we clipped twenty five minutes off the completion time. That night we developed the film again and found another disaster. The viewfinder that fitted on top of the camera was a Leica accessory of excellent German standard but the shoe on the Reid was badly engineered British; it gave a good eighth of an inch play either side of the parallel. With a 9.5cm lens at four feet we had cut every head off just above the eyes.

This time there was no excuse so we dumped the films and made up a dummy parcel with all the requisite paper work and sent it off to the War Office. There was no comeback and we heard nothing; the package was either lost or the War Office presumed the contents stolen. We were off the hook again.

Some weeks later I decided to photograph a total eclipse of the sun. In doing so I burned a hole through the back blind and melted a small hole in the aluminium pressure plate. The box wallahs at the War Office were very upset. From leaving Southampton to our demob two years later we had got through two Leicas and three Reids.

◆

I liked Jewish weddings because of people's kindness to me, always making sure I left with a parcel of food and a quid note in my pocket. It was my first experience of Jewish hospitality and my relationship with Jewish people became a lifelong love affair.

My record for weddings is five in one day and I was late at all five except the first. Fortunately, as it was the last Saturday before April 5th, the tax rebate day, the churches were fully booked so all the weddings were late themselves.

Every weekend there would be a dance to photograph, punters at tables, 2/6 a postcard. This was my least favourite duty because the dance halls were dark, the punters pissed and the split image finder on the old Leica only good in bright light. Another job entailed taking pictures of actors. Every few weeks a star performed at the Old Empire so my boss had an arrangement with the owners and we did all the publicity pictures. What a grand Variety Theatre that was; it's now a vulgar little arcade used as a short cut from Briggate to the market.

◆

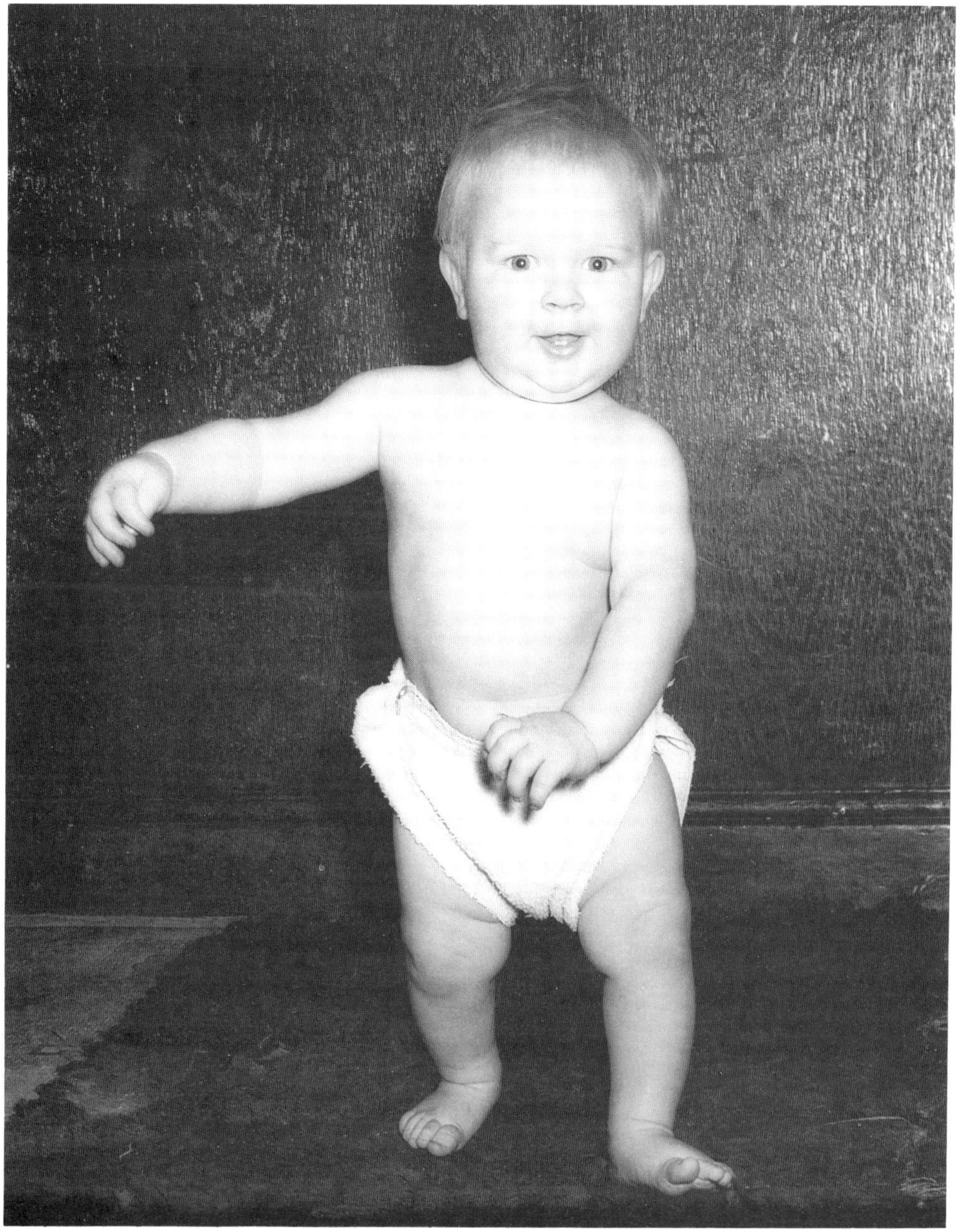

I was dropped off outside baby clinics in Halifax or on terraced streets in Barnsley and gave out Farley's rusks to young mothers. Then I'd take photos of their babies. Later in the week a salesman went round, just to 'show' the pictures. Of course the parents would ask, 'Can I buy one?' It was thirty bob for a 10 x 8 and twelve postcards. I took this one in Castleford. I propped the kid against a wall because he couldn't walk. He fell flat on his face on the peg rug as soon as I took the picture.

In 1957 when I was twenty three I started getting letters from musicians' agents asking if I could cover concerts as far afield as Birmingham and Leicester. Eddie Condon was the first big musician I was commissioned to do in this way. In the end I did all the Barber concerts and the tour of Sister Rosetta Tharpe. I liked her. She had a big reputation in the USA, a woman with tremendous presence and social confidence, a Gospel singer who could sing jazz as well. She also drank large glasses of milk at press receptions but these were liberally laced with four fingers of whisky.

Eddie Condon was an amazing guy and so was his long time pal Wild Bill Davison. They were both two bottles a day men. Bill told me that in his younger days if booze was short he drank Bay Rum Aftershave.

The Basie Band were next and played the St George's Hall, Bradford. I went every night with Black Bob and backstage became very friendly with the band. Some of the pictures from this particular occasion are amongst my favourites, although some of my negatives were, at the time, unprintable. I was a good printer but not good enough. Years later when experience caught up with ambition I managed to make some fine prints

◆

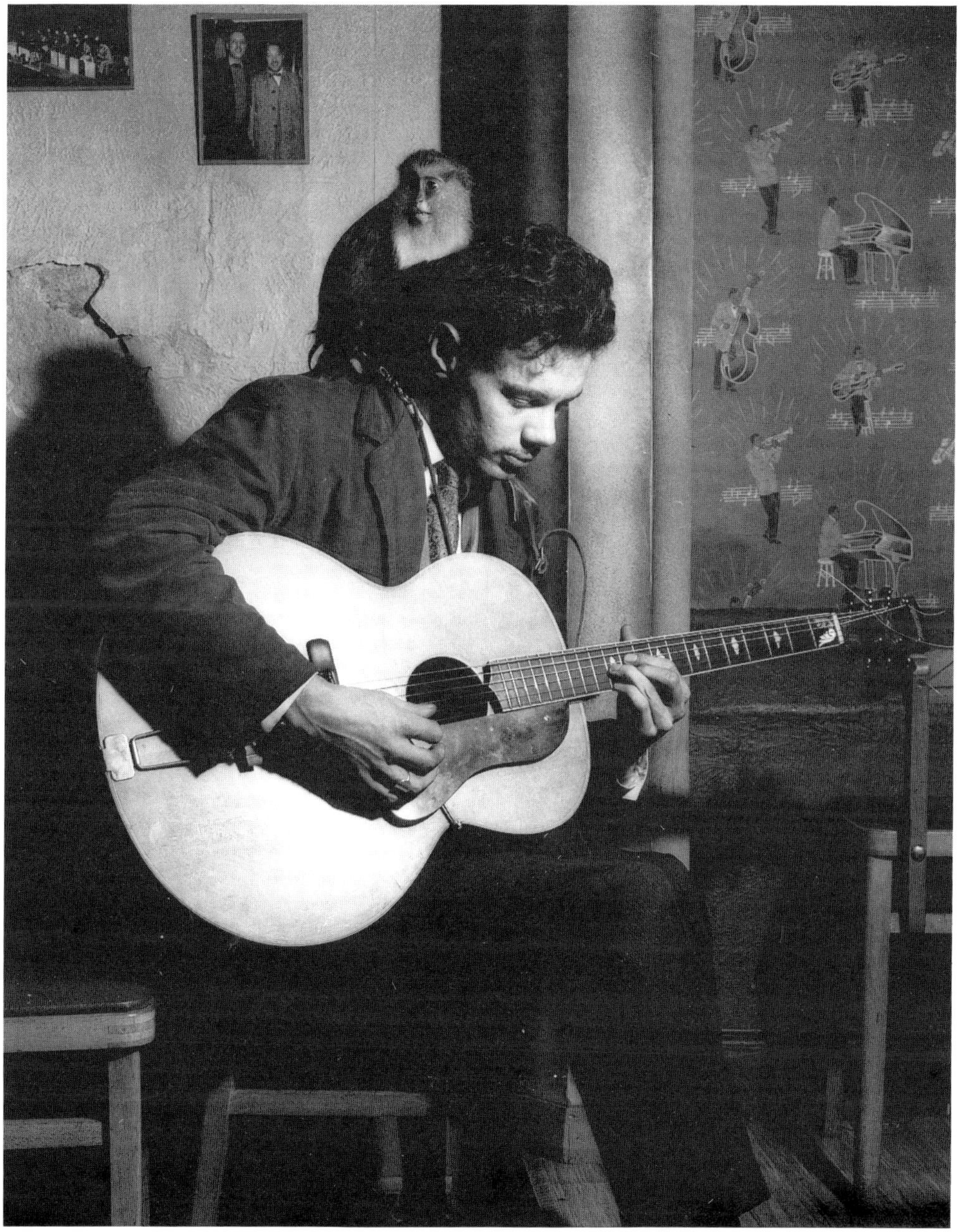

Johnny Booker of the Vipers skiffle group, 1955. The Vipers were one of the first groups to cotton on to the idea of bizarre publicity. They all had pet animals. Johnny had a grass monkey and another one had a Coati Mundi.

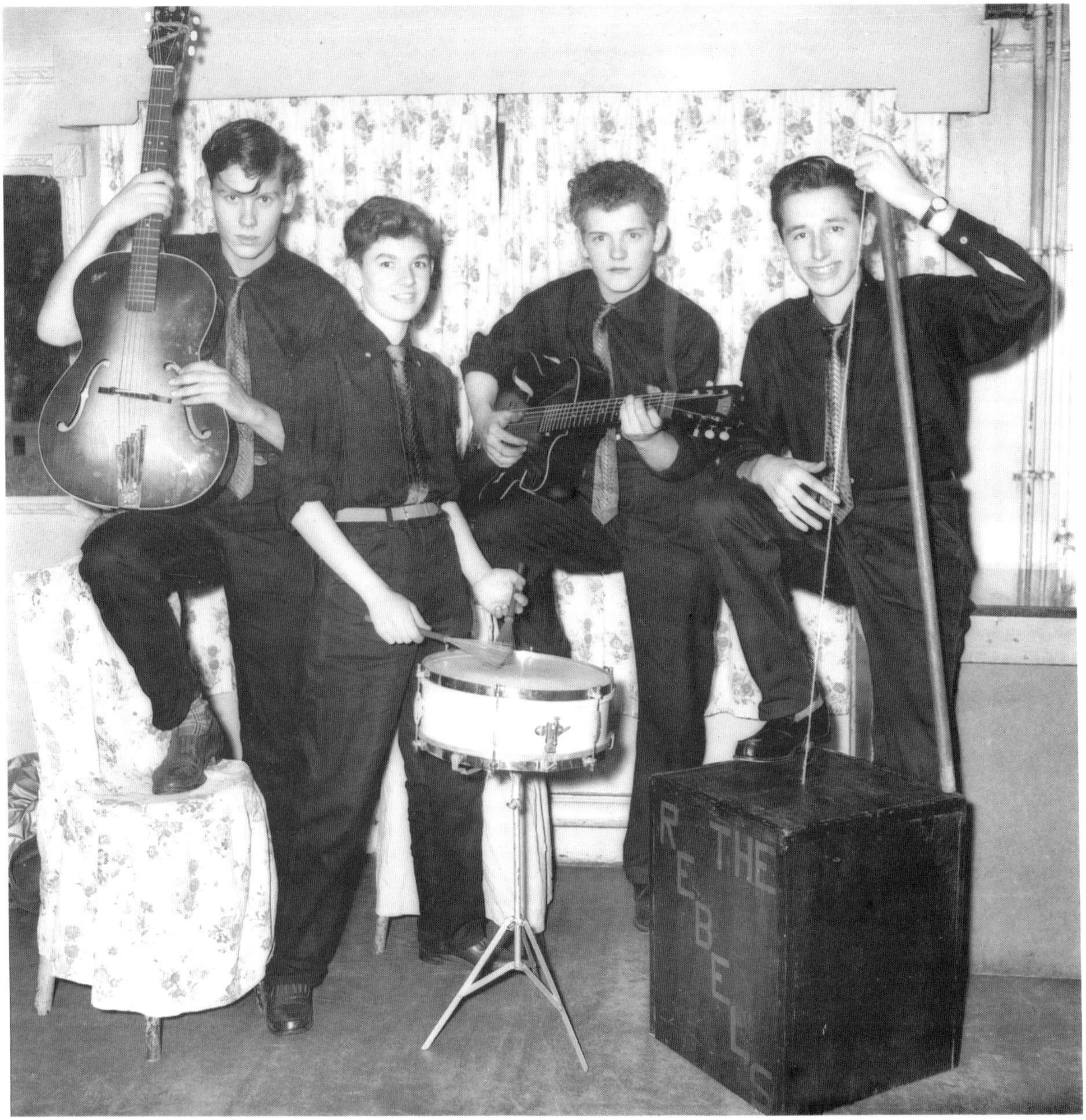

The Rebels. I often think the influence skiffle had on music in this country is underestimated. I used to watch Lonnie Donegan, Chris Barber's banjoist, entertaining at the interval during concerts. He did numbers like "Bring a little water" and "Rock Island line".

Some kids started copying the share croppers who had made guitars out of cigar boxes and a bass out of a tea chest. Skiffle became a bridge between trad jazz and the stuff kids in Liverpool were writing. That's how the Beatles started. Up to then music was written by Americans. In the case of 'The Rebels' they did one gig and were sent back to school.

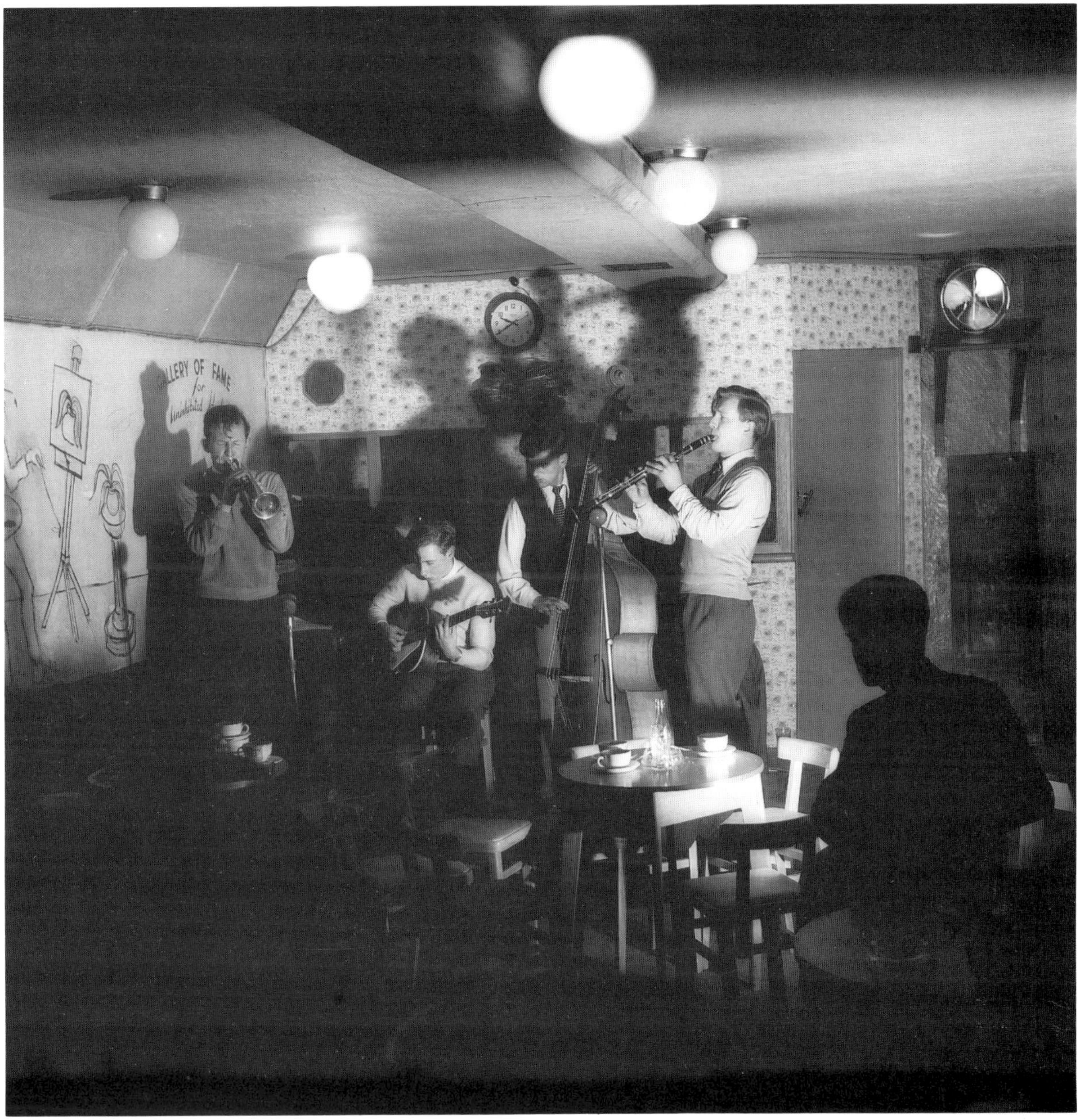

Studio 20 Leeds. The Devon Ramblers. Billy Bowskill is in the foreground on the right firing the flash. We didn't have a sync lead.

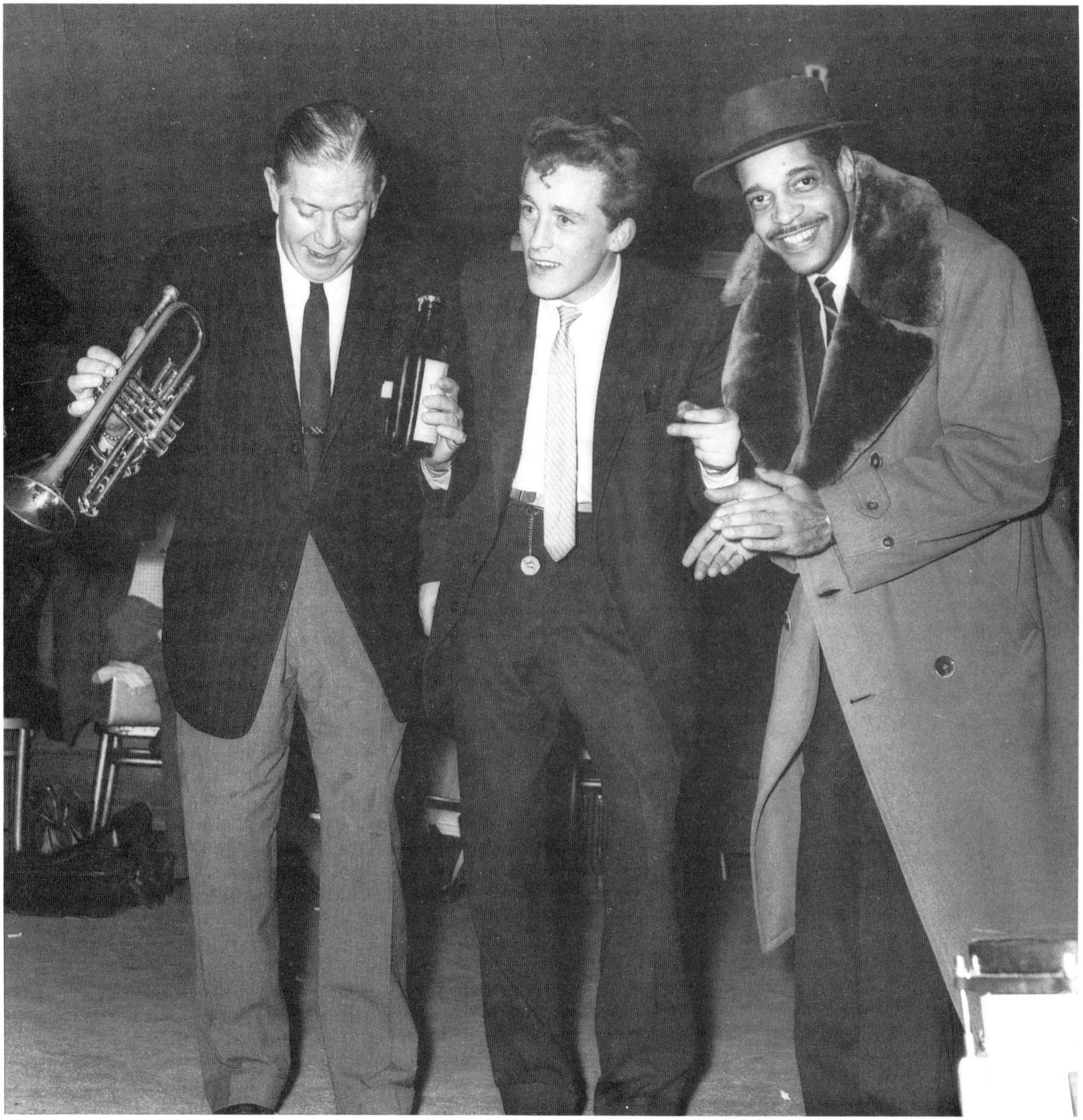

When Wild Bill Davison came to Bradford the Lord Mayor threw a civic reception and we all sat round drinking tea and eating Fig Newtons. I didn't think Bill was too chuffed, expecting something a little stronger. One of the councillors' wives was bending Bill's ear. 'Mr Davison, do you know what the Latin motto says on our coat of arms?' 'Let me have a think honey,' Bill said, studying the inscription. The room held its breath. 'I think it means all the whores in Bradford go to Leeds to get laid.' Revenge for the tea and Fig Newtons.

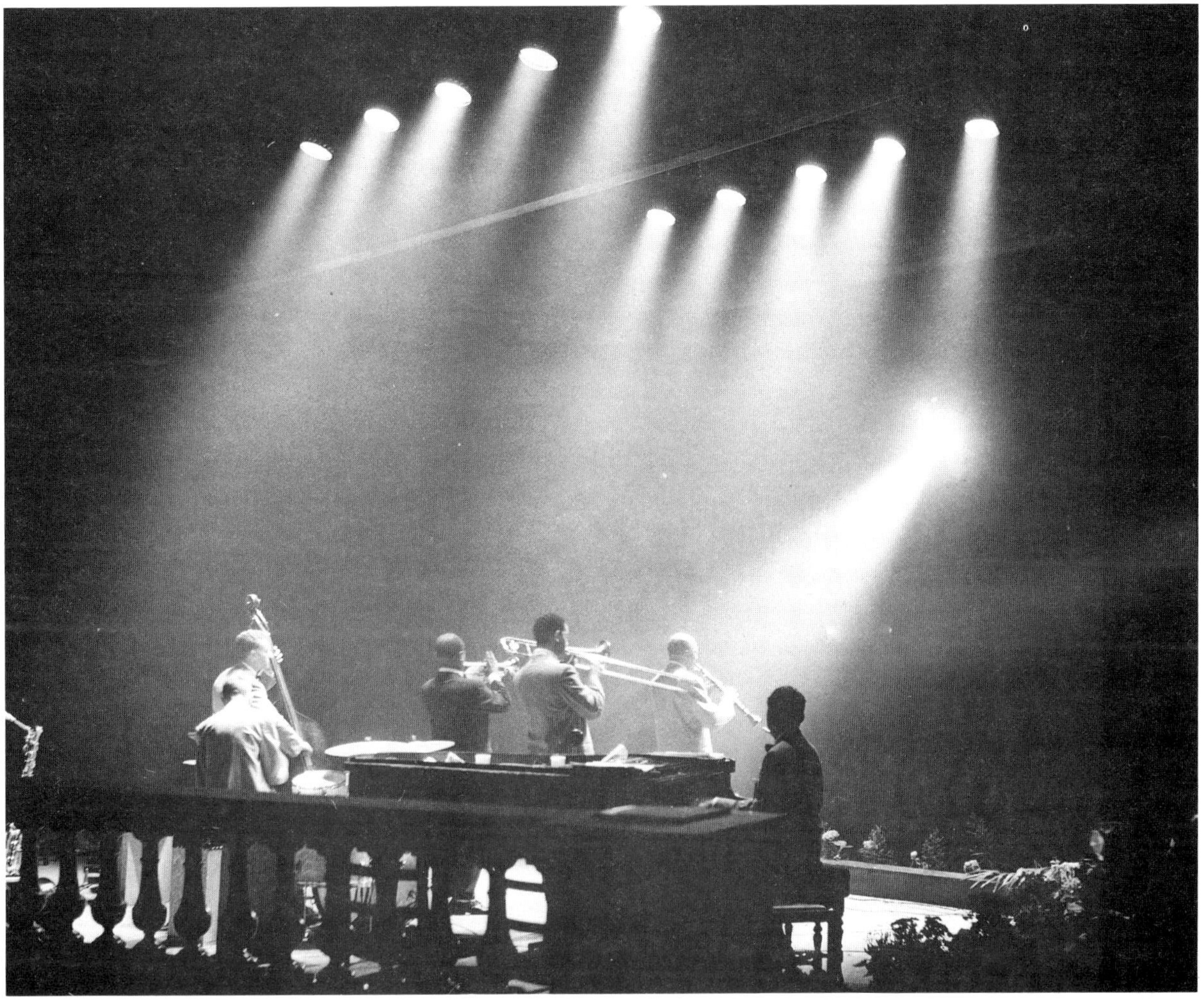

Louis Armstrong All Stars. Black Bob took us to Liverpool to see Louis Armstrong on his first British concert tour. Louis was obsessed by his bowels. On one occasion he wrote on a crisp bag for me. 'The more you eat the more you shit and the more you shit the thinner you git. Signed Louis.'

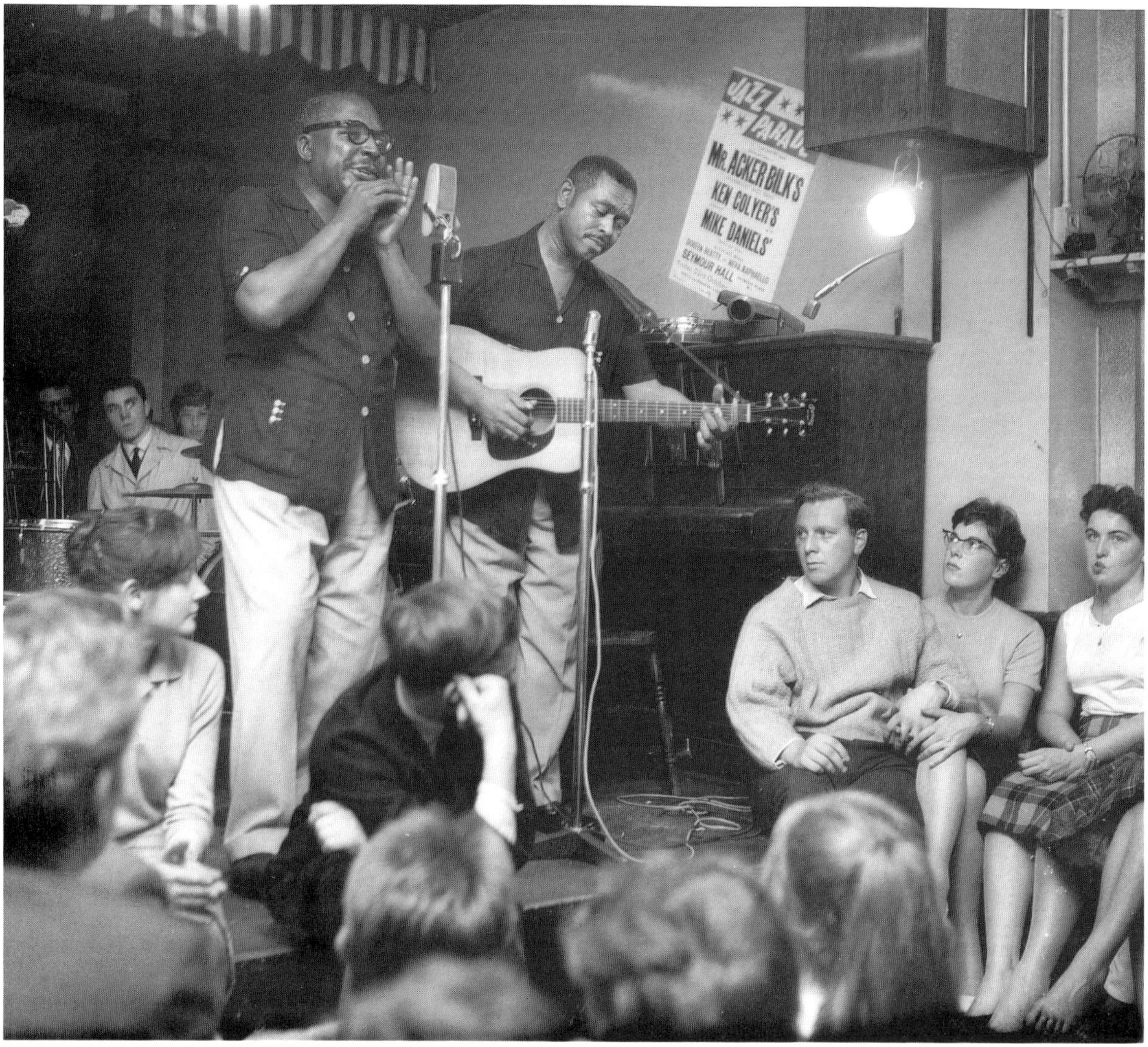

Sonny Terry and Brownie McGhee, 100 Club Oxford Street. The musicians' union ban on American musicians playing in England didn't cover "entertainers", so people like Sonny and Brownie as well as Broonzy and Muddy Waters were able to play.

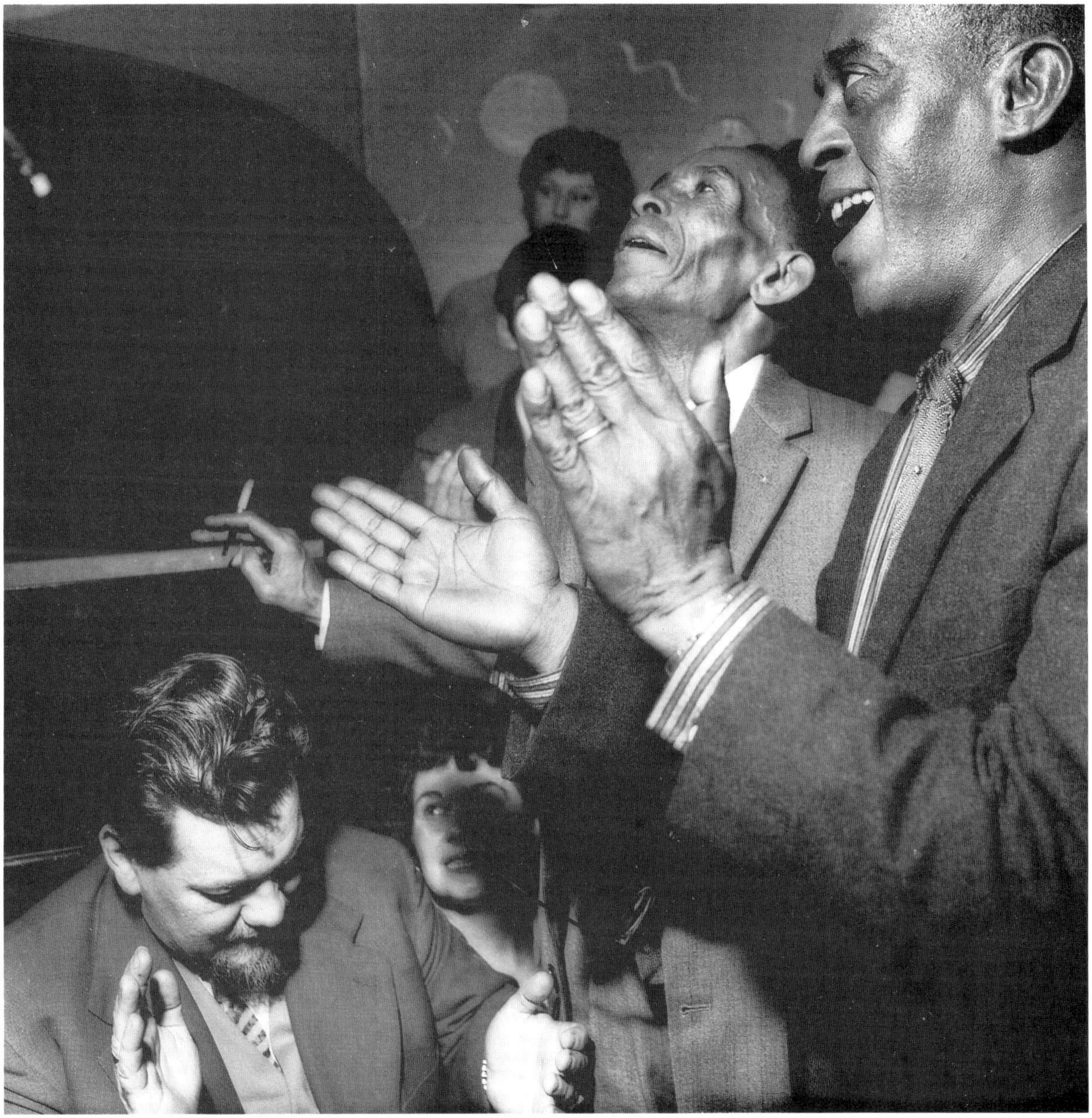

George Lewis in the Ken Colyer Club. ***Most*** *of the jazz clubs were within walking distance of my flat in Soho. The Colyer Club and the 100 Club in Oxford Street were a bit seedy, similar to studio 20 back home in Leeds. The Flamingo and the Down Beat on the other hand were up-market. It was in these clubs that I started to make my name.*

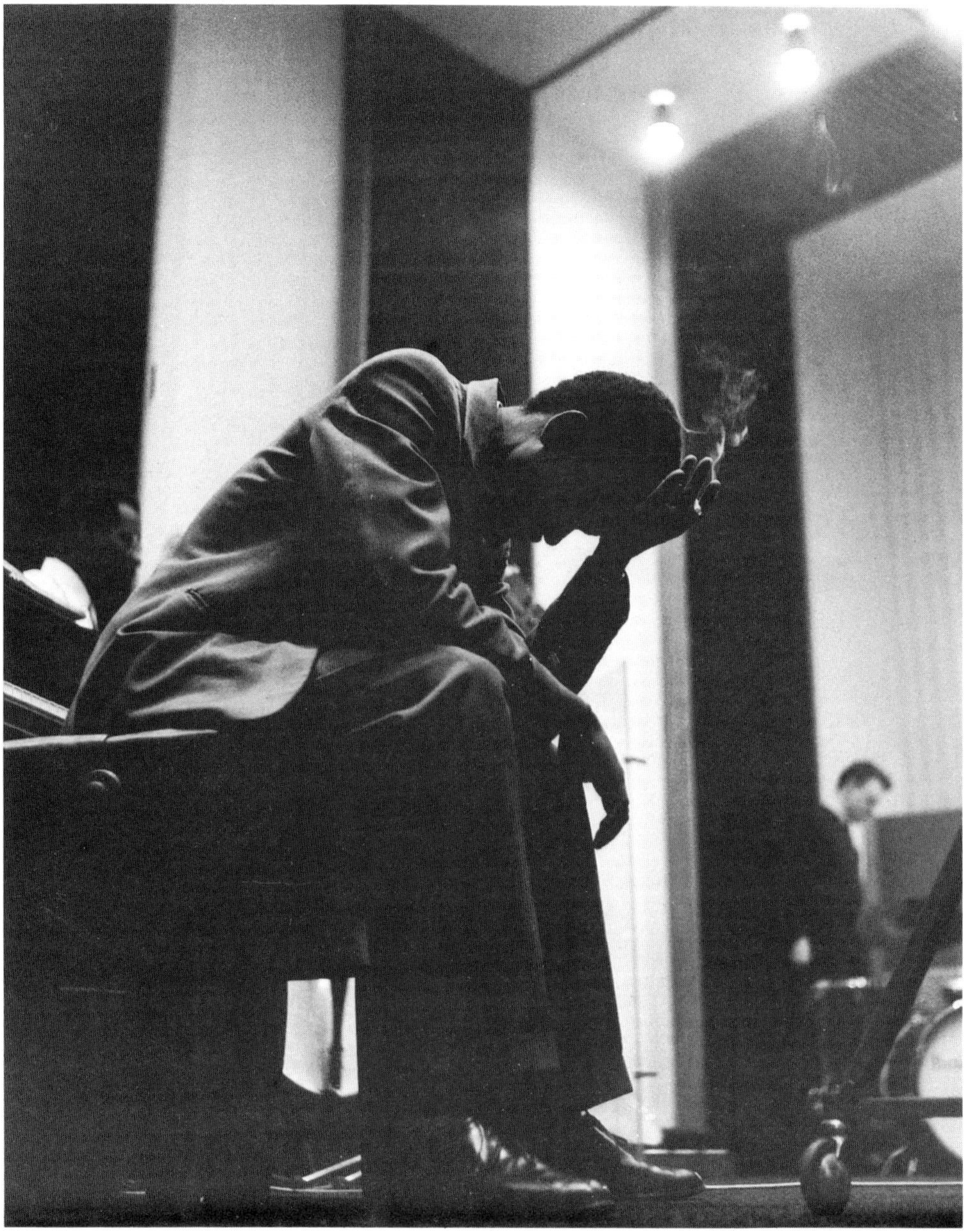

Joe Harriot at the Lansdowne studios relaxing during the recording of the E.P. Blue Joe. A series of my pictures were used for the record sleeve.

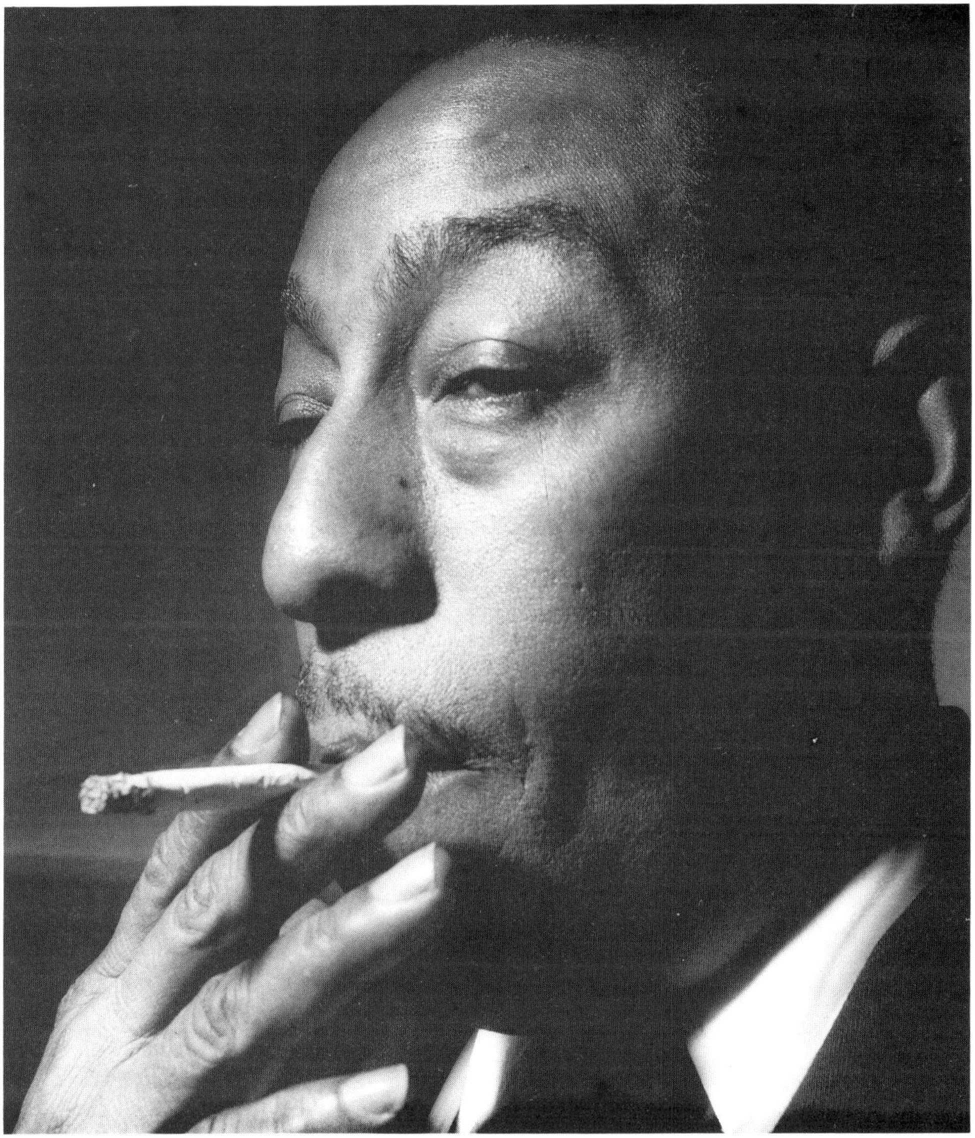

Johnny Hodges with a stick of Chicago Green. By the time I got to London dope was becoming fashionable. People stopped chewing benzedrine inhalers when the company that made them took the benzedrine out of them. Pity about that, they were quite nice with lemon gin.

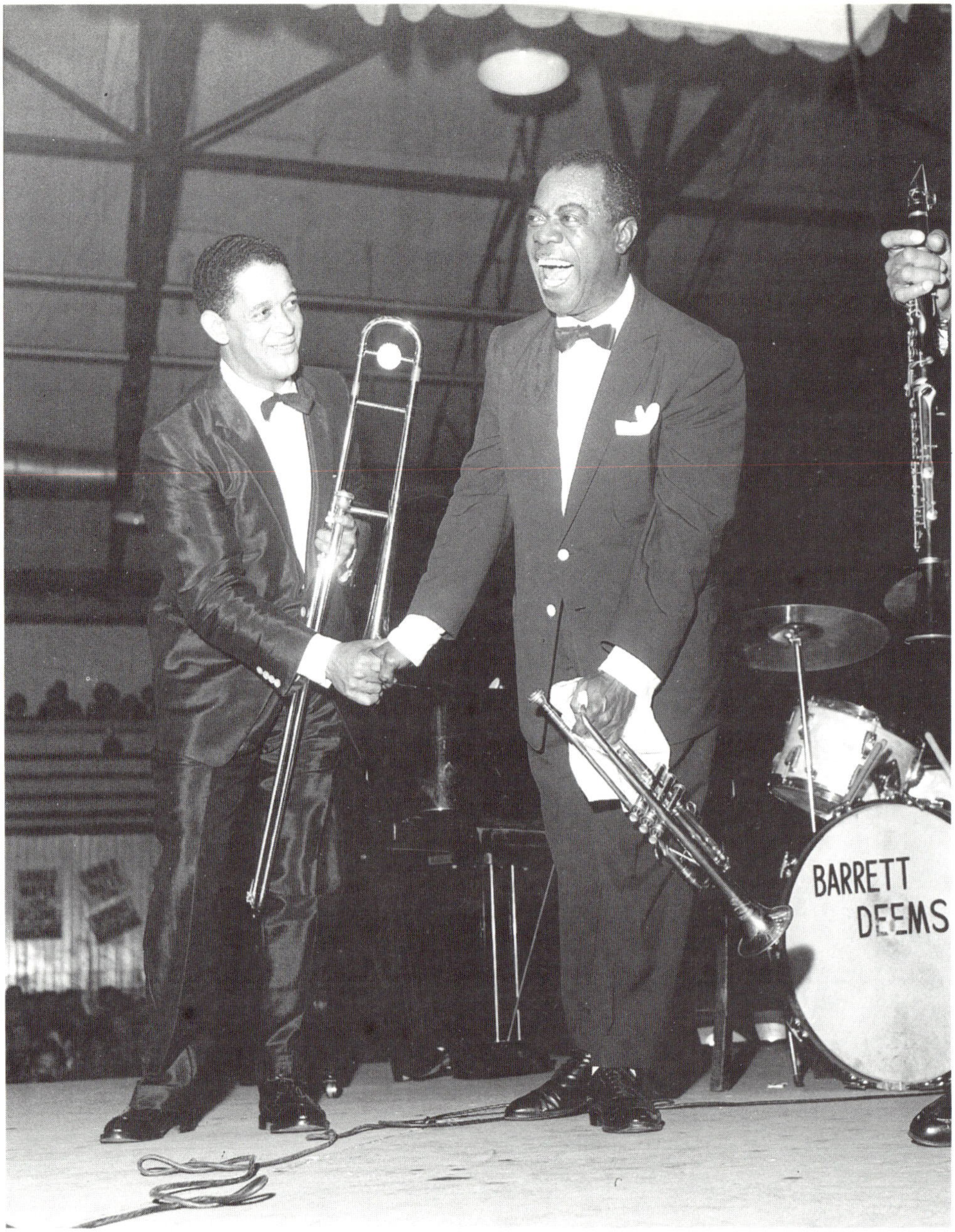

Louis Armstrong and Trummy Young at Liverpool. Louis was quite a small man physically. Always cheerful and chatty in public, in private he was tired and quiet. I took several pictures of him, but I don't rate them. He was the first superstar I ever met and I suppose I was overawed.

In 1956 Bob took me to a Big Bill Broonzy concert in Manchester and backstage we lashed into the VP sherry. On the way home Bob fell asleep at the wheel, the van left the road and dropped into a field, rolling over twice. I came to some distance from the van, lying on my back, with a strong tingling all over my body like an electric shock. I couldn't move. My Rolleiflex was clutched in my hand and I couldn't let go, my head was bleeding badly and a large piece of my scalp was hanging over my face. Bob crawled over to me, lifted my head and put a folded blanket under it. I passed out and came round in hospital.

A black face was peering down at me from the bed head and unseen hands were shaving my scalp with a dry razor. I passed out again. The sound of tearing cloth brought me round; my trouser legs were being ripped up the seams.

'Right,' said a voice, 'cut that overcoat off.'

'Not my bloody Crombie,' I shouted.

'We can't move you,' said a voice from the bed head.

'You will have to. That overcoat cost me fifteen pounds.'

So they sat me up and struggled me out of the garment which was thrown on the floor. Someone held my head and laid me out again. My arms were giving me hell; it was as if I was being beaten repeatedly on the funny bone. A nurse took hold of my shirt front and ripped it open. An involuntary gasp escaped from one of the nurses at the sight of my blood red army PT vest. It still had large scabs of molten nylon from the improvised lighting experiments. They thought for a moment my chest had been staved in. Whoever was shaving my head had now started snipping off little bits of tattered flesh. It was most uncomfortable and I protested in a hysterical babble of obscene army Arabic and York Road gutter slang. Eventually the lights in my head went out.

A hand touched my arm and a fierce shock skittered down one side of my body, I thought 'the swines are giving me shock treatment.' A voice asked quietly, 'Would you like us to call a priest, Mr Cryer?'

'No you can't. I don't want a bloody priest.'

'Could we have the name and address of your parents?'

'What do you want that for?'

'You've had a very bad accident and we must inform your next of kin.'

I asked the nurse for the time and a jolly black girl said, 'Three o'clock in the morning.'

'My old man's badly. You're not waking him up at this time just to upset him. You'll have to wait.'

An older woman who had just joined the group said, 'We can't wait,' and touched my arm. 5000 volts shot through my body, I screamed out and writhed about. My head wouldn't move as there was some sort of strap anchoring me to the bed head, my legs thrashed about and drips attached to my feet crashed over with the stands. Once more the lights went out.

Two days later I awoke in bed, flat on my back, encased from the top of my head down to my coccyx in plaster of Paris. There was a cage over my legs and two drips attached to my feet. The pain in my arms was dreadful. It wasn't located in the bones or the muscles but in the skin. I could even feel it in the hairs on the back of my hands.

As I became more lucid the pain spread from my arms until my whole body was suffused with a sort of electricity, constant, not pulsating. Had talking been possible I would have asked for help but the plaster round my head came down over my ears and under the chin, clamping my jaw tight shut. For days I lay drifting in and out of consciousness. My nights were filled with hallucinations. I remember Mickey Mouse was playing a trombone and leading a jazz band of cartoon characters across the ceiling, an image somehow familiar and not at all disturbing. My body felt as if it was glowing with a blue aura. The pain was constant and I was a tiny dot in the centre of the pain. Eventually this became the norm and didn't bother me so much.

To relieve the agony of contact with the blanket on my arms I took to sleeping with them pointing in the air at 90 degrees from my body. I even taught them to stay up while I slept. The skin on my hands was caked with oil and dried blood but eventually the skin cracked and flaked off in large scabs. There was no injury to my hands but as the skin dried it came off several layers at a time. My fingers were still totally paralysed.

◆

The chief surgeon made his rounds twice a week. Since I was in the death bed by the door he came to me first. He asked all sorts of questions which I couldn't answer as my mouth was still locked tight shut. The bed head was on foot high blocks and my body was sliding down in the cast so that the plaster cut open the flesh on my chin. A nurse noticed the blood running down the plaster and notified the head porter. He produced an electric saw and a couple of inches were cut from the plaster but because my jaw had been clamped shut for so long, now it was freed I couldn't open my mouth. Actually the nurses thought this a blessing because when I was in my delirium my ravings had been both obscene and blasphemous. Since the only bed available for me was in the women's ward, complaints to the Matron had exceeded all previous records. Eventually my bed was rolled out and transferred to the men's ward and some poor sod transferred to my vacant space. I met the man some months later and he blamed me for giving him the worst three weeks of his life.

Every day a truculent gnome gave me a shot of

penicillin. I know he tried his hardest to make it as painful as possible. I got totally disenchanted. One morning I said to him, 'If you don't quit I will crawl out of bed and ram the bloody needle so far up your arse your ears will get pierced.' This excited some interest and the routine was changed. All future injections were given by the ward sister, twelve stone and gentle as a lamb.

The plaster cast encased my whole head, consequently my head wounds couldn't be dressed and as a result I started to stink. By pressing my feet against the bottom of the bed rail, I could move slightly up and down in the cast. This made a squelching noise and caused waves of noxious gas to exude from the top of my head or escape out of the side of the plaster. This became a favourite pastime which was guaranteed to clear my bed space of unwanted visitors.

After a couple of weeks I had recovered enough to become bored. Lying all day staring at the ceiling unable to move became a nightmare. All the regular staff had cottoned on to my trick with the poisonous gas and therefore spoke to me from the foot of the bed. Nurses came occasionally and stood in giggling groups picking scabs off my feet and legs. I hated this but they told me it would prevent scars and they were right. Also the Lady Almoner fixed me up with prismatic glasses which enabled me to read a book propped up on my chest. The facility of a mirror also enabled me to see up and down the ward and carry on conversations with a bed on either side. The mirror was fixed on a servo arm at the bed head, which allowed me to watch TV upside down and backwards. My brain adjusted to this as it's second nature to a photographer anyway. During this period I learned how to stop my pulse beating or slow it down to five or ten a minute. This became a huge joke, particularly if the daily check was made by a student nurse.

◆

We were awakened every morning at 6.30am, breakfast came at 8.30am and as I had great difficulty getting to sleep before 1.00am this routine was a constant aggravation. One day, as the Matron was doing her ward inspection, I called out to her, an event which was considered by witnesses to be unprecedented, and asked why was it necessary to wake me up after a bad night to make me stare bog eyed at the ceiling for two hours while waiting for a brilliantine egg and a curly sausage. She glowered and foolishly came within range of my poison gas. She humphed, made a mental note to order me an enema and moved on. However, humanity prevailed and from then on I was gently awakened at 8.15am with a cup of tea and marmalade toast.

By now I was able to feed myself for although my fingers were still paralysed I could just about make a fist. The plate rested on my chest but finding my mouth was a bit of a problem and several forkfuls went either up my nose or down the sides of the plaster.

Then things got worse. About six weeks into my confinement the cast started to get tight around my stomach and, because there was a piercing pain in my side when I breathed, the ward sister arranged for a piece to be cut out of the middle of the cast. Inside they came across a plastic spool which was cutting a hole in my side. This was removed to my great relief but it was not the end of the problem. The Sister said I was full of shit.

'Do you mean verbally or physically?'

'Both,' she said.

Ten minutes later, down the ward came a nurse with an enema kit and worse, much worse, seven or eight young student nurses who were coming to watch.

Screens were put round, bedclothes removed and I was rolled over on one side, knees up. Having done this the Senior Nurse started telling the students how to give an enema. It appears that pegs have to be clipped somewhere on the rubber tubing to prevent the 1/2 litre of water forcing air into the lower bowel. Yet that's just what happened with disastrous results. The tube was inserted a good distance, and warm soapy water poured in, the large rubber bulb was squeezed and a quarter litre of air compressed itself into my lower bowel. The rubber tube shot out like a rabid snake under the pressure and leapt about squirting water all over the place. The nurses were hysterical, I was scarlet and then the whole procedure was repeated. When the tube was removed it occurred to the nurse that the bedpan was missing so a runner was dispatched to the far end of the ward.

'Run, girl, run!'

It was a long way down the ward from my bed. By the time the student nurse came back I was blue in the face and my gluteus maximus had gone into spasm. The nurses lifted me onto the bedpan, drew back the screens and left me to it. Nothing happened. I was so bloated in the plaster cast by now that breathing became difficult and in any case evacuating your bowels lying flat on your back requires a suspension of disbelief and a great deal of lateral thinking. I hadn't even started when the nursing sister returned.

'Have you finished, Mr Cryer?'

'No, I'm sorry love but-'

'Thwack!' a hand slapped down on the plaster cast and I thought I'd exploded, the sound effects were stupendous. The nurse was waving her arms about like she was conducting the Halle. It wasn't that, though, she was calling a pair of students to retrieve the bedpan and clean me up. The pan was almost full and for fear of spilling it took two to carry it.

The sudden and rapid removal of all the waste matter left me drained both emotionally and physically but 8lb lighter. From now on the plaster cast was too big and when the nurses were rolling me about I rattled around inside like a pea in a drum.

◆

In the next bed to me was Percy Aveyard, a baker with a badly injured thigh. We laughed a lot and played all manner of tricks on the nurses. The day Percy got out of bed was a hoot. It took two people to hold him for he fell about like a day old calf. I was watching in my mirror over the bed and laughing like a drain. This narked Percy.

'Just you bloody wait till it's your turn.'

It never occurred to me that there would be any problem for when the time came I would get out of bed and walk down to the lav.

'You watch me, Percy. I'll be down to the bog like a two year old.'

'Want to put some money on it?'

'How much?' I was thinking two bob or half a crown.

'A fiver.'

This shook me a bit. Five pounds was real money, it would buy 50 pints of beer or 35 rolls of film.

'You're on, Percy. I'll get out of this bed and walk unaided to the bog. That's a bet.'I couldn't lose. There was nothing wrong with my legs. Some weeks later the ward sister appeared.

You're getting up today, Terry.'

I could have wept.

'We'll just go and get a wheelchair.'

Percy snorted and alerted the ward as the sister swept out. I hooked my toes under the iron frame at the bottom of the bed and sat upright. A minute later I swung my legs over the side of the bed and jumped down. It was a long way. The bed head was on foot high blocks and the concussion nearly broke my bloody neck again. Clutching the bed rails for support I walked unaided to the bog and spent a luxurious fifteen minutes. Percy never coughed up the fiver.

Pretty soon I was buzzing about the ward helping with the meals and dishing out books. My fingers were still paralysed but I had adapted. Although when it was time for a leak a nurse had to get out my dick and put it away again. Not to have someone to help could be a disaster.

Once in Leeds Market, on my release, I had occasion to use the public lavs but found there was no way to unzip my jeans and the rest, so I asked a man in the next stall.

'Are you bloody joking? You bloody pervert.' His face was a picture of outrage.

'No I'm not bloody joking! Can't you see I've had a severe accident and it's left my hands paralysed? What do you think this plaster cast is, Scotch Bloody Mist?'

'I'll paralyse the rest of you if you don't sod off, you mucky bugger.'

On the way home I peed myself on the tram.

◆

Once I was mobile, hospital became quite a pleasure and because of my remarkable recovery I was treated a bit special by the nurses. The cast by now was much too big due to my weight loss, so they decided to put on a new one. On my way through outpatients we stopped the trolley at the lift. A woman sitting on the bench right by me was sobbing and wailing.

'What's up love?' I said. She held up a bloody stained, bandaged finger. 'You should worry. Look at me, I came in with a boil on my neck.'

She went hysterical and had to be restrained. The nurses were furious and shopped me to the ward sister. It took me days to redeem myself.

The new plaster cast was exactly like the old one but thank God all the stale peas and bits of fish were cleaned from my neck. The top of my head was a stinking mess. 53 stitches were left in but later removed by my hairdresser. I kept them for years in a wine glass but one day the cat ate them.

◆

At 0900 on a certain day I was told to expect a visit from Matron. She appeared with the Almoner.

'Mr Cryer, we are sending you home tomorrow.'

That didn't suit me; eight shillings a day sick benefit, three square meals, television, grapes. 'I don't see how it's possible, Matron, living on my own. It would be impossible in this plaster cast.'

'Can't you go to your father's?'

'We're not on speaking terms, Matron. He won't have me in the house.'

I distinctly heard her mutter to the Almoner, 'I'm not surprised.'

So my skive was extended another week or two until one morning out of the blue a telegram arrived by way of a friend.

'Jazz Shows London, Request you cover Floating Festival of Jazz leaving Tower Bridge Sat 10th 09.30 reply soonest.'

They obviously thought my ordeal was over and since expenses were up front, I shot off to the Matron.

'Excuse me, Matron, my father and I have made it up so it's alright to go home.'

She was well pleased. 'Tomorrow soon enough, Terry?'

'Terry,' for heaven's sake - she was pleased to see me go.

An ambulance took me to Leeds and stopped outside Dad's house. I chatted a minute or two to the driver and waved him off. As soon as he was out of sight I set out for my flat in Chapeltown and took stock. Sickness benefit for my stay in hospital totalled £50, my rent was 29/- a week. I paid promptly and that left £26. Black Bob had recovered from his minor injuries and was running his cafe-cum-jazz club so I could count on a little sustenance there but future rent was going to be a problem, even if I sat in the dark and didn't use the gas stove.

That night I collapsed into my own bed. I had to sleep on my back because the cast allowed no other position. I was quite used to this and it presented no problem, until the morning that is. In hospital there was a bed end for me to hook my toes under and a hand hold on a chain over my head. Sitting up was easy in hospital. At home there was neither. I couldn't sit up or roll sideways. Peggy in the flat next door had gone to work and she wouldn't be back until three in the afternoon. I was stuck and panic stricken. There was an urgent need for the toilet. By the side of the bed was a large lemonade bottle half full. If I could reach that there was some hope of solving one of the problems. That was accomplished after a lot of grunting. I drank the lemonade knowing that it would naturally create problems later in the day.

There was the sound of kids playing in the street. One must have fallen because there was a loud wail. Okay, so the world's full of problems but the only one which concerned me was how to direct a stream of urine into the half inch neck of a lemonade bottle while lying flat on my back staring up at the ceiling. It wasn't the best of operations but the planning was great fun. As the Dutch say, 'Putting up the tent is finer than the circus.'

Peggy came home at 3 o'clock and helped me out of bed and I staggered like Frankenstein to the lavatory. After that I slept sitting up.

◆

There was lots to do before my job in London; like cashing the expenses cheque Jazz Shows had kindly sent and having a nice bag of fish and chips from Cantor's Jewish Fish Bar. When I went into Cantor's Harold behind the counter, who hardly knew me, gave me the fish and chips and twenty Woodbines and pushed the money I offered back at me. Then without a word he served the next customer.

The steam train to London took six hours and I had to stand as far as Peterborough. My appearance in the underground train to Tower Bridge created something of a stir but by now people staring and even laughing caused no offence and occasionally I could get my own back by frightening cheeky kids.

The SS Daffodil was waiting at the riverside and the Jazz Show's people were checking passengers aboard. When they saw me they nearly freaked and in fact some of the front line musicians couldn't play for laughing because when I stepped forward to take a picture, my paralysed fingers couldn't press the

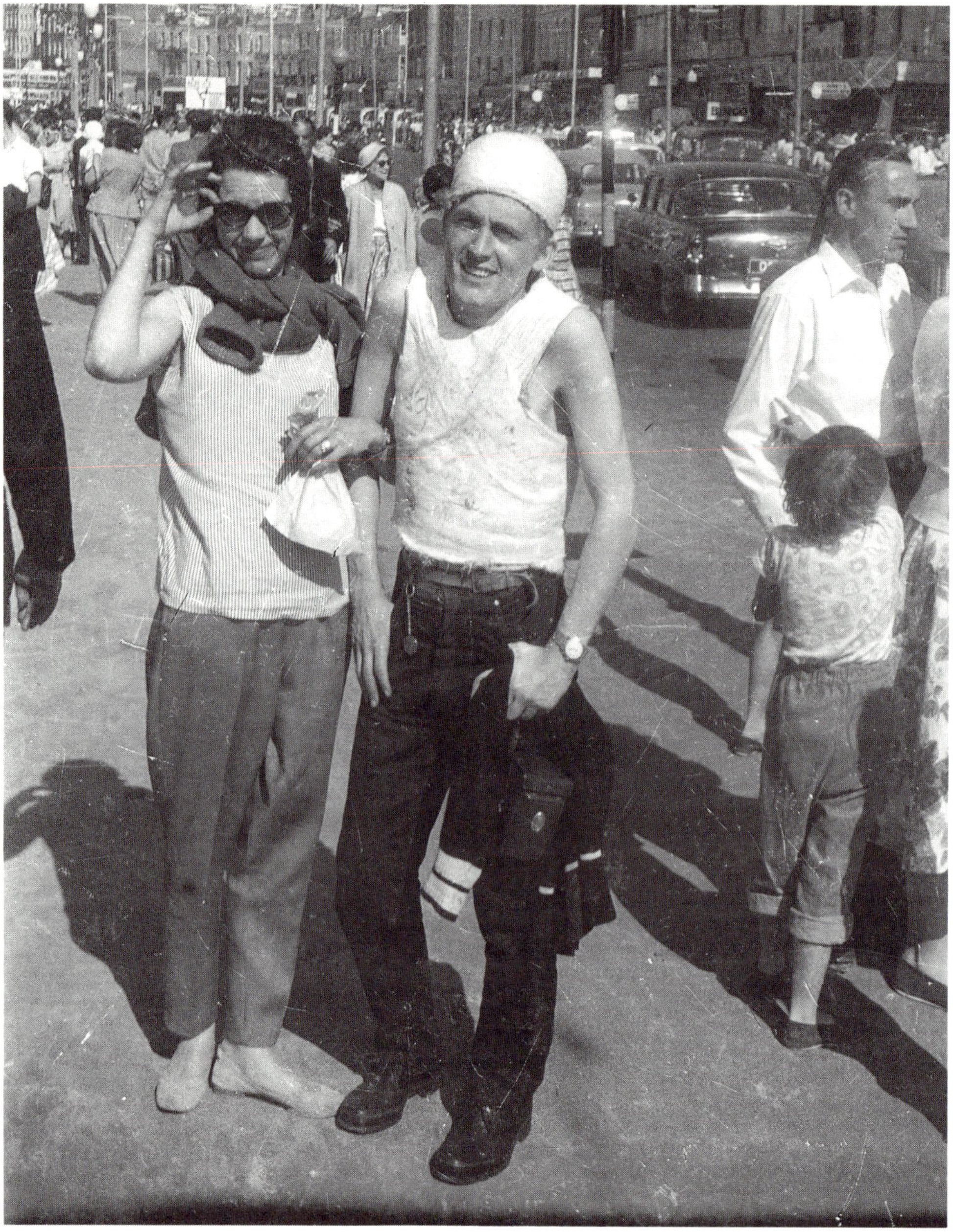

In my plaster cast on the day I arrived for the Jazz Shows floating festival. The organiser said, 'I hope for Christ's sake you don't fall overboard.' The plaster cast weighed three stones and had an iron bar up the back.

camera release button. In the end I had to fix up a rubber tube to the cable release socket, the other end was a rubber bulb which I held between my teeth. On biting down I fired the shutter. Not being able to bend my head to see into the waist level viewfinder, most of the framing was guesswork.

On my return home I developed the 10 rolls of film one at a time in a basin. They were surprisingly good, not my best but usable, and the revenue from the print orders enabled me to pay for an enlarger and stock of materials.

I staggered about Leeds in the plaster cast for another five weeks. I had paid my rent from the 30/- National Assistance money and with the shilling change bought a sheep's head which made excellent soup. All that time I lived on pressed brawn and soup made from vegetables which were scavenged from Leeds Market.

Towards the end of this period I met Ann who came to live with me. Ann's earnings as a school teacher improved my diet considerably. The plaster cast did nothing for my love life. Then one lovely day the hospital sent for me and removed the cast. Pasted in the album of my memory are the four smashing Geordie nurses giving me a bath.

◆

By the late fifties there was little going off in the Leeds jazz scene. No further jazz clubs were appearing and Studio 20 was beginning to go downhill. Wide boys had discovered it and started causing a bit of bother. At that time people began to chew the inside of Benzedrine inhalers. The law allowed you to take your own drink but Bob cottoned on that there was a bit of extra money to be got so he started supplying booze. He got caught by the police.

I sat in the balcony in my plaster cast during the court case. A copper came up behind me and said, 'Take that fucking hat off.' The defence lawyer stood up and said that the club was an important amenity because 'It attracts very important people, including Humphrey Lyttleton and his father.' He was supposed to say Humphrey Lyttleton and Chris Barber.

◆

Ann and I got married in 1957 and I managed to do a fair amount of freelance work, most of it from London, so we decided to move south. Although we left on spec with no address to go to, we dropped on a nice little flat in Lisle Street just off Leicester Square. The property belonged to Alf Kusnitzov, who I knew as Alf Harris, and his wife Sadie. They adopted us on sight. Alf was a generous kindly man who owned a string of greengrocer's shops around the West End. He ran these with his two sons.

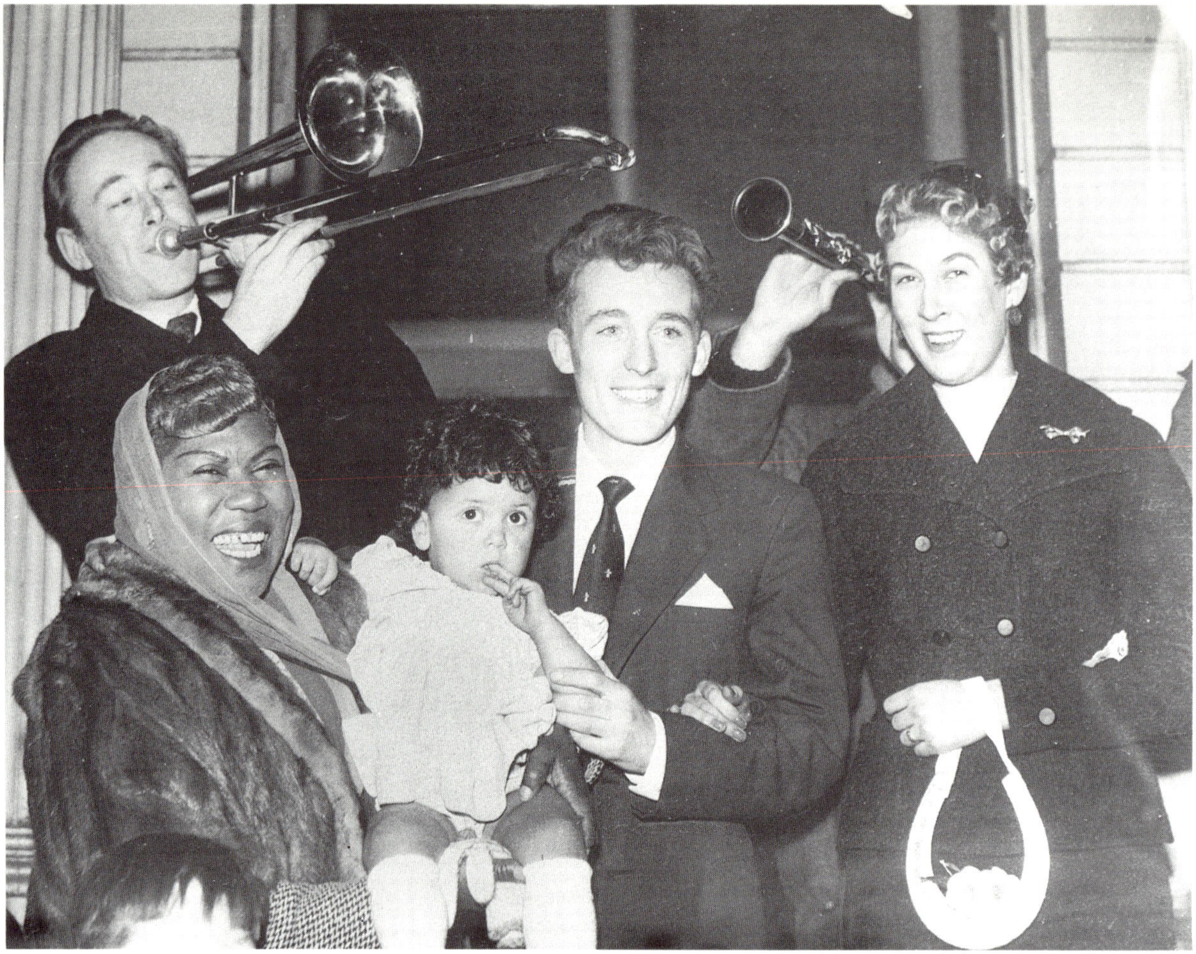

In 1957 while on tour with Chris Barber's Jazz Band and the great gospel singer Sister Rosetta Tharpe, Ann and I got married. We were quite happy just living together but under pressure from Sister Rosetta I bought a special licence. Rosetta was the Matron of Honour, Chris was Best Man and Monty Sunshine, Chief Usher.

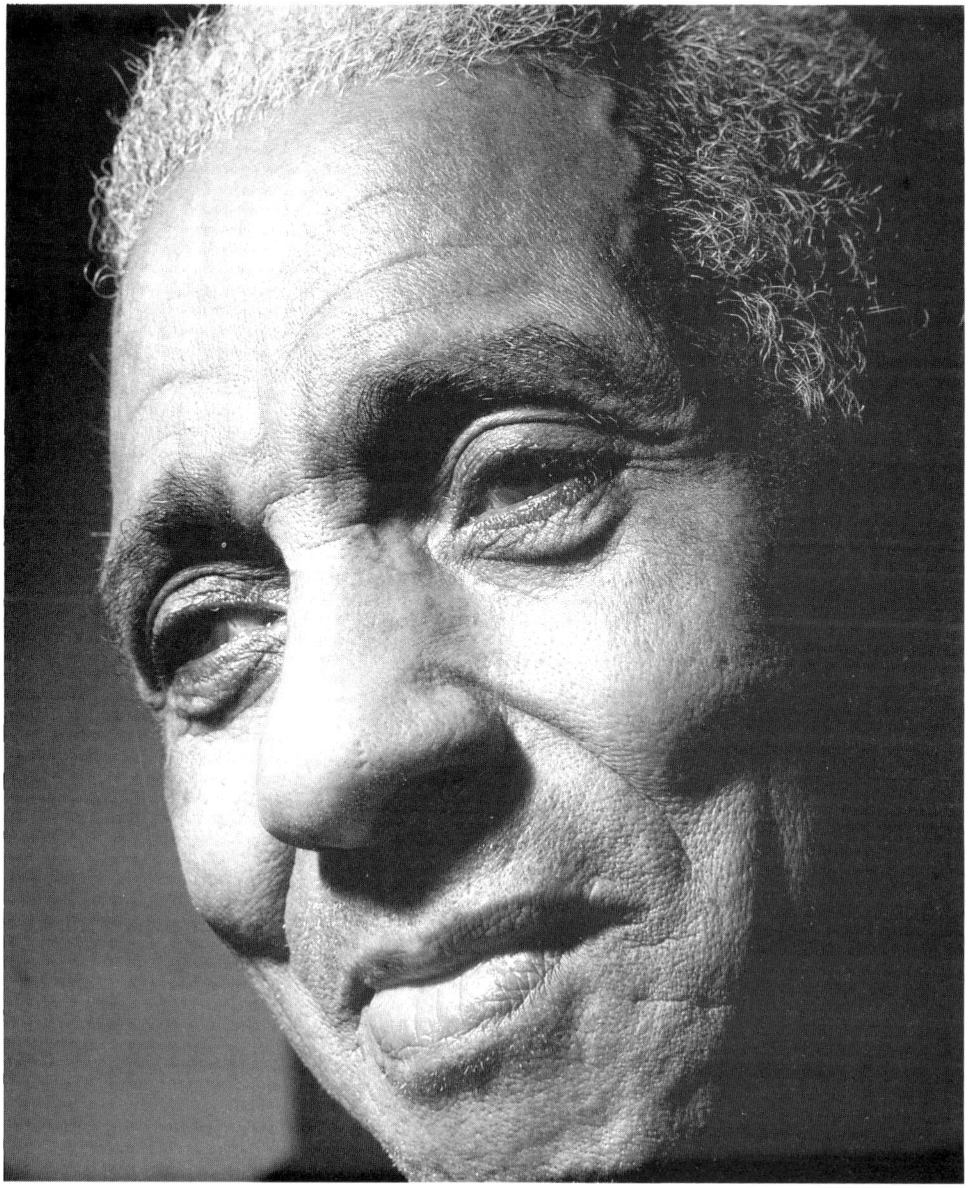

Alcide "Slow Drag" Pavageau. To take a photo like this with my Rolleiflex I had to get within 9 or 10 inches of his face. Because the camera is twin lens the parallax prevented me from seeing the image, so I had to guess the focus.

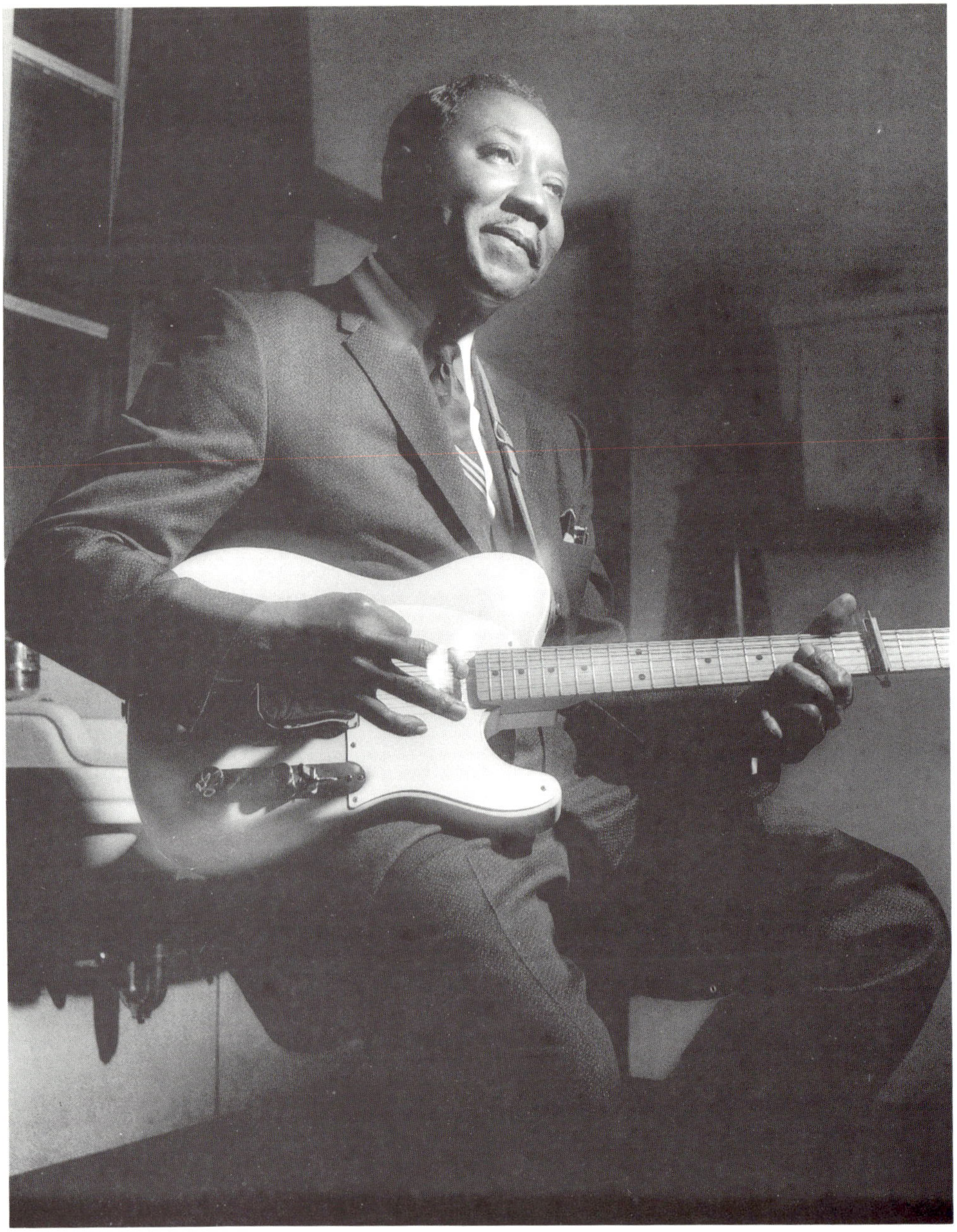

Muddy Waters. Wigmore Hall London. Muddy was a big influence on young white British kids in the 60s. In fact the Rolling Stones named themselves after one of his songs. These days kids know him because Levis used his music to sell their jeans.

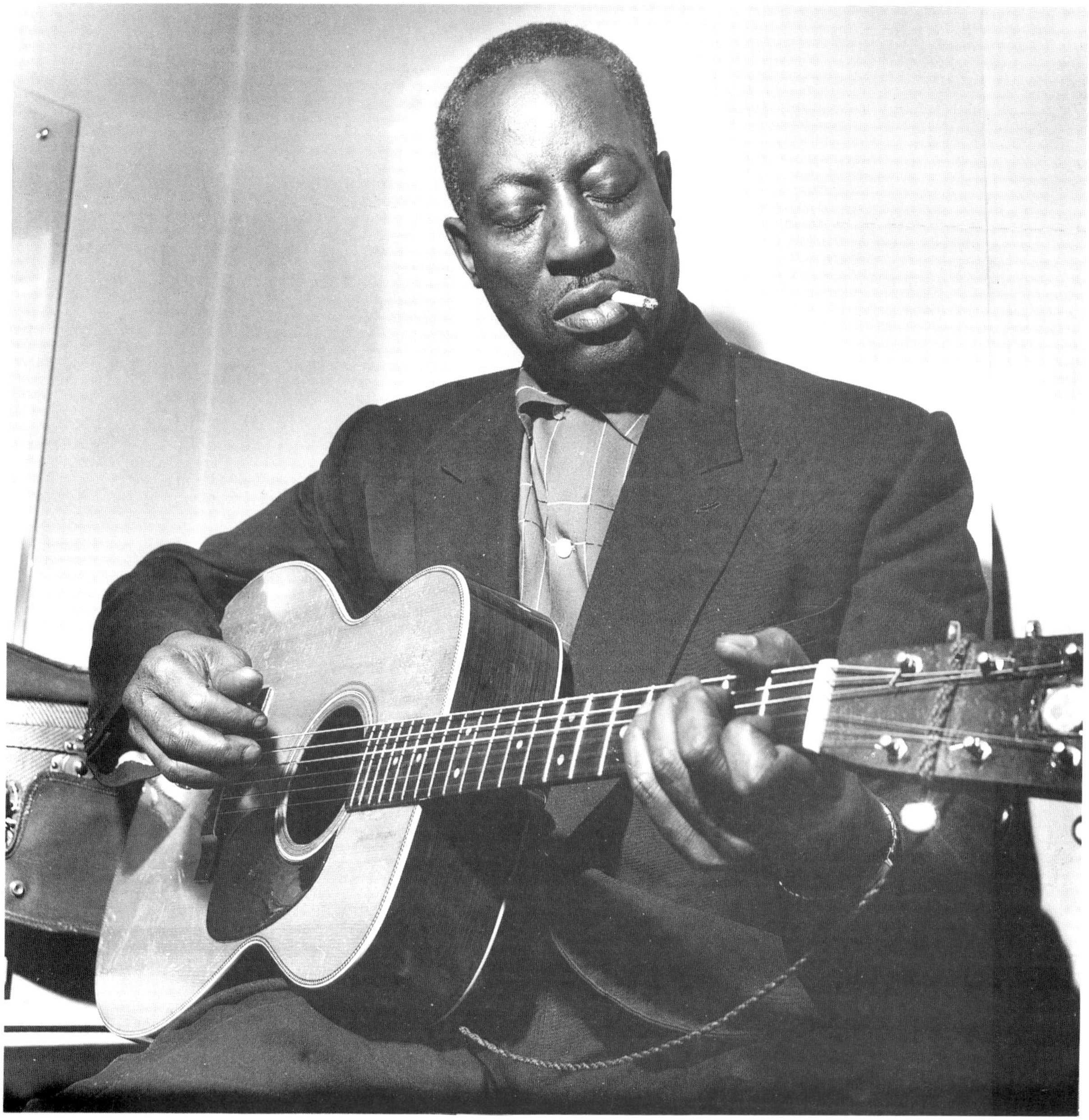

Big Bill Broonzy in Manchester. I didn't know it at the time but this was to be my last photograph for a long while. I broke my neck in a car crash on the way back from the concert. I developed this picture seven months later.

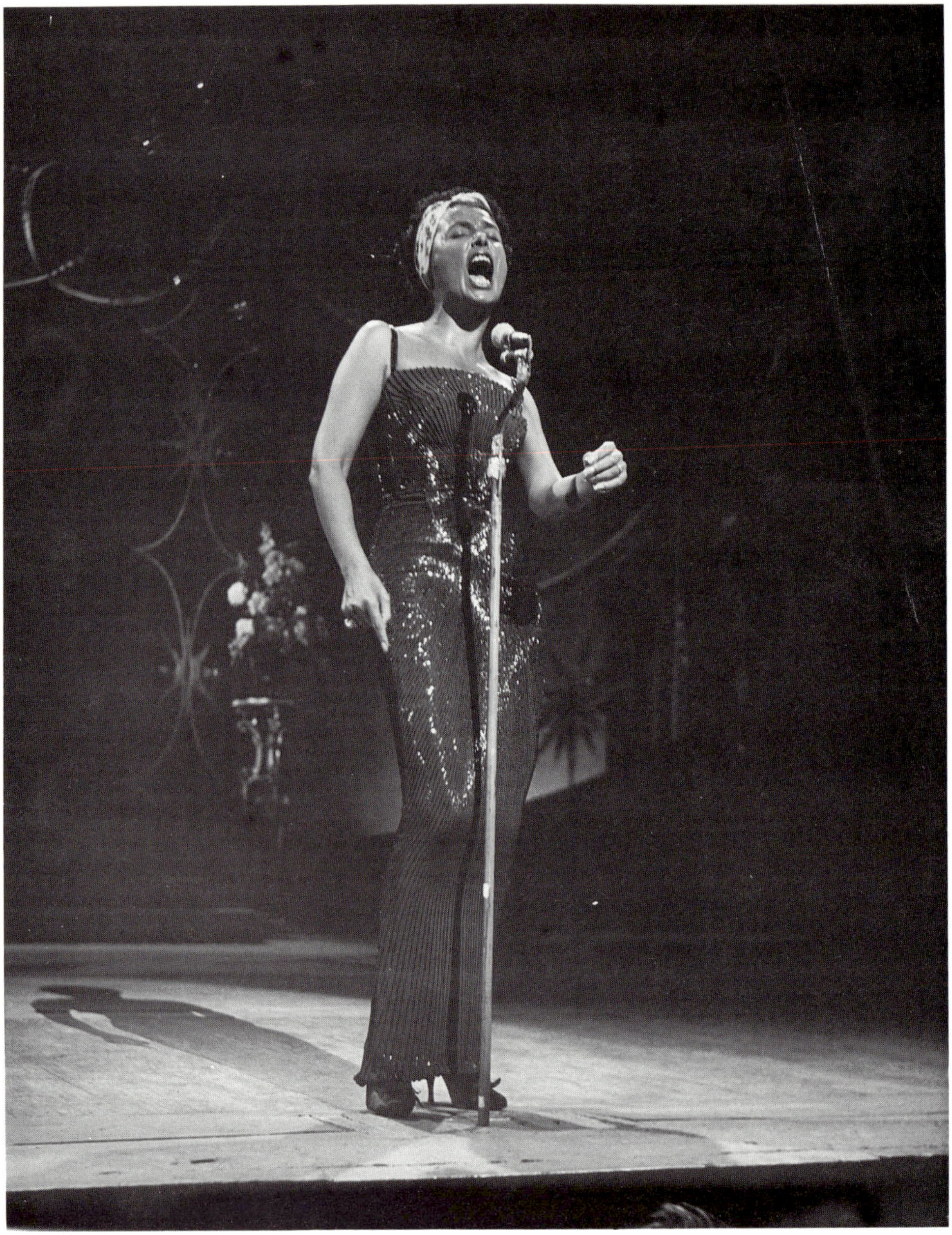

Lena Horne at the London Palladium. She was the most staggeringly beautiful woman I've ever seen. I photographed rehearsals at the Palladium every Sunday for the music press.

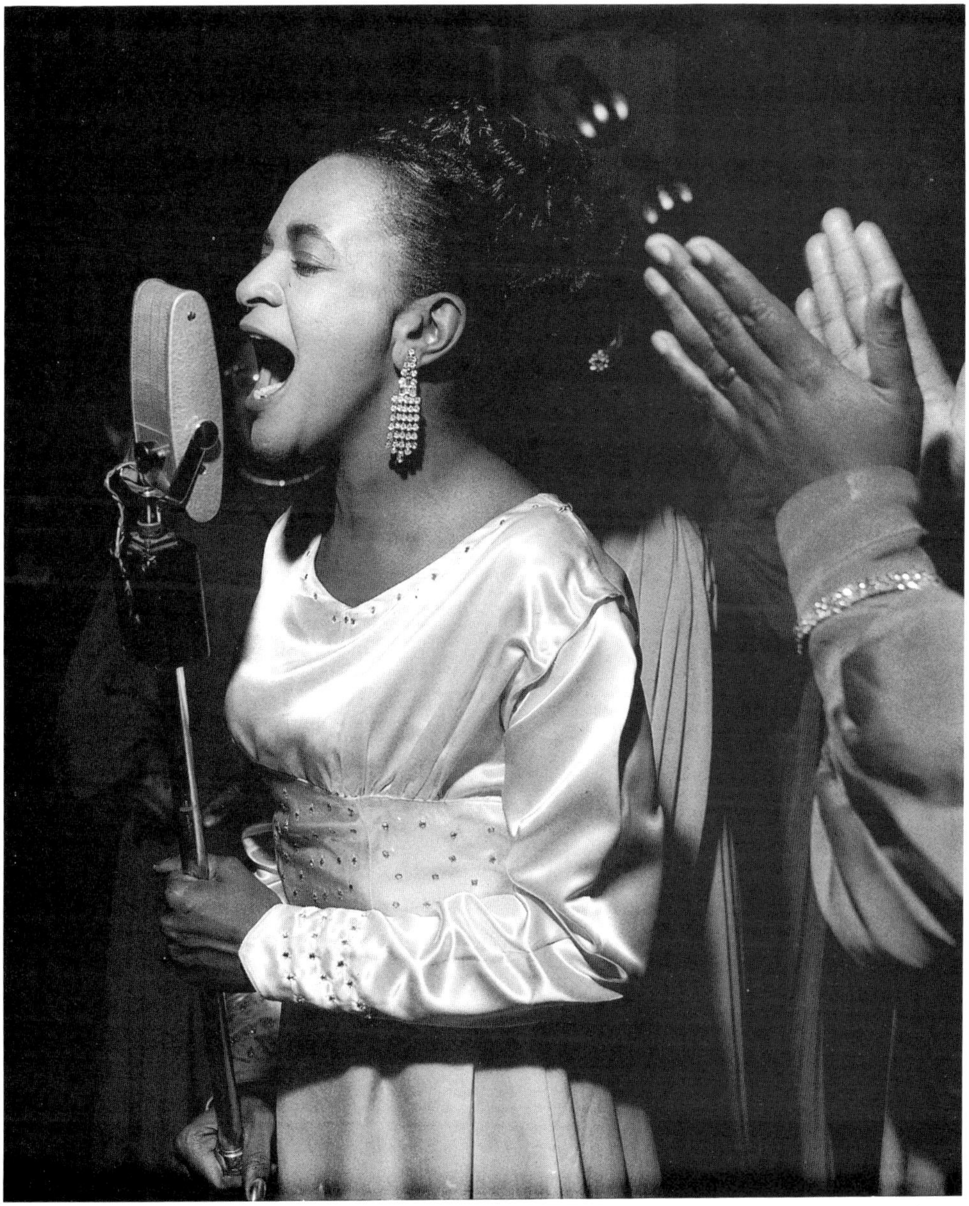

Clara Ward at the 100 Club Oxford Street. People went to the 100 Club for jazz, coffee and coca-cola. If you wanted alcohol you went to the Blue Posts pub round the corner.

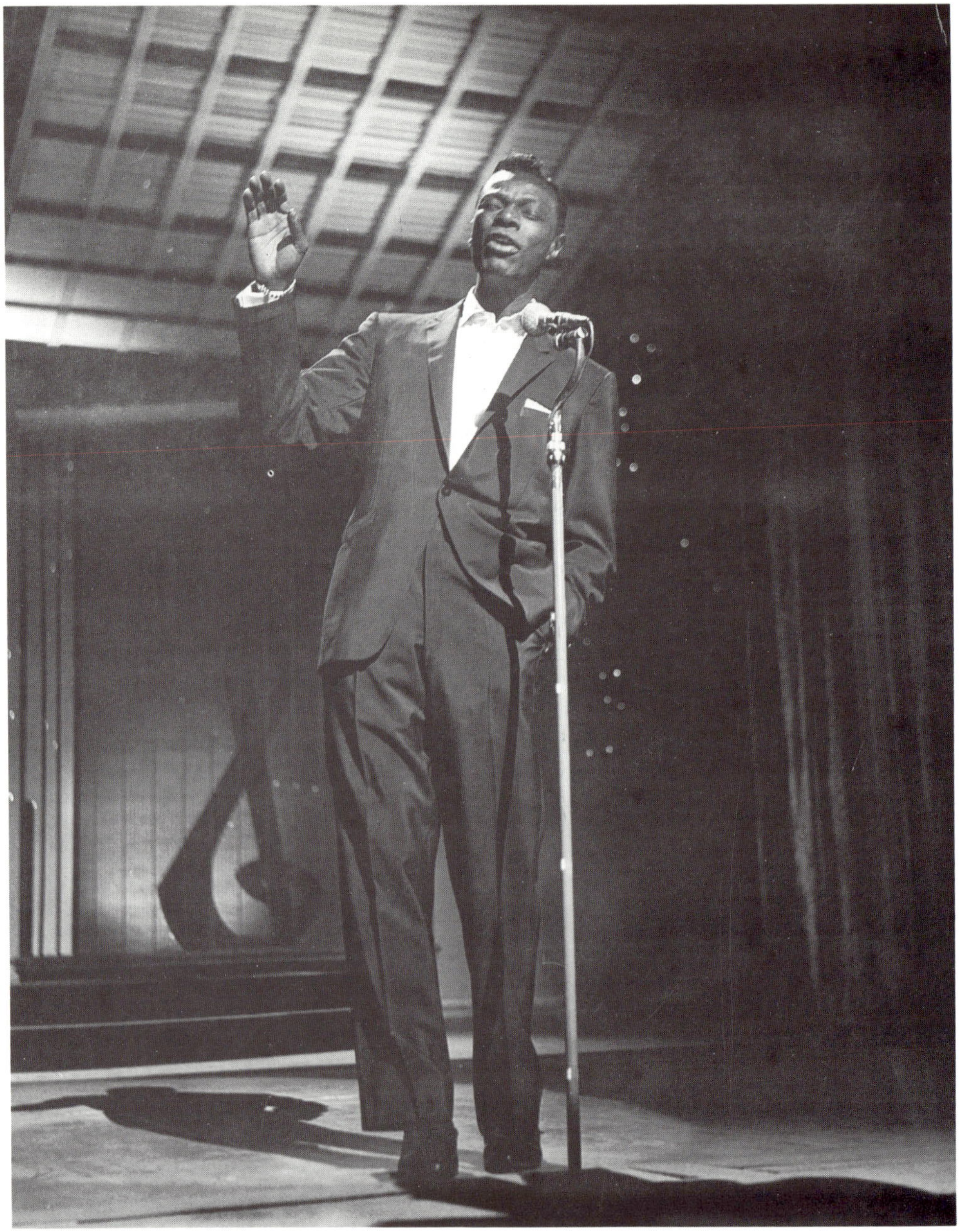

Nat King Cole at the Palladium. He was just as nice as the image he portrayed. Billy Bowskill once said to me, 'Even though he left jazz he never gave a bad performance.' True!

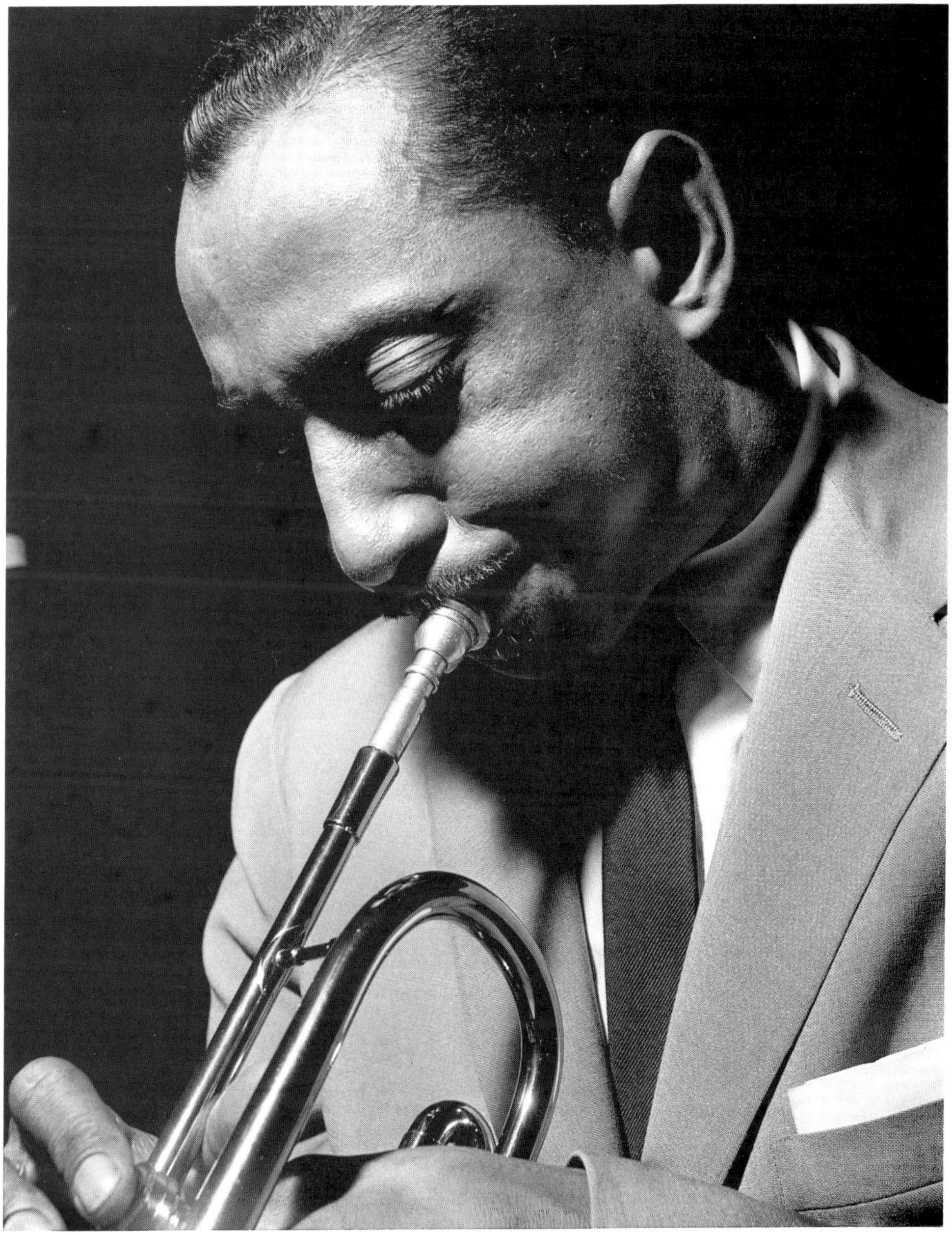

Joe Newman at a private jam session with the Ellington Band at the Flamingo Club, Wardour Street, London.

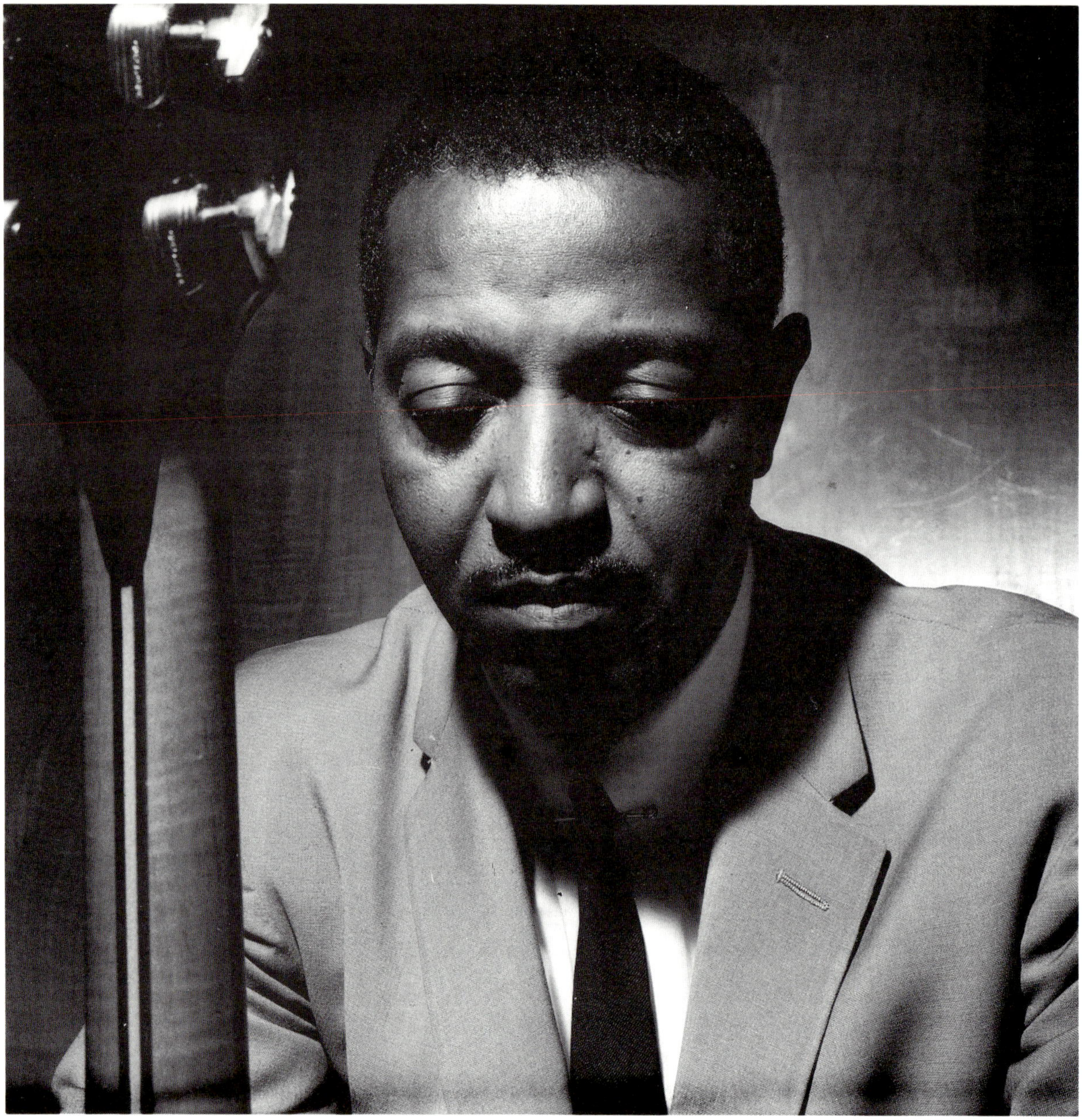

Freddie Green of the Ellington Band at the Festival Hall in London. Freddie probably didn't know I was taking this picture, he was sitting reading a book. I tried not to pose the jazz pictures, preferring the chance element. This stood me in good stead in later years when I became a press photographer – then you need to be a busker.

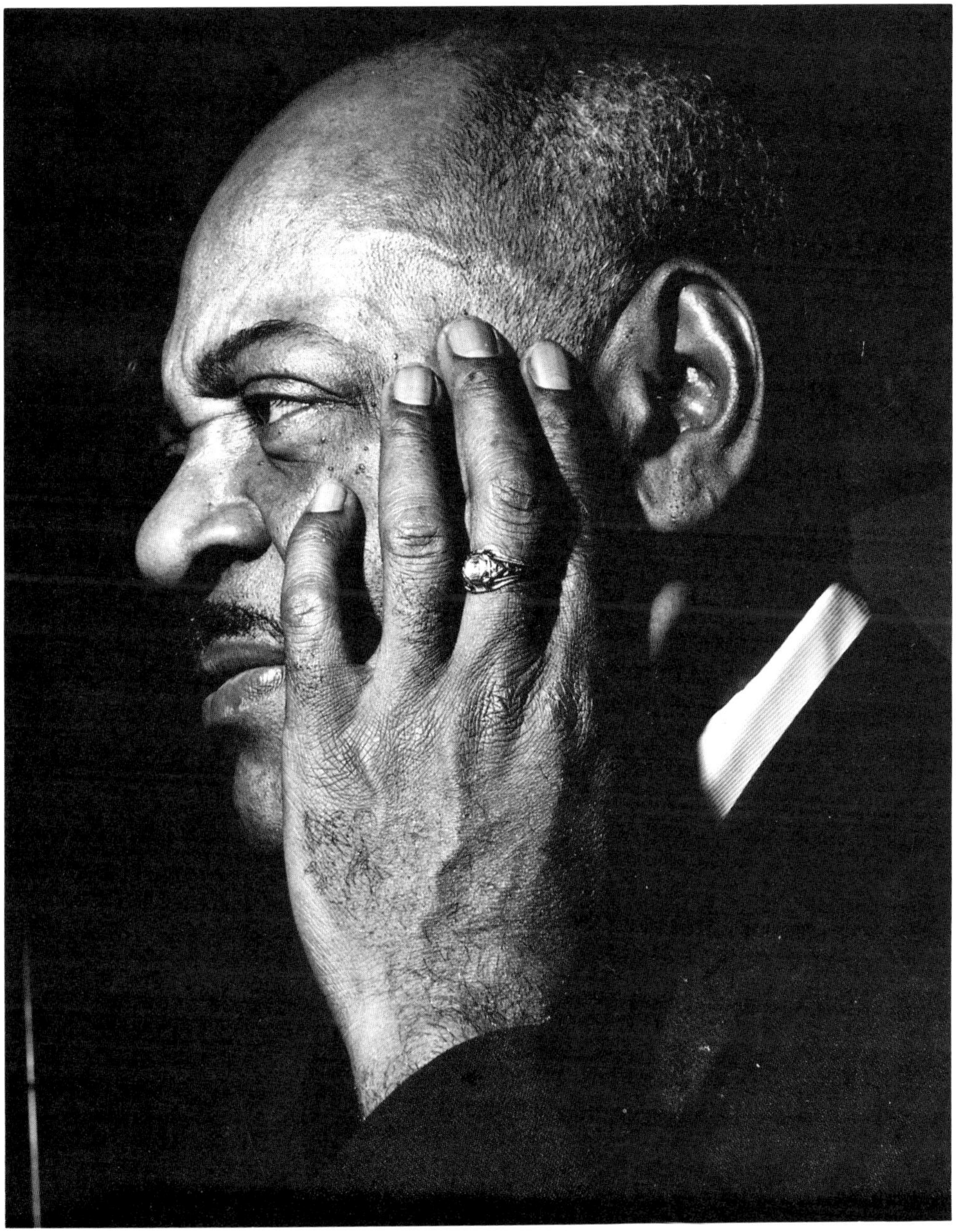

Coleman Hawkins at Bradford St Georges' Hall. Coleman was a stalwart of Norman Granz's Jazz at the Philharmonic shows. They came over when the ban on visiting American musicians was lifted.

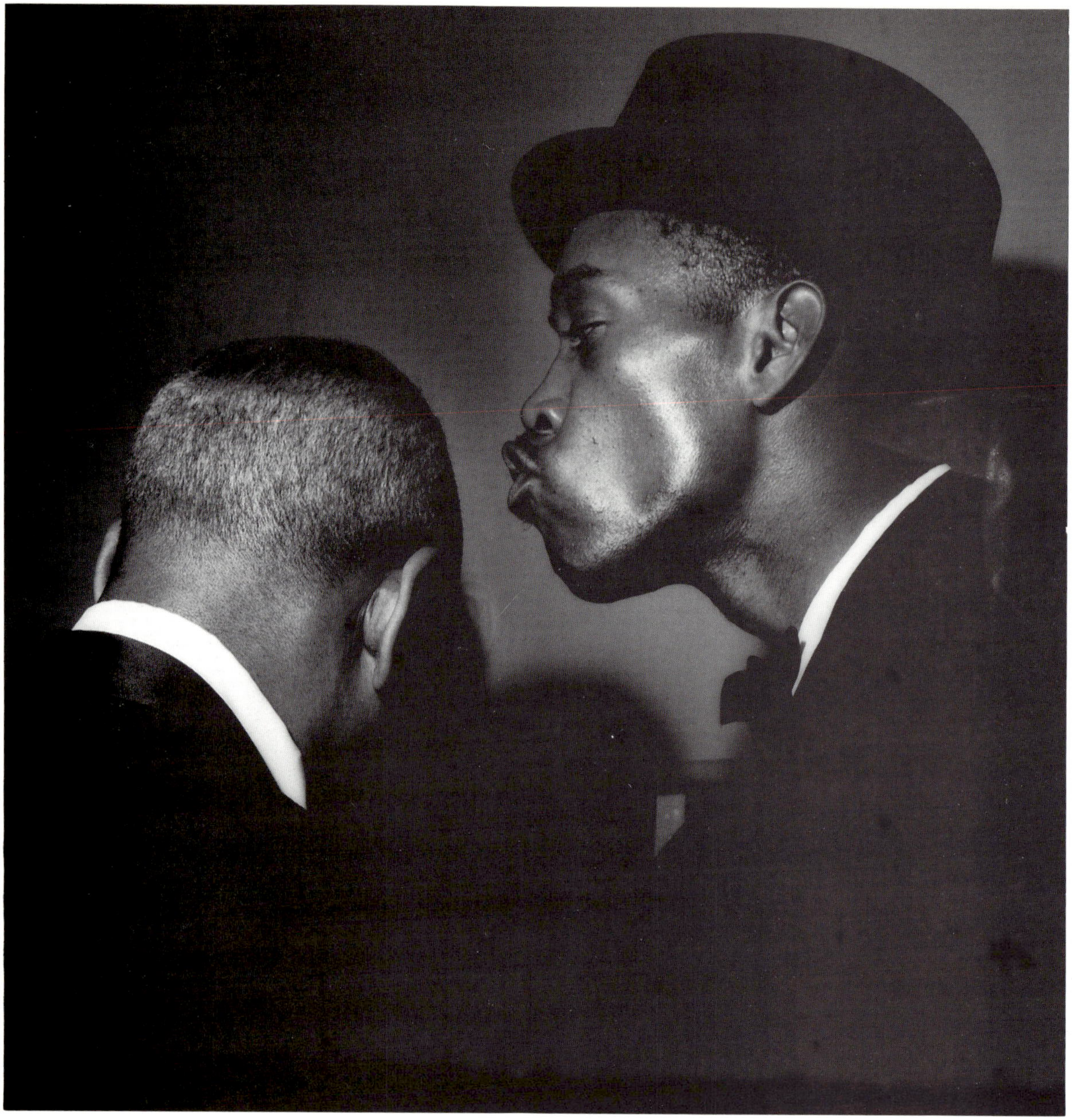

Coleman Hawkins and Sonny Stitt at the Gaumont State Kilburn. I took this one during Jazz at the Philharmonic's 1959 tour.

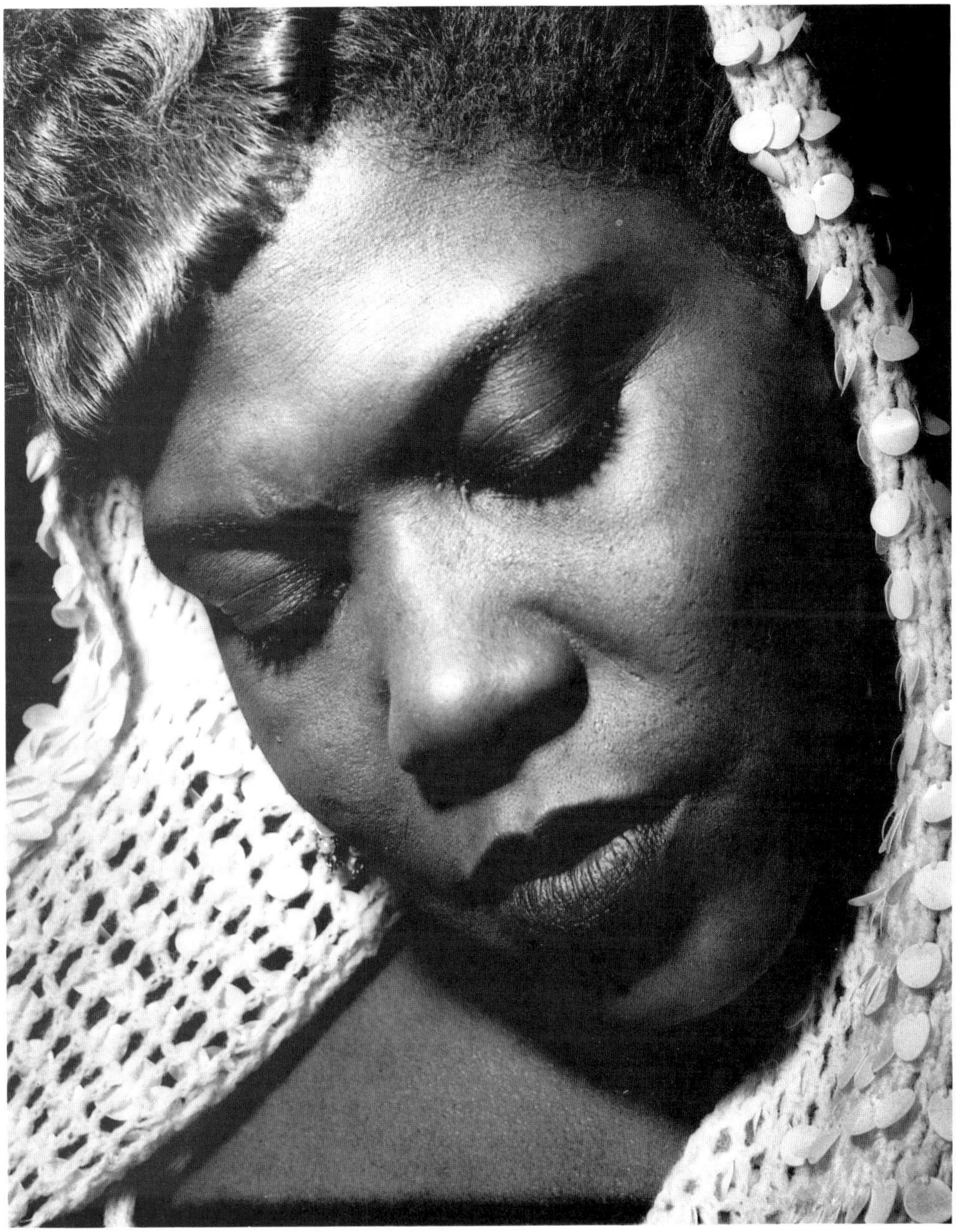

Sister Rosetta Tharpe. She gave me the best wedding present I could have imagined. A night in the Adelphi at Liverpool and a night in the Grand at Scarborough while she was on tour.

Alf's guidance was a major influence on my life and he was one of the few people whose advice I have ever taken. Sadie was an earth mother. During the war she had been a sergeant cook in the army and continued the career at home cooking meals enough to feed a regiment.

All my life I'd suffered from a bad chest. I had constant colds and bronchitis and my lungs bubbled like a waterlogged Hammond Organ. During one bout of illness Sadie fixed me with a mammoth hot drink composed of large quantities of gin, lemon, honey and an unknown ingredient of Russian origin. Next day I was totally better and I've never suffered since.

Living in Central London was great. Just up the road was the Cottage, 150 yards away was the Colyer Club, across Charing Cross Road, the Down Beat. Jazz at the Cool Canary, the 100 Club, the Flamingo and Ronnie Scott's, all within a short walk. When the Musicians' Union relaxed its ban on American bands these clubs were bulging with musical giants. Sonny Terry and Brownie McGhee, Muddy Waters, Dizzy, Wild Bill, Jesse Fuller, Paul Gonzalves, George Lewis, Jimmy Rushing, Johnny Hodges, Woody Herman, Kenny Clarke – I saw them all. After a concert they would drop into a club and almost without exception play into the small hours. I had a field day. Life was great.

Ann was working the box office at the Marquee as well as teaching during the day so even our finances picked up. My pictures appeared in Jazz News at ten bob a time and this money was supplemented with a day job in Wardour Street. My day job was taking soft porn pictures for two Jewish fellows who published magazines. The studio, which was really an attic, was located above a drinking club which they also owned. I worked with Martin Brooks who was my age and it was a dream of a job for a 23 year old. All we did was take pictures of girls either undressing or dressing. Sometimes they wore costumes - mortar board and suspenders, blackboard and cane, typewriter and specs – all Mickey Mouse stuff and quite tame compared with the rubbish allowed out today.

We also had the contract to print the *Wagon Train* stills for commercial television. On this job we produced 1500 10'x 8' prints every fortnight. Two of us printed all 1500 in a day by hand in very limited darkroom facilities. One day the owner of the company asked me if I would do three days' printing for a friend and on top of my wage, £10 a week at that time, he would give me £15. I said yes without thinking.

My new boss's premises were in a basement in Finchley Road. I reported at 8.30am. The owner showed me a pile of boxes containing 35mm films and a stack of boxes containing bromide paper. In all there were 5000 sheets. He wanted five postcard prints from each negative. I never thought to ask what the subject matter was. On the way out he locked me in the basement and promised to return at 5.30pm. That meant printing for eight and a half hours without a break. Why had he locked the door? The answer came when I looked at the negatives. They were quite obscene and he didn't want me to get caught doing them.

I'd seen plenty of smutty pictures in Egypt but they were period pieces shot in the 20s and, in spite of the subject matter had a curious charm which didn't offend. The pictures in this grotty little basement were crude and sexually explicit. The man on the films wore his socks and a little black party mask to hide his identity. I was at a loss what to do, so I got on with it.

When the man returned at 5.30pm I had printed just short of 4,000. I told him that was all he was going to get. He paid me off and I went home with a blinding headache and a distaste for crude pornography which has remained to this day. I am not against pictures of people screwing but it has to be done well. The ones in the basement were technically very poor and in bad taste.

When you're feeling down London is not always the best place to be. Oxford Street is a nightmare of commercial vulgarities with pickpockets, con men, three card tricksters, fashion and tat along its complete length. One Friday I was fighting my way back to the office through crowds of Christmas shoppers. There wasn't a taxi to be had, the buses were full and my progress was considerably hampered by the forty pound camera bag on my shoulder. Christmas decorations were hanging arrogantly from building to building and I was feeling well pissed off.

Outside the Academy Cinema, round a street vendor with a tray of clockwork Father Christmases, stood a group of people. On the pavement three or four of the toys were maniacally buzzing in circles round his feet. Approaching him I asked, 'How much?'

'Half a crown, mate.'

I gave him the coin and pointed to one on the floor which appeared to be more active than its colleagues.

'Can I have this?'

'You can have any, mate.'

So I stamped violently on the little bugger and squashed it flat. The people watching were outraged. I thought it was a really funny thing to do and it gave me no end of pleasure.

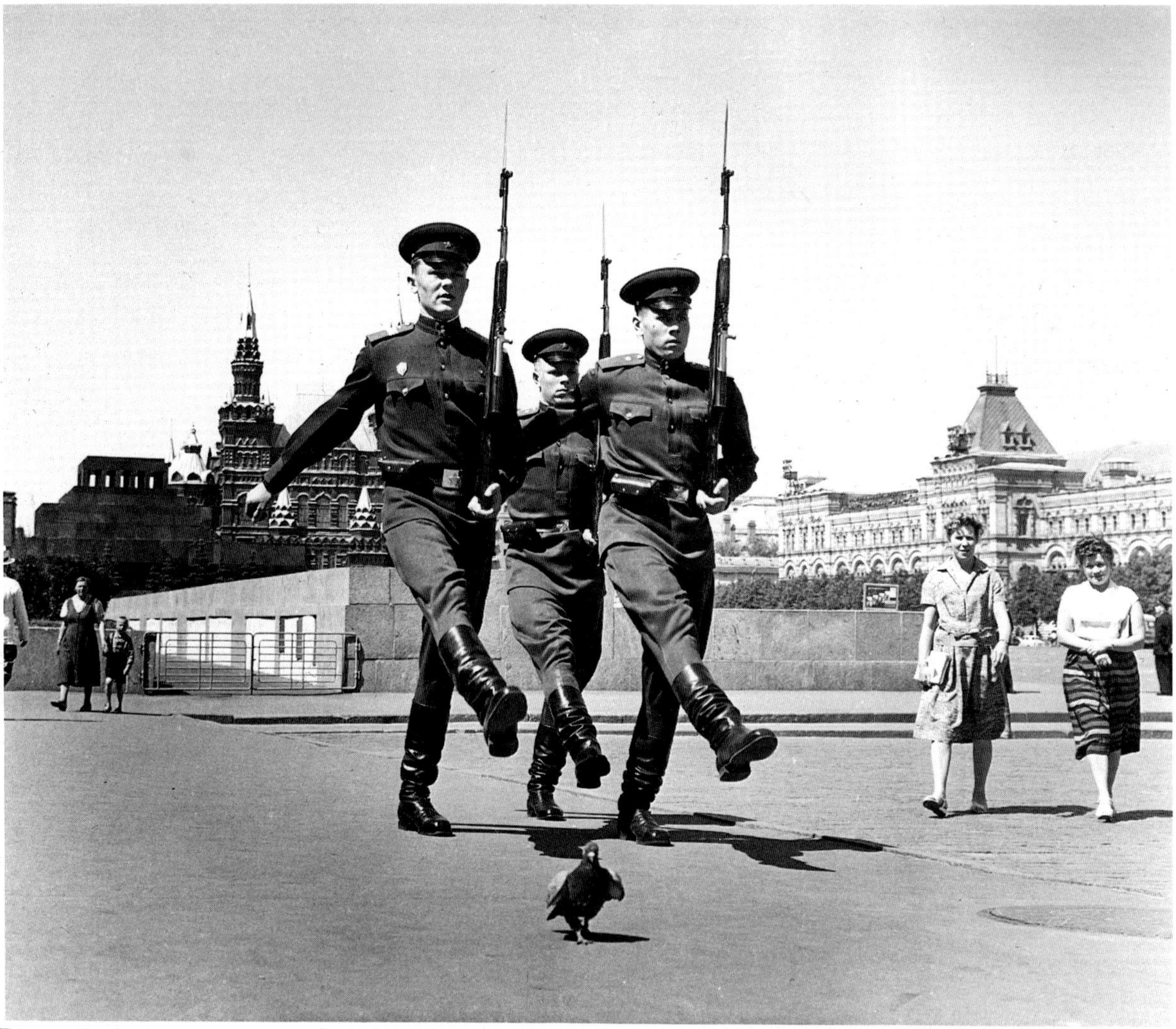

I have a photographic memory for almost every good image I've seen. I once saw a picture of some athletes at White City Stadium with a pigeon on the track in front of them. When I saw the pigeon in this photo eating scraps in Red Square it reminded me of White City. I ran round to the front of the soldiers, put my camera on the floor and clicked as everybody came into step, just before the pigeon took off.

I was having a rest in a cafe in Sokolniki Park, Moscow, with a glass of lemon tea without the lemon and thinking that it's funny but in over a dozen visits to Russia when I have ordered 'Chai citron' there has never ever been any citron, never, yet it's listed in the bloody menus in Ten Point Bold, when I was approached by two elderly men. One was very big and broad, the other small and darker; both wore fedoras with wide brims. By their gait I could see that they were not your ordinary muzhik. They indicated the vacant seats. I got on picking my way through a caviar and black bread butty. Obviously they wanted to sit down. This gave me a chance to exercise my only Russian word 'Da'. They sat and we struck up a conversation which involved on my part a lot of arm waving. They had little English but were two lovely old lads and obviously found something about me amusing because they were gently taking the mickey.

I felt at the time that they were a bit special but couldn't think why. Anyway we parted company good friends. Later in the day I met an English aerospace engineer over for the Industrial Exhibition.

'Saw you at the cafe today, Terry. Do you know who those two men were? The bigger man was Tupelev, father of Russian aviation, and the other was Mykoyan, designer of the MIG jet.'

I was in Moscow in 1961 for the first of the industrial exhibitions Khrushchev had allowed in from the West. From a news point of view this was hot. Russia had been a closed shop to photographers since the war.

◆

'Terry we've got a little job we think would be just up your street. Come up to the board room.' This was Mike Newmarch, the boss of my department. 'We're going to send you to Moscow.'

I was dumbstruck and terrified. The department had five photographers, all English, all highly competent. Why were they sending me, the department lackey? Of course now, when I think about it, their choice was obvious; being a freelance on two pounds a day, my services were expendable. 'We are sending you with a convoy of lorries. You are signed on as a lorry driver's mate. We have a contract with the company for pictures and feel it would make a good picture story.' Mike went on, 'When you get to Moscow you will attend the Industrial Exhibition and do such pictures as the exhibitors request plus any news pictures you come across.'

After four years of Catholic indoctrination, daily readings of Kravchenko's *I Chose Freedom*, stories about rats in cages tied to your head, starvation, beatings; Russia was high on my places to avoid. Looking at it another way I had never worked as a proper photographer. The army service didn't count, babies, door to door, a few weddings, all a far cry from Fleet Street. This doubt and lack of confidence has never left me.

I decided to ask Alf Harris.

'Go, Terry, it's the chance of a lifetime.'

'But Alf...'

'No buts Terry.' Sadie joined in, 'You can bring me back a pair of schtivells and a fur hat.'

'What's schtivells, Sadie?'

'Boots, putz, boots, knee length.'

'Sadie, I don't want to go. I want to learn this job slowly.'

'What's with pictures? You've got a camera, press the button, you've got a picture.'

My mind worked overtime trying to think of a way of getting out with honour. I didn't and went.

The point of departure was Shoreditch. A convoy of five pantechnicons and a Thames van was sent off by the Mayor of Shoreditch with the wives and children of the drivers cheering. It was all quite moving. We took the ferry to Antwerp and drove through the night to the German border. Getting the convoy through customs took several hours so we had to cook up at the roadside. The drivers had brought masses of camping equipment and food and we supplemented the fry up with bags of chips from a mobile cafe. Here I learned for the first time that the Brits haven't a clue when it comes to chips.

The Thames van had only two seats so I had to sit at the back window on a first aid box. This suited me as it gave unrestricted access to my equipment. The function of the van driver and partner was scouting. En route there were many low bridges which had to be avoided. On one occasion in Germany we had no alternative route other than a low bridge on a tram track. Unless we watched out the overhead wires would just touch the lorries' roofs. The cockney lads let the tyres down on 40 wheels and we scraped through with an inch to spare.

On our way through Belgium and West Germany I took lots of snaps and posted them home every evening. Passing through Check Point Charlie from West to East, I took pictures of the Eastern side as instructed, guards, buildings, the lot. Of course, this is strictly verboten but my confidence was picking up and I was determined not to fail. Most of the shots were made through the rear window of the van. I was on my second roll when a guard spotted me. He shouted to his mates and they came on like gang busters.

'Raus, raus.'

'OK, OK, Kraut.' The last word under my breath.

'Photograph verboten. Raus.'

I dived out of the van with my Rolleiflex.

'Passport bring.'

They took me into a little hut and demanded the film in my camera. I wound it on, clicking off the unexposed frames, with camera focused at about four feet and pointing at the guards as they took the film and the passport. My passport contained no visa for Moscow as I was in a block-visa held by the senior member of the crew. This perplexed the guard a little and he spoke to the senior officer, then handed it back to me and said in French, 'Bonne chance.' With this he pointed to the door and smiled. That smile worried me.

Back in the van, Colin the driver asked me if I wasn't a bit sick at losing my film.

'No, when the Kraut shouted I dumped the camera and picked up my spare. The first frame I exposed I took in a lav in West Germany. It's of some graffiti. The rest will show underexposed pictures of the guards looking into the camera.'

'What was the graffiti?'

'Oh, just the word bollocks.' He laughed and banged his foot down. We weren't out of trouble yet, there was another half a day to go before we were out of East Germany.

We crossed over the River Oder into Poland and pressed on into Poznan for the night. The lads went out on the town, I stayed and brought my captions up to date. From now on the film had to be stockpiled as posting them to London would be hazardous.

To travel through the Polish countryside was to step back in time; barns with grass roofs, crop cutting with scythes. We didn't see one tractor and most of the field work seemed to be done by women, a cheerful lot who shared our food when we stopped for a cook up.

We pressed on to Warsaw. The city had taken a fearful battering from the Germans and was mostly rebuilt, quite a lot in Russian Grotesque, although many of the historic areas had been skilfully rebuilt in the original and looked splendid. I didn't knock about with the lads in the two days we were there as my brief was to get as many library stock photos as possible. What I did manage to find, however, was the old ghetto area. One of the gates was still standing, the top wreathed in barbed wire. In the middle of the ruins was a memorial to the Polish resistance, a few house bricks placed in a heart shape with a jam jar in the middle. The jar held a few wild flowers.

We set off at sunrise for the Russian border a distance of about 200 miles, and reached it late that afternoon, crossing the River Bug at Brest Litovsk. Our hotel took its name from the river I thought as we booked in.

The Russian side of the border was very depressing, no more than a collection of grotty buildings and a few wooden houses but the population were amazed and delighted to see us. The last convoys they had witnessed were German coming and, later, going.

Through Byelorrussia the roads are narrow, very straight and very uneven. They pass through no towns or villages for these are set well off the road. Let's face it, the Steppes are a little boring.

We headed north for Minsk and stayed

overnight, then Smolensk, then Moscow. The first sight of Moscow is awe inspiring and after many visits this city still remains my favourite place. The hotels on the other hand were not outstanding. Although we were booked into a brand new one which had opened that week and was not intended for non Russians, the rooms had no hot water. Our drivers refused to put up in it. Miraculously the Intourist guide managed to put us up at another new place, where the toilets flushed boiling water.

Luckily the hotel backed onto Sokolniki Park, the place where the exhibition was sited, so I could get there on foot. As there were many stands to photograph before my press work started this meant I could get there before the crowds. So every morning, avoiding the red hot pipes descending from the flush box, it was a 6.30am call, shower, lavatory, and out the door for 7am spot on. A fifteen minute walk to the site, ten minutes begging the guard to let me in and I was off working.

Showers were communal in the hotel as were the lavatories. Neither had doors and as our party had the whole of this corridor to itself we got into the habit of walking around naked. One morning I waltzed into the ablutions and was staggered to find it filled, literally filled, with naked and half naked Mongolian women. There wasn't one under 14 stone. What was I to do? My first impulse was to dash out looking foolish then I thought maybe these people share facilities. There are no doors on public lavatories in the centre of Moscow, you can be sitting there having a brown thought when the loo lady casually wanders up, offers you two bits of bog paper the size of a large postage stamp and asks you how you're doing. Confronted by the Mongolians I decided to brazen it out and sauntered in saying, 'Good morning ladies.' They were very friendly and amused at my eight stone milk white body, something about the same size as the largest one's left leg. Big as they were, they were very handsome. I drew the line at using the toilet but showered with them every morning for a week.

One afternoon as I was leaving the hotel they were all getting onto a bus with husbands, most of whom were smaller than I was. Seeing me the men came across laughing and pinned a small medallion on my jacket. I found out later that the showers and toilets were ladies, the gents being in the other wing.

On the opening day of the exhibition, the place was really jumping. Premier Khrushchev was to do a tour of all the pavilions so naturally there would be tremendous photo opportunities. Apart from the press pictures there was plenty of PR. Every stand he visited, every handshake, was a potential bonanza. There was only one drawback. I was unofficial. The exhibition organizers had tied up the photographic rights with The Financial Times, part owners of the show. Their man Brewster had already got his beady eye on me.

The opening ceremony was the usual; speeches,

marching bands and girls in regional costumes. Inside the hall the BBC had set up cameras to do the first live broadcast from the USSR to the UK. In order to play safe I stayed just outside the door of the main hall from which the VIPs were to start their tour. Khrushchev arrived with a party of VIPs and I started walking backwards into the hall. The cameras had started rolling and the first pictures to reach the UK were of me bumping backwards into the presenter. Years later my stepmother told me that she'd shouted to my dad to tell him that I was on television. Dad came galloping out of the lavatory with his trousers round his ankles but he was too late. A few minutes later Brewster pointed me out to the KGB men saying in a loud voice that I was a lorry driver's mate. The hoods hustled me outside but five minutes later I was back in and shooting, making sure to keep in front of the party. There was one shot which was an absolute gem. On a Lancashire boot manufacturing stand was a pedestal with two boots from the Crimean War. The light and distance from the aisle were just right. I waited and as Nikita passed with his head exactly between the boots he turned my way and I cracked off a shot. It was the last one on the roll. I flipped the back of the Rollei open and pulled the release knob, all this on the run. I needed to keep up with the action.

Life was against me. The spring in the back of the Rolleiflex is meant to push the spool up sufficiently to give quick access for reloading. At this critical point it sprang too much and the unsealed film fell to the floor and unrolled itself, fogging all the frames. Khrushchev saw what happened and laughed like a drain. The incident also attracted the attention of Brewster. Once again he got me put out of the building and once again I got back in. It was getting more frantic. There were four more halls to go and a lot to catch up on.

One of the exhibitors was a company who made laundry equipment but unfortunately they couldn't get it operative as the Fire Marshall would not allow a pipe carrying kerosene into the building. As Nikita was passing the stand, a girl stepped into his path and asked if he could pull rank and do something about it. The girl's Lancashire accent flummoxed the interpreter but he managed to convey the problem. Khrushchev turned to a man in his party and said, 'Get it fixed.' Then turned to the girl and said, 'Eto budet rabotat zavtra i pervoe chto vy mozhete stirat eto trusiki Mikoyana.' This translates as, 'It will be on tomorrow and your first article to wash will be Mikoyan's underpants.' A lovely man, Khrushchev; pity he made such a cock up of the administration.

The tour came to an end and a large crowd had gathered round the party in a corner of the building. There was no way I could fight my way through because, let's face it, you can't get heavy with the KGB.

In my early morning visits to the site I had recced all the buildings and knew my way about. I occasionally had a glass of tea with the cleaning ladies in this very building so I knew there was a small balcony a few feet above the crowd which led off from the cleaners' storeroom. Within seconds of getting to the area this knowledge allowed me to go up the stairs, into the storeroom and out onto the balcony. The VIPs were just below about ten feet away. The British Ambassador was presenting Mr Khrushchev with a set of golden goblets and they were toasting each other. I cracked off a couple of shots. As I was finishing the KGB bodyguards looked up in horror. From their manner I decided I'd better be long gone. As luck would have it there was a police car off-loading at the park entrance. A ten dollar bill changed ownership and the driver ran me across town to the Associated Press office. There were no processing facilities at the AP but I had brought all the necessary chemicals so I dish developed the films in the bathroom.

Within one and a half hours I had dried them with methylated spirits, run off a few prints and sent the goblet shot on the wire to London. It was in all the nationals. We scored ten to the opposition's one.

◆

After a couple of days the English newspapers started to filter through and we saw that every publication carried my pictures. It was not just the goblet one. I had scored for Lansing Bagnel, ICI, Pye, the Iron and Steel Federation, Lucas, Distillers Co, AEI and Bendix. There were also several feature pictures. This batch attracted more commissions and the pressure increased. ICI flew out a couple of models and the Daily Express requested a fashion feature.

Now fashion was not my strongest subject and still isn't but the very nature of the locations gave the pictures a lift. This project also managed to get hauled up by the police when we placed a leggy model in front of some Russian shopping ladies. One of the ladies wandered into the photograph and then complained that we were insulting the Russian people and reported us. As a result we were bundled outside and told to stop taking pictures.

This incident allowed the Express to have a field day. They blew the thing up beyond credibility and ran the story for two days on the lines of 'British photographer and models arrested in Moscow.' The fact was we weren't arrested; but then the Daily Express was never averse to having a go at the Reds. For my part I was very angry because I felt that it put me in a dangerous position. The Russians had behaved very well during the incident but I felt that there was a list at No 2 Dzherzhinsky Prospekt and my name was on it with a red line underneath.

Wiring photographs through the Russian Telegraph Service was becoming difficult and expensive, though whether this was because of the increased volume or sheer bloodymindedness, God

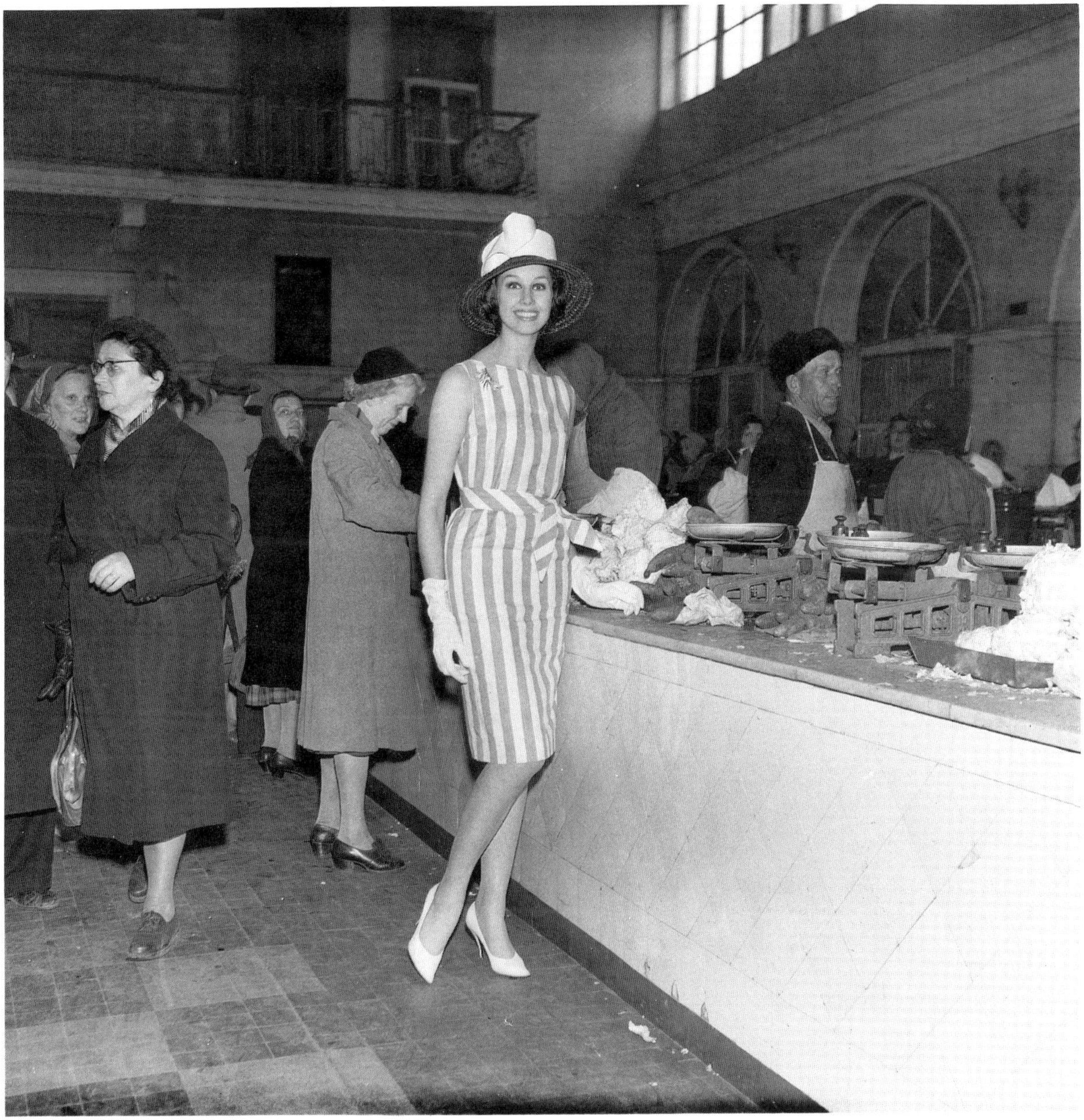

Fashion photograph for the Daily Express. The lady on the left complained that the lady in the middle was embarrassing the Russian people, which of course she was. We all were.

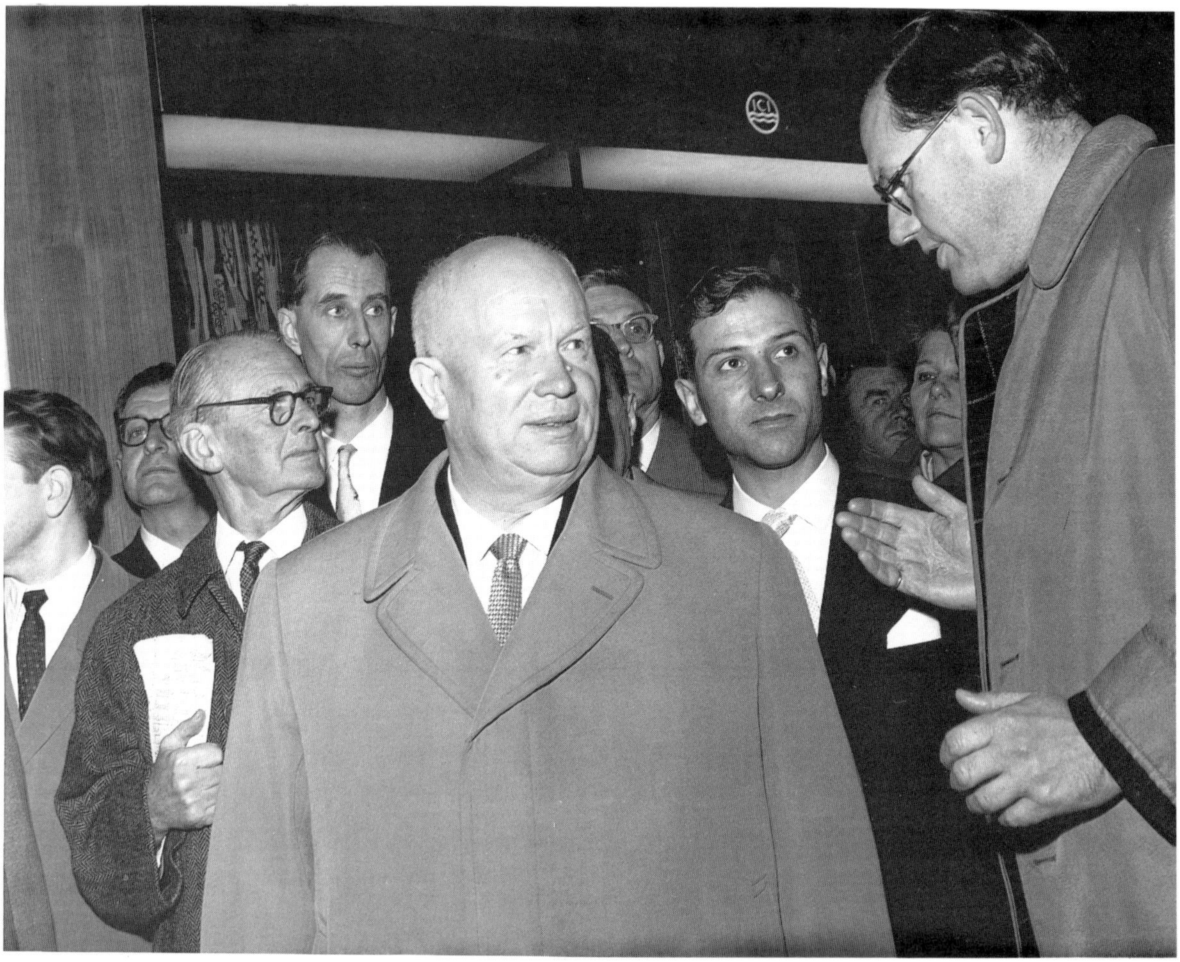

Reggie Maudling and Premier Khrushchev. This picture was commissioned by ICI. Khrushchev never actually visited the ICI stand, so I took a photo of him near another stand and painted in the logo.

only knows. Fortunately I had a contingency plan. Before leaving the UK I had obtained a list of all the English personnel going to the exhibition from Clarksons, the travel agents handling the flights and hotel bookings. Someone was leaving every day so all I had to do was make contact. Most of those leaving early carried films for me. In all the time the only package that went missing was carried by the fashion editor of the Daily Express. Her office was only 250 yards from the Associated Press in London; she said she'd posted it!

◆

Moscow is a bizarre place and has the most peculiar effect on visitors. They either patronize wildly, get drunk and fall in love with the floor dragon guarding the hotel corridors or cut their wrists on the steps of the British Embassy. It is a city where there are no half measures. It has more drunks than Glasgow twice over and more art galleries than London, Paris and New York put together. I'd sooner spend a week in Moscow than a fortnight anywhere else on earth.

At the end of my third week I decided that enough was enough. My health was starting to deteriorate. I'd been working about sixteen hours a day and not eating properly. A touch of bronchitis was also slowing me down considerably. It was time to leave while still ahead. Getting a flight was no difficulty, as I had softened up the Intourist girls with a few goodies, but I was worried about my camera case for it was filled with rolls of exposed film which the Russians were quite capable of confiscating. This plus the fact that there was one more job to do in an airport where photos were strictly forbidden.

'Oh, Terry, when you're leaving make us a quick snap of the Rothman's ad at Sheremetevo.'

'OK, Mike.' Mike Newmarch was the Chief of Wide World, part of AP's library service.

'By the way, Terry, don't draw too much attention to yourself. The Russians might not like it.'

Sheremetevo, the international airport, was a fairly primitive place compared to Heathrow or Kennedy but the Russians were very sensitive about airport security. In fact most people played safe by packing cameras in their suitcases and avoiding any confrontation. I couldn't do this as there was a picture I needed. The main building apparently contained the only advert for western goods in the whole Soviet Union, a sign for Rothman's cigarettes. Associated Press had been commissioned to get a picture and the Russians wouldn't allow it.

In those days people catching flights out were ferried to the airport in large chauffeur driven limousines, usually one for each passenger. I would have been happier to share as I'd spent the last three weeks on my own, being hounded by the exhibition organizers and treading very thin ice with the law. Paranoia was beginning to take hold.

I checked my baggage at the flight desk, keeping a tight hold on my camera case which always travels with me. The Rolleiflex round my neck raised a few eyebrows but nothing was said. My money was checked and paper roubles converted into sterling then it was on to Immigration. There the man took one look at my passport before his eyes did an Eddie Cantor. There was no entry visa or exit visa, just a visitor's permit. He was obviously well perplexed. How did I get in without a visa? This wasn't possible. He reached for a phone. I felt sick. My background insisted that the authorities and the police were not to be trusted in any country and here I was, apparently illegal, in the capital of Totalitaria.

The man kept banging the phone up and down trying to get through to someone but he was having no luck. I knew what the problem with the passport was. I'd entered the country on a block visa with the lorry drivers so my passport didn't need one. Somebody in the UK had presumed my exit would be with the drivers so I didn't get one to leave. It was simple but I thought it better to keep that to myself otherwise I might have to stay another three weeks at least and leave with the lorries. The man failed to get through on the telephone and called for a senior. The two held a heated discussion which went on for about twenty minutes until the senior got exasperated and wrote in my passport, stamped it, handed it to me and said, 'Sadites po bystree na samolet.' – get on the plane quickly.

'Do svidanya tovarishch.' – bye bye comrade, I replied.

I was out of his office like greased lightning and into the main hall. There two air hostesses panicked me along. The flight had been held on the tarmac thirty minutes but now it was loaded and ready to go. As I rushed along I saw at the end of the hall the poster, about thirty feet square, Rothman's Cigarettes. This was it. With my camera set at infinity and the shutter at 125th with full aperture, a complete stab in the dark, I had to take it. There was no way I could get out an exposure meter and start measuring the light values. I would create enough attention as it was. I had to distract people.

Just a few feet down the hall there was a woman sitting at a desk. As I passed she offered me a paper carrier bag containing leaflets and a few small badges, a souvenir of my trip; a free gift.

'Spasibo, luv,' I said smiling. I had the answer. Moscow in 1961 was 'uptight city.' No native would be seen to take money and restaurant tips were usually turned down with a look of disdain. Wheels could be lightly oiled with a ballpoint pen or a bunch of flowers but money could only be accepted in private. Diving into my pocket I took a handful of small coins the exchange wouldn't take. I threw them on to the table but the money bounced and scattered onto the floor. The woman and both air hostesses stooped to pick it up. I turned and with the camera at waist level clicked the shutter.

◆

Mike Newmarch met me at Heathrow and we shot off to the AP to look at press cuttings. In the three weeks we had scored 34 national publications, 250 regionals, eight magazine features and massive PR sales to industrial companies. ICI alone had ordered 2750 10' x 8' prints from my fashion pictures for their fibres division. I acknowledge now that my success in Russia gave me a false estimate of my abilities but I didn't see it at the time. There is a lot more to photography than the Kodak slogan 'You press the button, we do the rest.'

As a reward for my work in Moscow I was taken on on full salary, although still maintaining my freelance status. Within two days of my return I was bundled onto a 1st class BOAC flight to Uganda to illustrate a book for American Catholic primary schools. From then on the assignments came thick and fast. Sweden, Germany, France, Greece, all the Iron Curtain countries, South America; these were all PR and advertising jobs, although some, like the Russian trips, bridged over into the news category. PR photos quite often have the same urgency as hot news and must be got back to the UK PDQ. So often I took a portable enlarger and chemicals and did the processing in hotel bathrooms. In capital cities prints can be wired from telegraph offices or sent by friendly travellers on aeroplanes.

This is a last resort as the reliability can't be guaranteed. A photograph I took of the soldiers and pigeons in Red Square was published all over the world, though ruined in most cases by bad cropping. It won the Encyclopedia Britannica Award for 1961. The resultant publicity did me no harm and the work came in thick and fast. The AP sent me all over after that.

I was hardly ever at home and that's when Ann and I split up. She wasn't exactly a home body but she did need a home around her and she wasn't getting one. I was devastated and spent months in deep depression. Then in a fit of pique I told the AP to up stick the job. I was getting ripped off anyway. Think about this. If one of my own personal pictures was put on the wire to foreigns they paid me £3. The photograph got published in dozens, sometimes hundreds, of papers but there was no further payment. To add to that I was on 24 hour call seven days a week and quite often worked a 16 hour day for a basic £25 a week. It was dog's work. There were five photographers in the department and we all got less money than the salesmen.

Six months after I left, the department closed down. This may have been because I took most the big clients with me. I didn't hang around long. It took a few weeks to get organized then I joined forces with Mike Marchant, a salesman from the AP and we started our own business.

The first job was for the Gulf Oil Company in Holland, a wonderful country for disappointed lovers, and there by a windmill behind a Gulf petrol station I met my lovely Johanna Maria De Jong. Her name sounded to me like a peal of bells, the pain melted away and I fell instantly in love. After spending a few days at her parents' house I took her back to England where we married three years later.

That was in the mid sixties, the profligate sixties. Advertising and PR skyrocketed at this time. It was not uncommon to shoot two jobs a day and run a print order of 500 10' x 8' from each. When a foreign job came along Johanna went home and stayed with her parents. It was an ideal arrangement.

◆

I had many good clients, - J Walter Thompson, Young and Rubicam, ICI, United Africa, Bensons - but my biggest was Gulf Oil Company. Throughout the sixties I worked for them all over the world; oil rigs, seismic exploration in the Nigerian swamps, refineries, banquets, petrol stations, the lot. The longest I was away from them was the three weeks I spent in South America for the Steel Company of Wales. In three weeks I also did all the South American countries finishing in Rio.

You have to watch your back over there. Once a taxi driver tried to hijack me into a Favella shanty town. I'd booked him to run me up into the mountains above the giant statue of Christ. When we got there I shufftied the taxi meter. It took me less than thirty seconds to see that a picture wasn't possible because of the ozone. Getting back in the taxi alongside the driver I saw the meter had shot up to four times the amount of cruzeiros. The last time this flanker had been worked on me was in Rome and the driver didn't get away with it on that occasion.

'Wass ist der geschaft?' I said, using German as there were so many of them in Rio.

'No understand Mister.'

'Oh you speak English. What's with the meter?'

He lapsed into Portuguese so I swore in Arabic. 'Kasumuk, clifti whaller, enta zie el zeft.'

The argument looked like turning nasty and we were quite isolated up in the mountains. 'OK, OK, take me back to Copacabana. We'll let the police settle this.'

He rolled the car onto the road and screeched off down the hill but as we neared the foothills outside Rio he suddenly shot sharp left into a collection of shanties and stood on the foot brake. This looked dangerous so I gave him a mighty smack full in the face, grabbed my camera case, fell out of the car and legged it down the road. Wilson the Wonder Athlete would have come second best the way I was shifting. On reaching my hotel I instantly booked out and took the only flight going west. It happened to be to Nigeria. There I picked up some work for the Nestle Company, Unilever and Gulf Oil.

When my department at AP closed down some

of the old team joined up with me and Mike and we formed a cooperative operating out of the City. We shared many clients in the financial centre, Lloyds, the Mansion House, Guildhall, along with most of the country's leading manufacturing giants. Then round about 1967 Gulf went into motor racing. This worried me a bit as I'm not a sports photographer and I didn't like cars. It also meant using 35mm which I hated and telephoto lenses, technology quite new to me. My living had been made so far with a Rolleiflex and a Hasselblad. Both cameras were unsuitable for car racing.

Our first few races were quite successful. With our connections at the AP we got many pictures onto the wire service and Gulf got lots of publications world wide, which was the object of the exercise. Some circuits were well equipped. At Nurburg Ring in Germany, for instance, there were darkrooms behind the pits. This meant we could issue prints to the press all through the race. This impressed Gulf but they wondered why we couldn't do the same elsewhere.

There were no darkrooms elsewhere so I made one. In the late 19th century photographers took portable darkrooms into the field, sensitized the plates on site and used them wet. To enable them to see what was going on, a small panel of red glass was let into the side to admit safe light. As Gulf were expecting something like 200-300 prints per race an 8 inch square of red glass would be inadequate so I designed and had made a six foot cube of orange plastic which fitted over an aluminium frame. It was a giant safe light. I could get inside and work in broad daylight. Power for the enlarger was provided by a Honda generator. It worked a treat and gobsmacked the opposition.

On the occasion we used it at Le Mans the Gulf Oil top brass showed up along with account executives from Young and Rubicam. They stood outside the tent to await the miraculous appearance of handfuls of 10' x 8's and as we had just won the race the pace was frantic. During the Le Mans 24 hours I shot a film every hour or so, developed it, printed it in less than 30 minutes and delivered prints to the press office. I did this throughout the entire race. I kept going on cans of beer, about the only time I drank whilst working. Often the beer would take effect and the need for a leak would become urgent. Rather than close everything down and walk or run 200 yards to the lav I peed in a jug and emptied it down a nearby drain. On this occasion I just handed the jug through a door flap and said, 'Here, empty these chemicals, Mike.' Mike wasn't there but the Executive Vice President, Grady Davis, was. Grabbing the steaming jug he scurried off to empty it.

We won the Le Mans two years running with the same machine, a GT40, the last of the great sports cars. Gulf eventually went into partnership with Porsche but without the same success.

◆

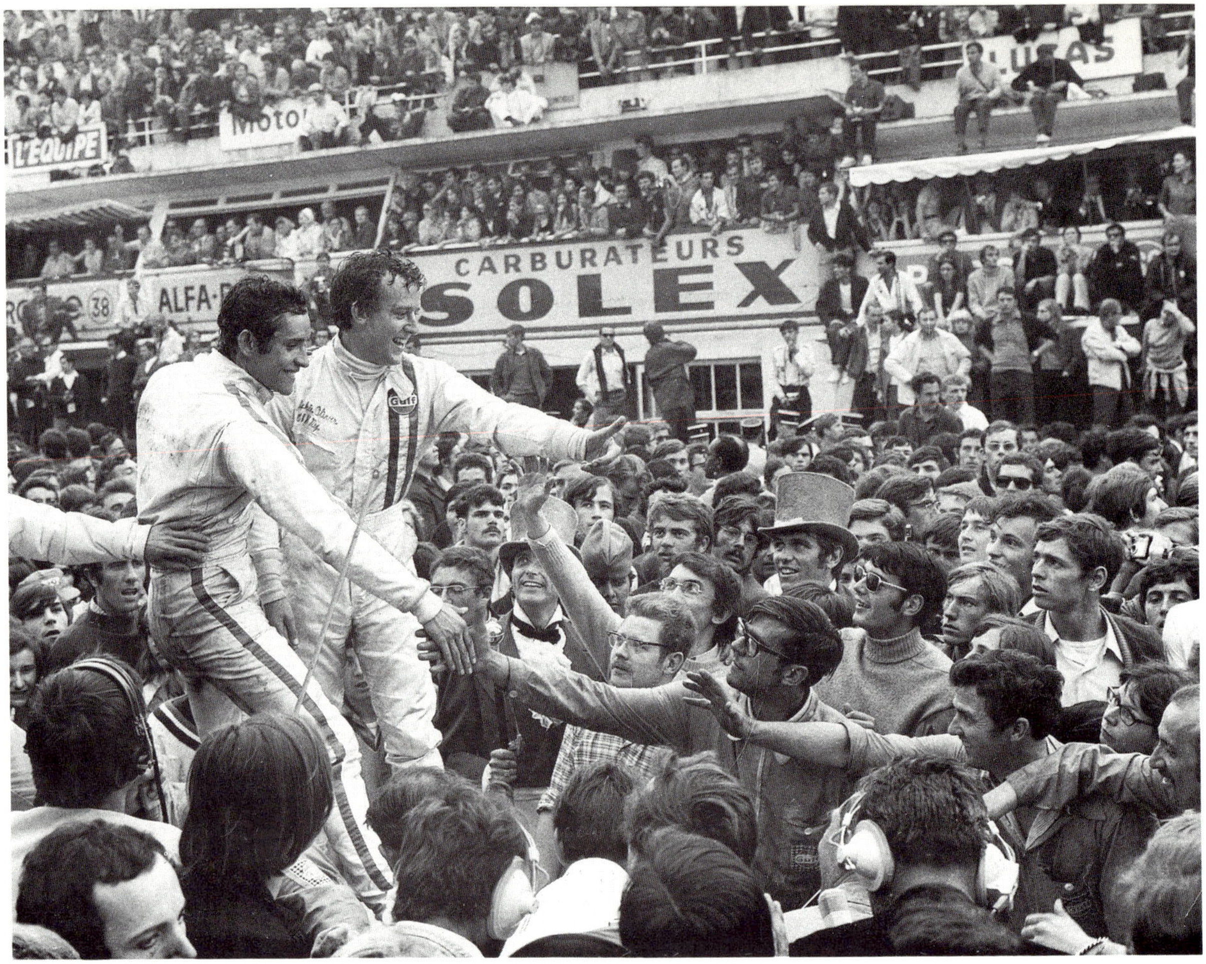

Le Mans 24 hour Race. Champagne days. I used to get hotel chefs to cook me special meals and Gulf Oil picked up the tab. Two men lifted me up to get this shot and it made every racing paper.

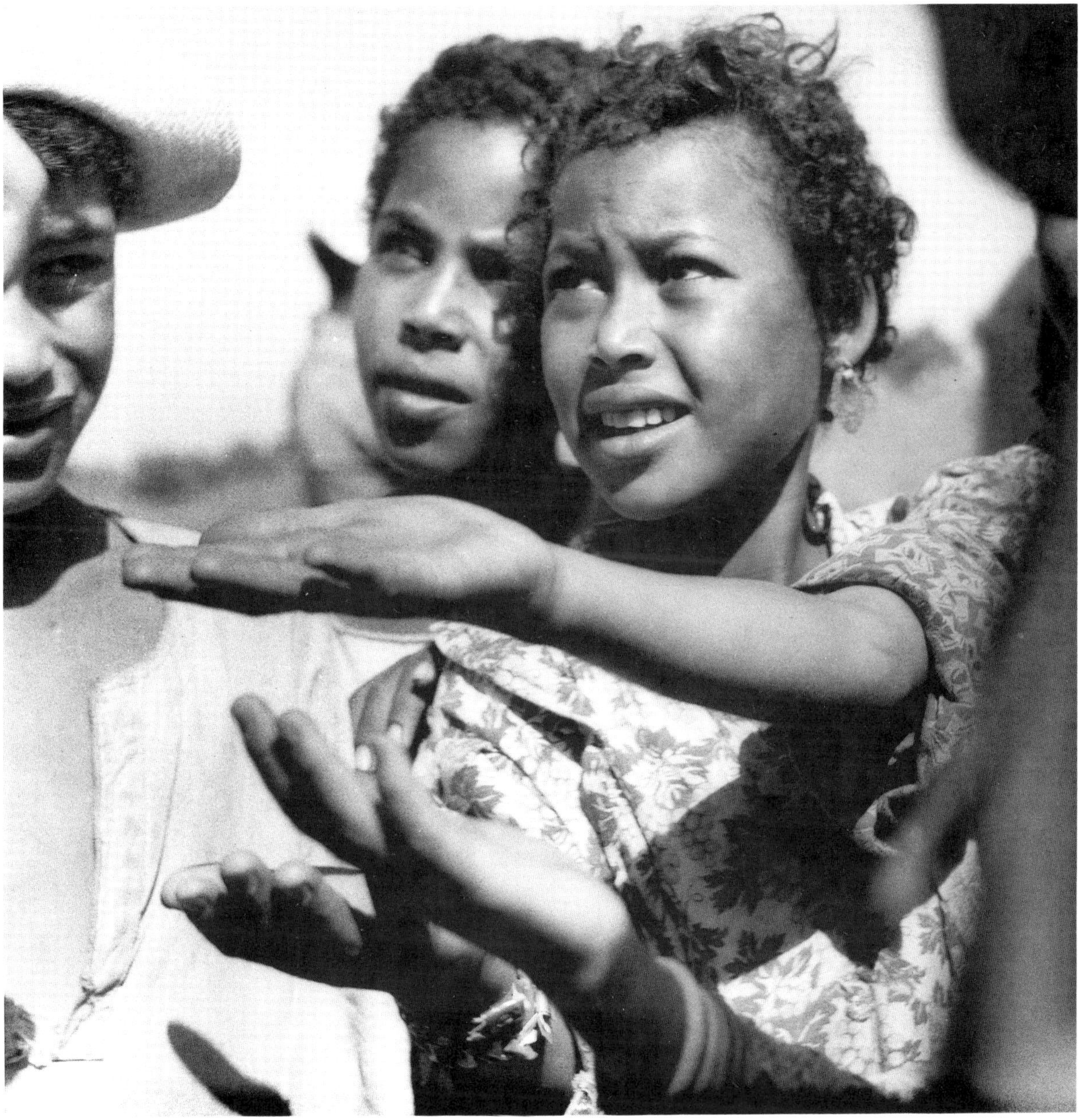

Ismailia, Egypt 1953. Wherever soldiers went kids followed shouting, 'Baksheesh', much the same way as we had followed American soldiers pestering them for chewing gum.

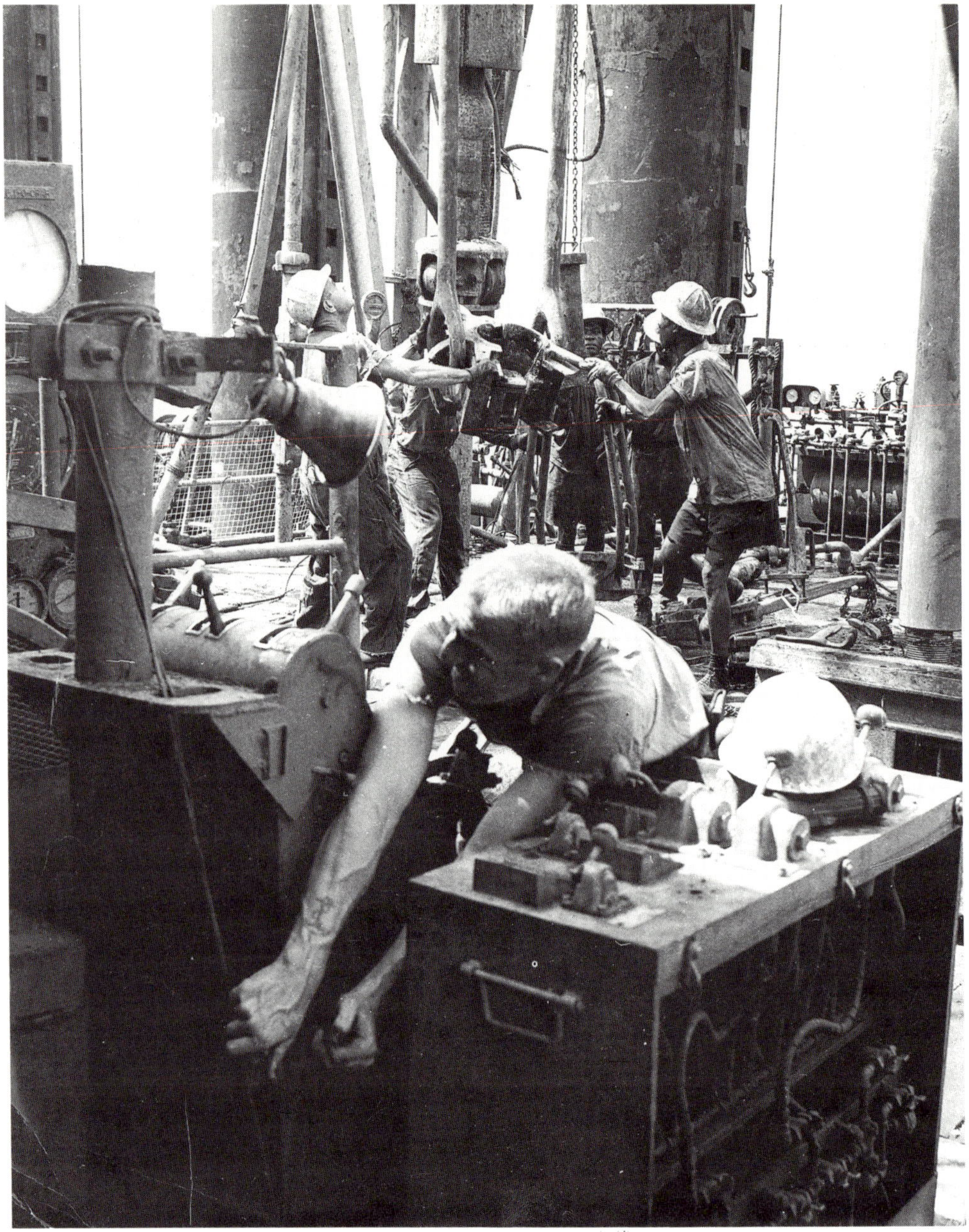

Drilling for oil at Escravos Bar, Nigeria. I had a big account for Gulf Oil and did two or three jobs a week for almost ten years.

In the early '60s I made friends with Keith McCartney and started going to Liverpool and was more or less adopted by Auntie Ginny, the family matriarch or 'control'. She got that name because when she answered the phone she would say, 'control'. Ginny was a lovely gentle woman of sound practical common sense and kindness. The extended family, which was huge, relied on her advice in all matters; pregnancies, birth, marriage, make up, food, parties and pot. When she went to London to the premiere of *A Hard Day's Night* she took Paul McCartney, her nephew, a box of Manx Kippers and half a dozen black puddings.

I started to photograph the family at various parties and weddings and kept it up for seventeen years. My last visit was in 1990 to Ginny's funeral but on this occasion I left my camera at home.

◆

During my first trip to Russia in 1961 I discovered through the Embassy grapevine that a reception was to be held at a government dacha up in the Lenin Hills on the outskirts of Moscow. Attending would be the Russian premier Brezhnev, several members of the Politbureau, a squabble of British MPs and several businessmen from the UK. The press were excluded and the location not published. I just had to attend.

Taxis in Moscow are as scarce as rocking horse road apples and even if you are lucky enough to get one you couldn't guarantee that he'd run you up into the Lenin Hills. I've never actually been in a Russian taxi. I've joined queues for one only to be told to 'sod off' or the Russian equivalent. I took a bus to the outskirts and set off walking.

The Lenin Hills, while not quite as big as the Yorkshire Dales, do cover a fair bit of ground. I was banking on seeing large black cars all gliding in one direction so that I could follow them. After about an hour I was ready to give up. My camera case was heavy and my stomach aching from hunger, when a large black Zil pulled up just ahead of me. It had a MOC number plate, KGB, bad news. I was thinking I'll plead ignorance and ask them not to overdevelop my films this time, when a window rolled down and out popped a head. Bloody hell, it was Reggie Maudling.

'I say, are you British?' Cheeky sod, what did he think I was?

'Yes, sir. Press photographer.'

'Are you going to the reception?'

'Yes, sir.'

'Can you show us the way?'

'I think so, sir.'

'Get in,' he said.

I did. The car slid forward. We drove down long avenues of trees, behind which, hidden by walls, were government dachas confiscated from the privileged rich at the time of the revolution and now reserved for people enjoying the same privileges. The driver, a Russian kept turning to me, the quizzical look on his face indicating the need for directions. My Russian was limited to food, drink and political platitudes so the best I could offer was 'Pryamo tovarishch', straight on comrade. Reggie Maudling, very impressed by my fluent command of the situation, settled back in his seat and read a folder of papers.

Fortune favours the brave and as we floated past a large dacha set well back from the road I noticed in the drive several Zims, a Roller or two and a Jaguar. The driver stopped on my instruction, reversed and drove through the gates. Two soldiers on guard, seeing we were flying the Union Flag, presented arms.

Reggie and I walked up to the entrance like old friends. There we were met by a delegation of Russian bigwigs who shook us both by the hand. At least it was the right place; my stomach had been heaving during the journey at the thought of being rumbled.

It was a grand reception. Despite austerity in the Soviet Union the big wheels did things in fine style; tables groaned under lavishly prepared delicacies. Beluga caviare came by the bucketful, as did smoked sturgeon, Siberian crab, salmon, iced soup, an endless flow of good Georgian wine, vodka, and brandy. It was like a page out of Mrs Beaton. I was starving. The only food to pass my lips in the past twelve hours was a disgusting sausage I had shared with some girls in the Gum Stores staff canteen. It would have been bad form to attack the food before anyone else. I wouldn't have done anyway as my pictures always came first, regardless of the temptations.

By the time people got round the food I'd shot eight rolls of film, all of British businessmen talking to Brezhnev or other important ministers. My pocket was bulging with business cards and firm orders for long print runs. I also knew there would be extra revenue from the newspapers if I could get the pictures out. By the time I felt it would be acceptable to dive into the food, most of it had been scoffed but there was plenty of Beluga left. Caviare was always slow to go at these Russian functions. I suppose the natives regarded it as commonplace and it appeared the Brits didn't like it. I did, although the liking took a lot of practice.

On this occasion the exquisite fish eggs were in five hundred gram portions in glistening crystal bowls, nestling in beds of crushed ice. It took me about twenty minutes to eat the lot, along with three slices of sour black bread, half a decanter of wine, a couple of vodkas and two oranges. The oranges were pure luck. In Russia oranges were so scarce they were regarded as exotic and were always the first to disappear into Russian pockets at any function.

The oranges came in useful, I traded them for a lift back to my hotel. The day had been a great success so I treated myself to a night at the Bolshoi.

◆

In April 1961 Gagarin circled the earth in Vostok 1. It was a colossal achievement considering that the previous generation was largely illiterate. The Russians had been very secretive about the operation and had up to then not issued any pictures. The May Day parade was coming up and it seemed logical that this was the occasion to show the space capsule for the first time thereby achieving a huge press scoop and massive PR. It made sense to me that Vostok was in Moscow but finding it would be a problem.

I rang London and spoke to Eddie Gilmore of the Associated Press. Eddie was a Pulitzer Prize winner and had spent some time in Russia and knew Moscow inside out. He advised going back to the Permanent Exhibition as this was the most likely place. Of course it wasn't that simple to speak to him. Most or probably all phone calls in and out of Moscow are listened to, so we had to hint and pretend we were talking about other matters. This was the first time since the war the Russians had allowed in large numbers of foreigners and they were very twitchy. I left it a couple of days to quieten down and set off to the Park.

The area covered by the Exhibition Halls was about thirty acres, each building in the architectural style of the region represented. I had visited most of them shooting library material so knew full well that if Vostok was anywhere it would be in a place inaccessible to the public. There was a building set back in the trees and in the thirty minutes I observed it it had no visitors. It was a large hall with no windows, the double front door was about fifteen feet high and there was an elderly man not in uniform but holding a rifle standing on the approaching steps. This had to be something good. But how to get in? A full frontal was out of the question so I approached from the back and found an open door. The corridor was dark with two doors left and right and a large door at the end. Groping my way down the corridor by the light of my cigarette lighter, I pushed a door open and entered a large room. My lighter by now was getting hot and running out of gas but just before it did so I made it to the large double doors and stood there, shaking with excitement, still not knowing what was in the room. As I wasn't carrying my flash gun, I had to produce light somehow. The chance of finding a light switch was quite out of the question. The door would solve the dilemma if I dare open it. Was it worth it? I'd already had trouble with the law, shooting fashion for the Daily Express in an out of bounds area. The British nationals had run the story for two days and embarrassed the Russians no end. Was it worth the risk? The worst that could happen would be deportation which would leave the job unfinished and create all manner of problems for the AP Editor in Moscow. On the other hand personally I didn't give a toss for him as he had been no great help to me. The thought of not completing the assignment didn't bear thinking about. So I stopped thinking and gently eased one of the doors open about nine inches.

The old lad with the shooter was still on the steps with his back to the building. Sunlight streamed through the gap. I turned and at the far end of the room, about fifty feet away, was the blessed space vehicle with a huge printed board at the side of it. The light wasn't sufficient to make an instantaneous snap and I couldn't even get a reading with my light meter. It would need a time exposure and my tripod was at the hotel. Standing about twenty feet from the space capsule was a five foot plinth with a bust on top; it may have been Lenin but I couldn't quite make it out. It was an ideal support for my camera. The angle was not quite right but by wedging my press card under its front the elevation was perfect. I made three exposures at full aperture; ten seconds, twenty seconds and thirty seconds. Subsequently I found that the ten second exposure, although very dense, was printable.

Unfortunately the picture was never used although it was the first to reach the West. AP's reason was that publishing before the official Russian picture would deprive them of much needed hard currency and cause severe trouble for AP's operations at their Moscow Bureau. My action might even get their editor kicked out on some trumped up charge.

Disappointment was shortlived. My picture of Russian guards in Red Square won the Feature Picture of the Year in the Encyclopaedia Britannica Press Awards. Better than a kick up the arse, as I said at the time.

◆

My second trip to Russia was in 1964. My partner Mike Marchant and I were on our way to Moscow for the Agricultural Fair. From there we were going to drive down through the Ukraine to the Black Sea, then back over the Transylvanian Alps through Hungary, Austria, then home. We took most of our meals by the side of the road, as we'd brought along plenty of food and a primus. The trip was mostly uneventful and in Moscow we were booked into the pre-revolution Hotel National just off Red Square in Gorkogo Ulitsa.

The fair was in Sokolniki Park with many countries exhibiting. The only other photographer there was from my old company AP so there would be plenty of work to go round. During the day we put in about ten hours and at night about fourteen. Moscow in 1964 was having its own swinging 60s and although the plainclothes police were buzzing about like flies round a cow's arse they left the

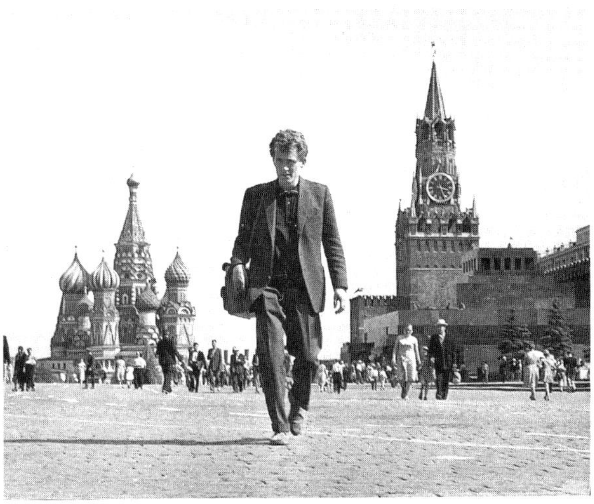

Red Square 1961. On my way to take fashion shots for the Daily Express.

I had an agreement with Tupperware for publicity shots both on the journey to Moscow and during the time I spent there. Mike, my partner, took this on our balcony overlooking Red Square. Lenin's Tomb is just above my right hand.

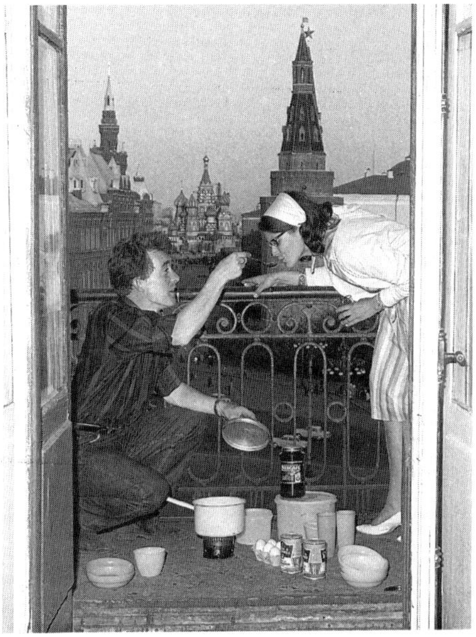

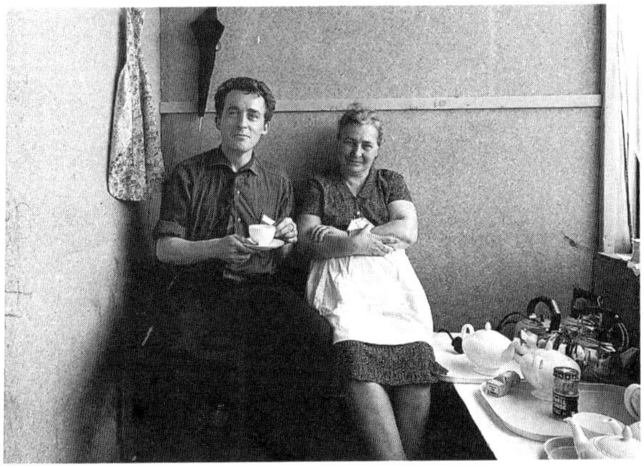

I took tea regularly with the cleaners at Sokolniki Park.

visitors alone and watched from a discreet distance.

Mike and I got through so many large wads of Monopoly roubles that we realised that we had better stop spending or get some more. In those days the exchange rate was about five roubles to the pound but on the black market it was fifteen or twenty. Using the black market was very risky. While we were in Russia a factory manager was executed for fiddling meat. He ran a pie factory and had adjusted the machinery filling the pies to give three or four grams less filling on several thousand pies a day. In that way he could syphon off quite a bit which he sold. Eventually he was caught, tried and executed. Although the Russians didn't execute tourists and we had gone on a tourist's visa, they had a habit of hanging onto foreign dissidents caught red handed in case they wanted to swap for one of their own held in a UK prison. We kept their people probably for the same reason.

There were money changers about and one night at the Bolshoi we made contact and arranged a meet at Sokolniki. The next night we picked up two lads at the arranged spot and Mike drove around while I negotiated. The younger of the two was called Alex. I noticed that every few minutes he turned and looked out of the rear window. 'What are you looking for, Alex?'

'Secret police. They're everywhere.'

'If they are secret how do you expect to spot one?' I felt that he was just winding us up to gain a psychological advantage.

'All the police drive cars with a MOC or MOK number plate. Look we give eight rouble for one pound sterling.' 'No, we want fifteen.' I looked out of the rear window. 'Is that one of the cars?'

There was a MOC right behind us. The other lad slid down in the seat below the window but Alex screamed, 'Faster, faster,' slapping Mike on the shoulder. He was shuffling back and forth like a kid trying to get a go-cart started.

Mike slammed his foot down and we shot forward. I thought Alex was going to shit himself. I've never seen anyone quite so agitated. There was very little traffic on the roads in Central Moscow in those days so the sight of a large silver Fort Estate burning rubber at eighty miles an hour, being chased by a clapped out Russian Zil, attracted quite a lot of attention. We raced about the streets for a good twenty minutes, the Russian car keeping up with us at a discreet distance.

It soon became obvious that they didn't want to catch us. They had our number and consequently knew which hotel we were at so they could grab us any time. They were obviously waiting for us to drop the two lads. This we did outside Gorky Park. As soon as they were out they were off like greyhounds. Seeing them, the cop car screeched to a halt, two busys leaped out and shot off after them but the way the lads were shifting the coppers had no chance.

That was them, what about us? They knew who

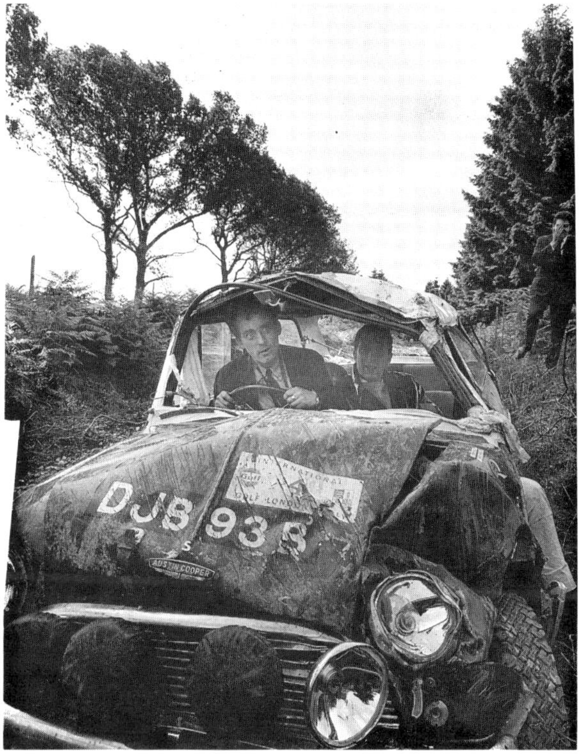

Mike Marchant, my partner in business, and me at the Gulf 2000 mile motor rally.

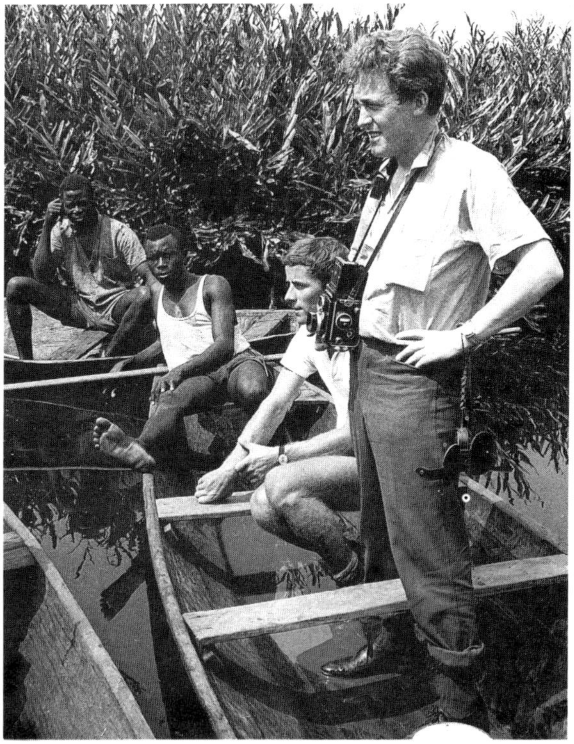

With a seismic exploration team in the swamps of Nigeria. I spent two days in a hollowed out tree trunk. The swamps were thick with mosquitos but they never seemed to bother me. After being brought up with bed bugs in Leeds and insects in Egypt you get used to things like that.

we were so every time we went out in the car they followed but made no attempt to speak with us. Having got lots of good shots of Khrushchev at the Trade Fair and picked up a decent amount of PR work, we decided to leave for the Black Sea, setting off at about 6 o'clock in the morning. If there was any such thing as a street map of Moscow we didn't have one. All that Intourist had provided was a sheet of white paper with a black circle representing the capital and a straight line to another dot called Kursk, then another to Kiev. The dots came every three inches and marked petrol stations. The 'map' was hand drawn in biro. The petrol stations were about one hundred miles apart.

There are several bridges across the Moskva. We had been given the name of the appropriate one to cross and told to drive south. That was the sum total of our instructions but of course we had the map.

In the back of the car we had camping gear, large supplies of food and a jerry can of petrol. Being sure you can fill a gas tank in Russia is second only to divorce as an anxiety creator.

The central Russian uplands are pleasant but there are no interesting villages to pass through as they are all tucked out of sight, well off the road. Occasionally we stopped and had a cook up, once sharing our food and French brandy with a farmer, but we only saw about four people in four hundred and twenty miles.

Then outside Kursk, a town where a great tank battle took place in World War Two, we ran out of petrol, ironically just outside the gates of a petrochemical refinery. An old man standing at the gate with a rifle and fixed bayonet on his shoulder 'arrested' us. He took us to the guard room and from there we were picked up in a car and taken to the local police station. There were no English speakers on hand so we were put up on camp beds and two interpreters were flown down from Moscow.

While we were hanging about we showed the police chief our map and tried with sign language to enquire where we had lost our way. He pointed to a spot about thirty miles south west of Kursk. Mike laughed, drew a circle and wrote Oops! I took the pen and added ski. There was now a Russian town called Oopski. We both laughed but not the copper. He didn't get it so when he was out of the room I snipped the cotton and removed the badge from his hat. Mike nearly had a fit. I've still got that hat badge.

Next day the two interpreters said we were to go to Kiev, where we would stay the night. Then on somewhere else, but didn't say where. Why Kiev? It's the opposite direction to Moscow. Mike and me were understandably nervous.

Next morning we set off again and most of the day the sun was behind us, which meant we were moving west and slightly north. When we stopped in a forest for a leak I told Mike what I thought. 'We're going to get away with it. We're going to Brest Litovsk, it's on the Polish border. Otherwise it would be Moscow. They're going to kick us out.'

Mike said, 'We haven't a visa to re-enter Poland.'

'Who cares, I'd sooner be banged up there than here.'

My suspicions proved correct and we were driven straight to the Russian border post on the River Bug and showed into a small room. Out of the window we watched as they dismantled the car; wheels off, seats out, linings removed, my camera case was taken away.

Two heavies came in the room and took Mike away. I was told to sit at the table with the two KGB hoods opposite. They kept their fedoras on. They had questioned me for about twenty minutes when a man came in from the next room with three glasses of Russian tea and they gave me one with a biscuit. On leaving the man who brought the tea left the door open and through it I could see Mike standing in his underpants. The tea man went up behind him and quite suddenly ripped off the pants.

'Oh my God' I thought, 'he's a shirt lifter.' But he was only looking for hidden papers. They later strip searched me but allowed me to remove all my own clothing myself.

After tea, the interrogation continued and followed the usual pattern; one man played the heavy bastard while the other was more caring, friendly and spoke English. The heavy one spoke a mixture of Russian and German. After a time the friendly one put the 'map' on the table. His partner, who was obviously senior, jabbed a finger like a dill pickle on the small circle west of Kiev. 'Vas is das OOPSKI?'

It needed no translation. I nearly wet myself. How can you explain humour? Christ, the circle on the map was the approximate position of the petrochemical plant. At this point a man came in with the twenty or so films I'd shot, including some grossly overdeveloped negatives and a lot of close ups of Premier Khrushchev. They were impressed. Eventually Mike and me were taken out to the car. It had been rebuilt and packed without a sign of having been tampered with. The friendly one handed us our passports.

'The bridge there leads to the Polish check point,' he said, pointing down the road. 'I suggest you get over it as quickly as possible.'

But Mike wasn't going to settle for this, 'What about these meal tickets and hotel voucher paid for and not used? We want a refund now.'

'Bloody hell, Mike,' I said, 'don't push it. Let's get going. Bugger Russia, bugger the meal tickets, let's get into sodding Poland.'

Mike said, 'I want a refund now. It's part of the Intourist contract.'

He wasn't going to let go but the exasperated KGB man had had enough. He went into the building and returned with two bottles of Russian champagne and some tins of caviare and smoked sturgeon, which he thrust into Mike's hands. He snatched our coupons and said, 'Get going quickly.' So we did. The Polish border guards let us through without ceremony. They had probably been coerced by the Russians.

For about an hour we drove through the countryside then we were stopped by a policeman. He saw the Russian goodies on the back seat and asked to see our passports. Of course we hadn't got either exit or entry visas for the period but seeing him keenly looking at the champagne in the back we decided to treat him. For an hour the three of us sat at the roadside eating caviare and drinking appalling champagne, washed down with good French cognac. We left behind a very happy, very drunk copper.

After the Russians deported me I started to send postcards to the KGB from various parts of the world. Their address was number 2 Dzherzhinsky Prospekt. One of the messages I wrote was, 'The White Rabbit has left the hut, please advise.' Another was, 'The Eagle has landed.' Later, I enlisted the help of several friends in this jape. We must have driven the KGB director ape-shit.

◆

By the late '60s I was becoming disillusioned working for the sake of money, doing rubbish jobs that paid well. I was crucifying myself and as a result photography was no longer a pleasure.

One morning Keith McCartney and me went to his cousin Paul's house in St John's Wood for a game of cards. Paul was having breakfast with John Lennon when we arrived so Keith introduced me to John.

'What do you do then pal?'

'I grub around taking pictures.' I underlined 'grub'.

'Are you any good?'

'Not any more,' I answered, suddenly wishing I hadn't said it.

'That makes no bloody sense. What do you mean not any more?' He seemed quite offended.

'I used to be good but somehow or other it's just gone.'

'Look pal,' he said, 'If you're ever any good you're always good. You might squander it for a bit but it's always there. You've just got to find it.'

Although I didn't exactly warm to Lennon, his words made a great impression. Later that day I passed the Time Life Building and on impulse went in and ordered a full set of the photography books they had just published. They were inspirational, full of work by the masters: Weston, Eugene Smith, Stieglitz, Brandt, Coburn. They gave me heart and a renewed passion.

◆

My reawakening interest in photography led me into a period of experimentation with Victorian print processes. Our relocation in Iver, away from the attractions of London's West End, was ideal and our newly arrived daughter Kelly provided a perfect model. One or two friends, although interested in my work, were critical and complained that I was wasting my time, but it was important for me to try to understand the mystery of the photographic process. Why did I have an overwhelming drive to make pictures? What did the Frenchman Niepce feel when he looked at the world's first photograph? My photography was instinctive. I was technically very limited, being a self-taught freelance, and needed to know how and why things worked.

I was also a real family man who wanted to stay as close as possible to his wife and child. In 1970 my second daughter Danielle was born and I was more and more reluctant to be away from home for long periods. Fortunately, motor races, apart from Le Mans, were twelve hour events, so we could be in and out in three days. This job gave me plenty of time to freak about with my babies and continue with experimental work.

By 1971 signs were beginning to appear in the country of a severe financial crisis. Clients started cutting back. A friend from ICI Fibres publicity told me she had been made redundant. I didn't know what the word meant. In my day it was called the sack and you got sod all but now as the middle class were being included the term was redefined. Being self-employed, the danger of getting kicked on to the scrapheap didn't pose a threat, but I was having to work twice the hours to remain solvent. Fortunately I'd bought the house at Iver for cash so not having a mortgage I was under less pressure than most people. My partner Mike did have a mortgage and, coupled with expensive tastes this led us to do more and more rubbish jobs for quick and easy cash. In the end I refused to work after 5 o'clock, preferring to be home with my family. This led to disagreements in the company and Mike and I fell out. Mike started a company on his own and I stayed with the cooperative.

Living outside London we became less enchanted with the capital. I still went into the office but apart from the odd visit to Kettner's Restaurant, we kept it at a distance and instead we made frequent trips to Yorkshire and Liverpool. In 1974 when my third daughter Julie was born we started thinking about moving north, and in 1975 we sold the house and did just that. We stayed a few weeks in Leeds and looked for a house in Harrogate. We found one eventually on the Duchy Estate, a fine big Victorian house with ten rooms, not including the butler's pantry which was my darkroom.

◆

I signed on at the dole office and they directed me to the DHSS because there was some problem

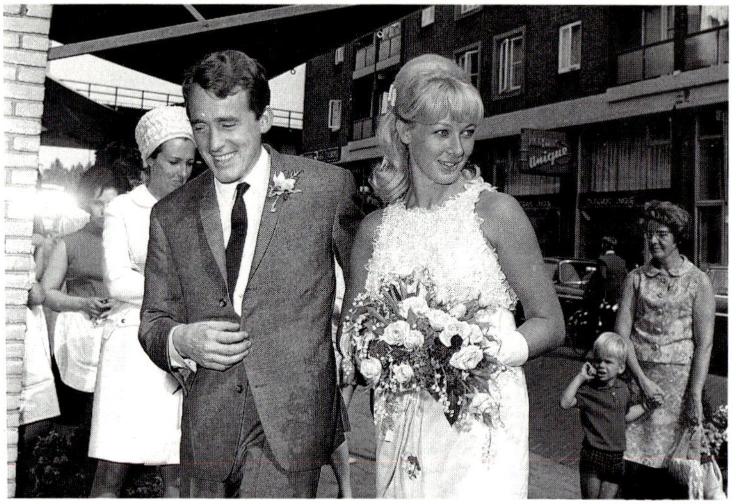

My second wedding. Johanna Maria de Jong and me in Rotterdam. The whole ceremony was held in Dutch. All I had to say was 'Ja' – 'I do'.

My three daughters, Danny, Kelly and Julie 'freaking about' as fairies.

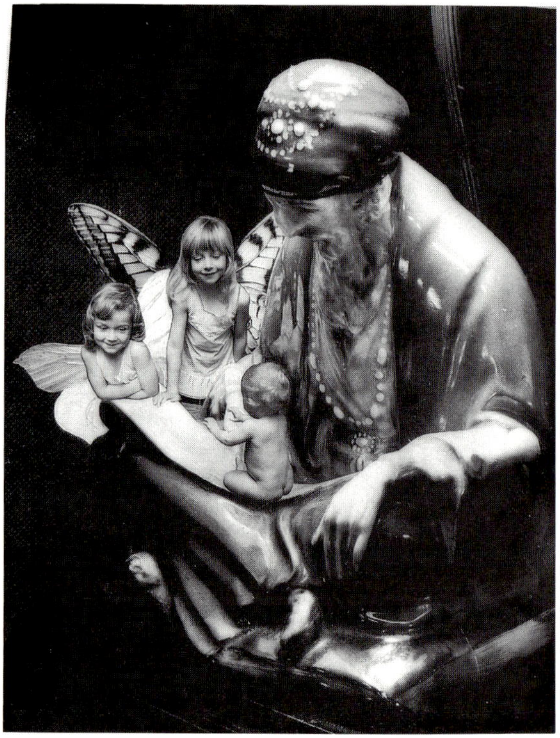

about me being self-employed. The girl at the desk was confused or bemused by my convoluted stories of holding companies, co-operatives and limited companies, but signed me on and I got paid for a week what I'd earned in London for an hour. I'd taken a chance but I have to say I wasn't sure my mind was quite prepared for the experience.

After a few weeks I was called to attend an interview at the same office.

'Mr Cryer, we have investigated and find that you gave up your job. Therefore you are not entitled to unemployment benefit.'

This was an older woman with a blue rinse. I was in deep shit. 'What can I claim then?'

'You cannot claim from us until you are working again. You are prepared to accept work, are you not?'

'Yes, if a decent job crops up.' I thought it would be a good idea to show willing.

'What do you do with your time? Why don't you look for a job?'

'Well...' This was going to be tricky, I was back behind the Iron Curtain. Then I thought sod it. 'My time is mostly spent doing experimental printing, trying to get my skills back.'Even I have to admit that this sounded a bit trite but it was the truth. She looked at me as if I'd just flicked a bogey at her. 'Mr Cryer, you can't expect Her Majesty's Government to support you while you play about at home.'

Bloody hell, I thought, you old cow. Being creative is like having a monkey on your back. 'Hey, love,' I knew she wouldn't like that. 'When did you last pay to go into an art gallery? Lowry came to this town some years ago and the dealers wouldn't give him houseroom.'

'That's beside the point, Mr Cryer.'

'Maybe so but I've grafted for 28 years at the hard end and I need a bloody rest.'

I got out of my chair and left. My cheque arrived a couple of days later.

Two or three months passed and we received a home visit. They obviously didn't believe that anyone who lived on the Duchy could possibly need charity. At one point our daily entered the room.

'Is this Mrs Cryer?' the social worker said, looking up.

'No, love, that's our cleaning lady, Mrs Burton.'

The woman sat down but didn't bat an eyelid. Having a daily in Harrogate is as natural as having electric light.

◆

When I was fourteen I'd applied to the Harrogate Herald for a job as a trainee photographer. I didn't receive a reply. Twenty seven years later one came asking me if I would like to join the staff. Things move slowly in Harrogate. The request was strangely flattering and I accepted.

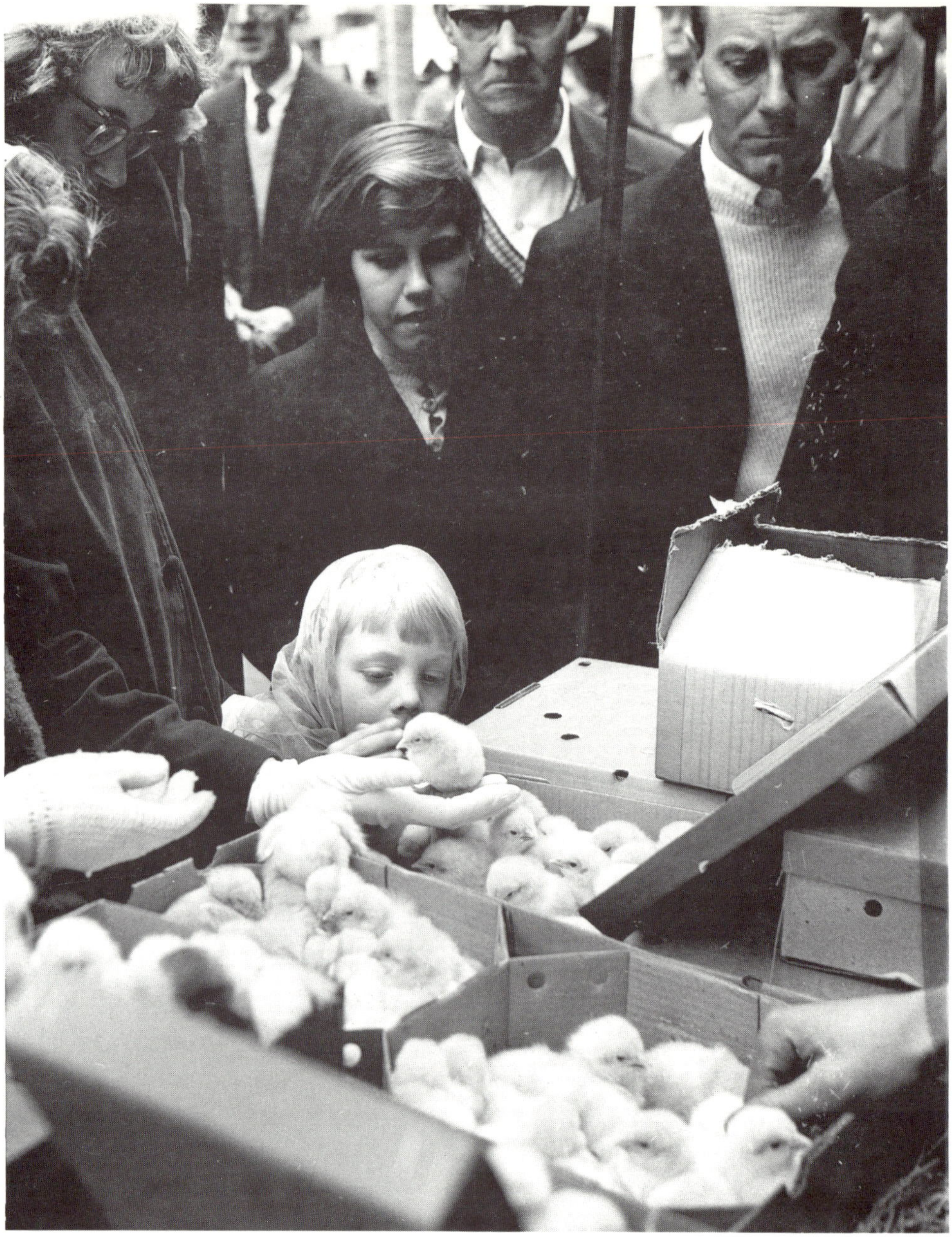

I was walking round Petticoat Lane in London around 1959 and I was attracted by the woman in white gloves doing her shopping.

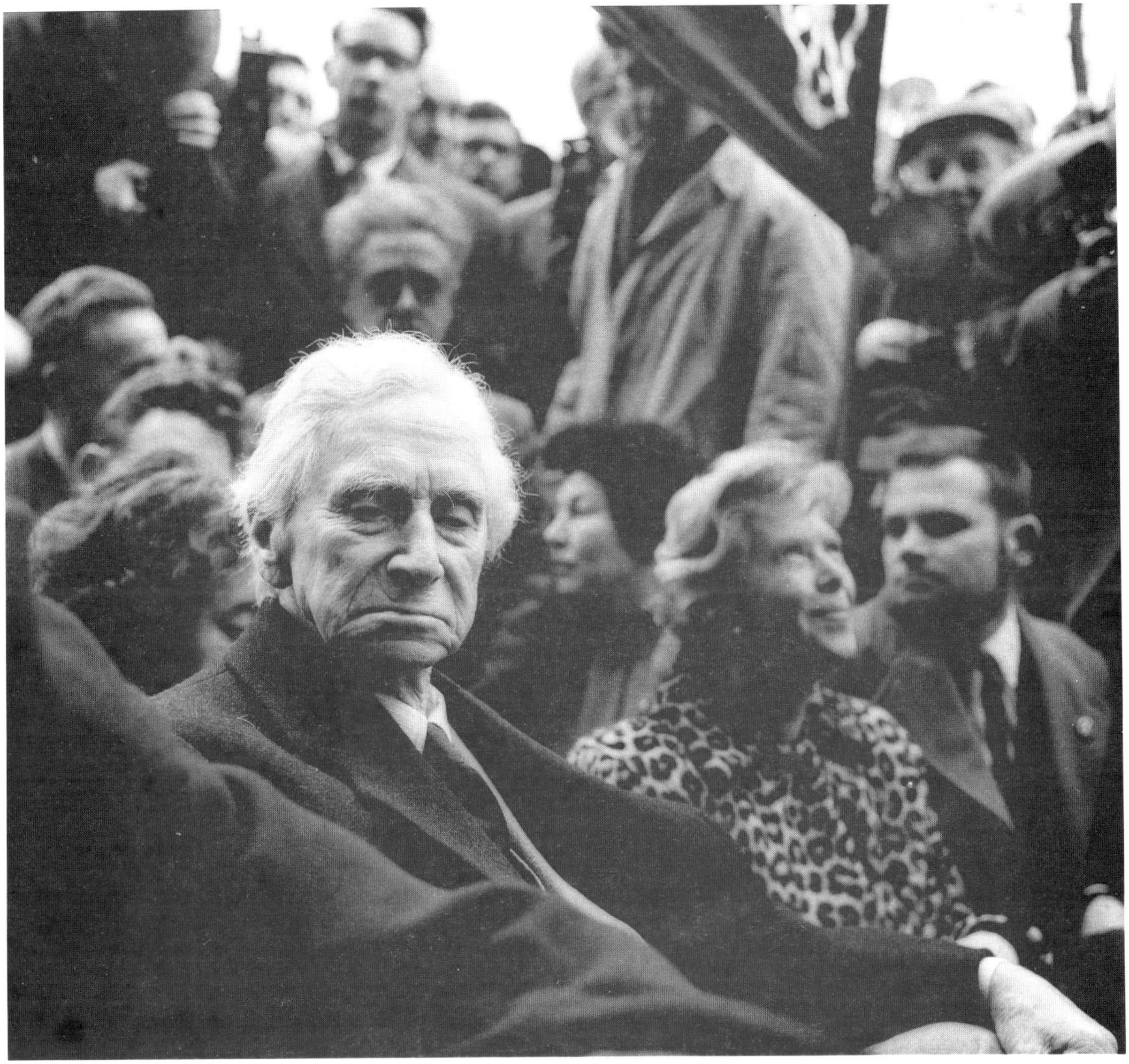

Bertrand Russell in 1961. A vintage year. Bertrand sat down outside Downing Street and I won the Encyclopaedia Britannica Award. This picture is now in the Humanities Collection at Houston Texas.

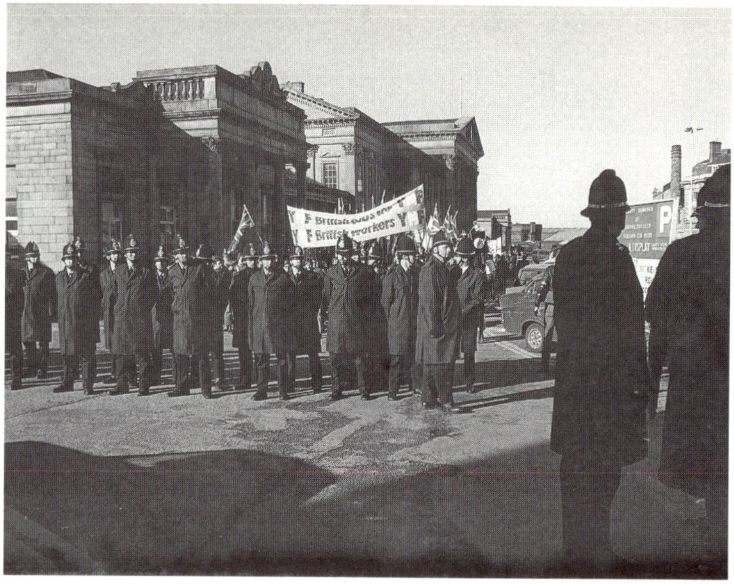

National Front March in Huddersfield 1982. I like to photograph demonstrations as they help me to keep my eye in. You need to be quick off the mark. I still do weddings for the same reason, unposed pictures at weddings need a quick eye.

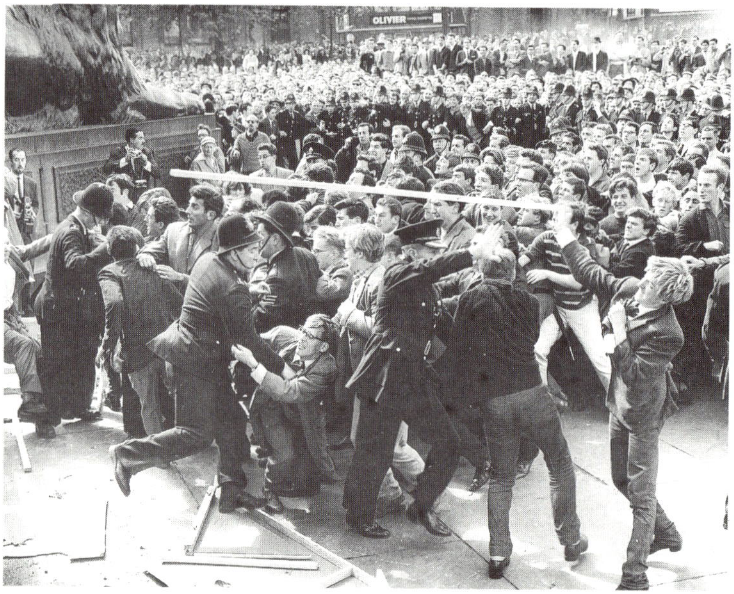

Anti – Fascist Riot in Trafalgar Square 1962. I made a half page in all the nationals with this. I stood up on one of the lions to take the picture. The Daily Express photographer is on the ground underneath the other lion and he missed the picture.

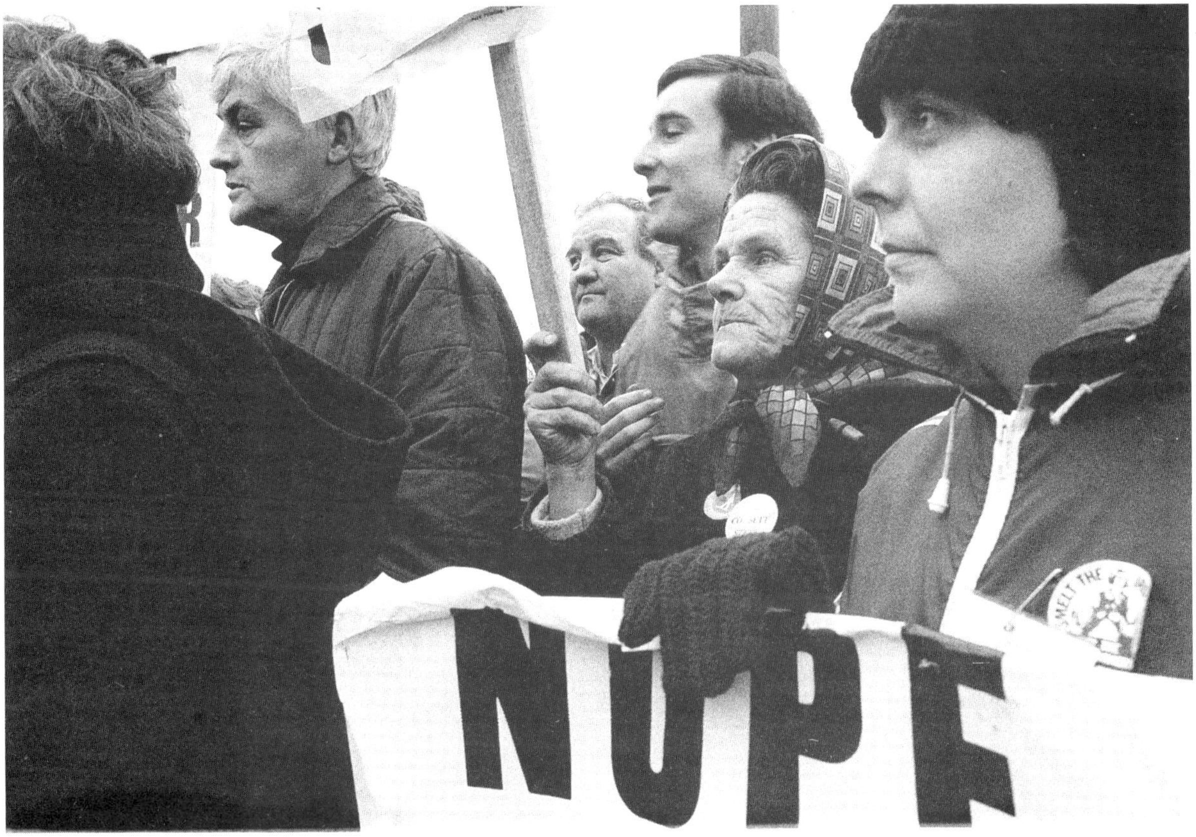

Consett steel strike taken for Trident Television. Their franchise was coming up for renewal and they wanted some publicity shots.

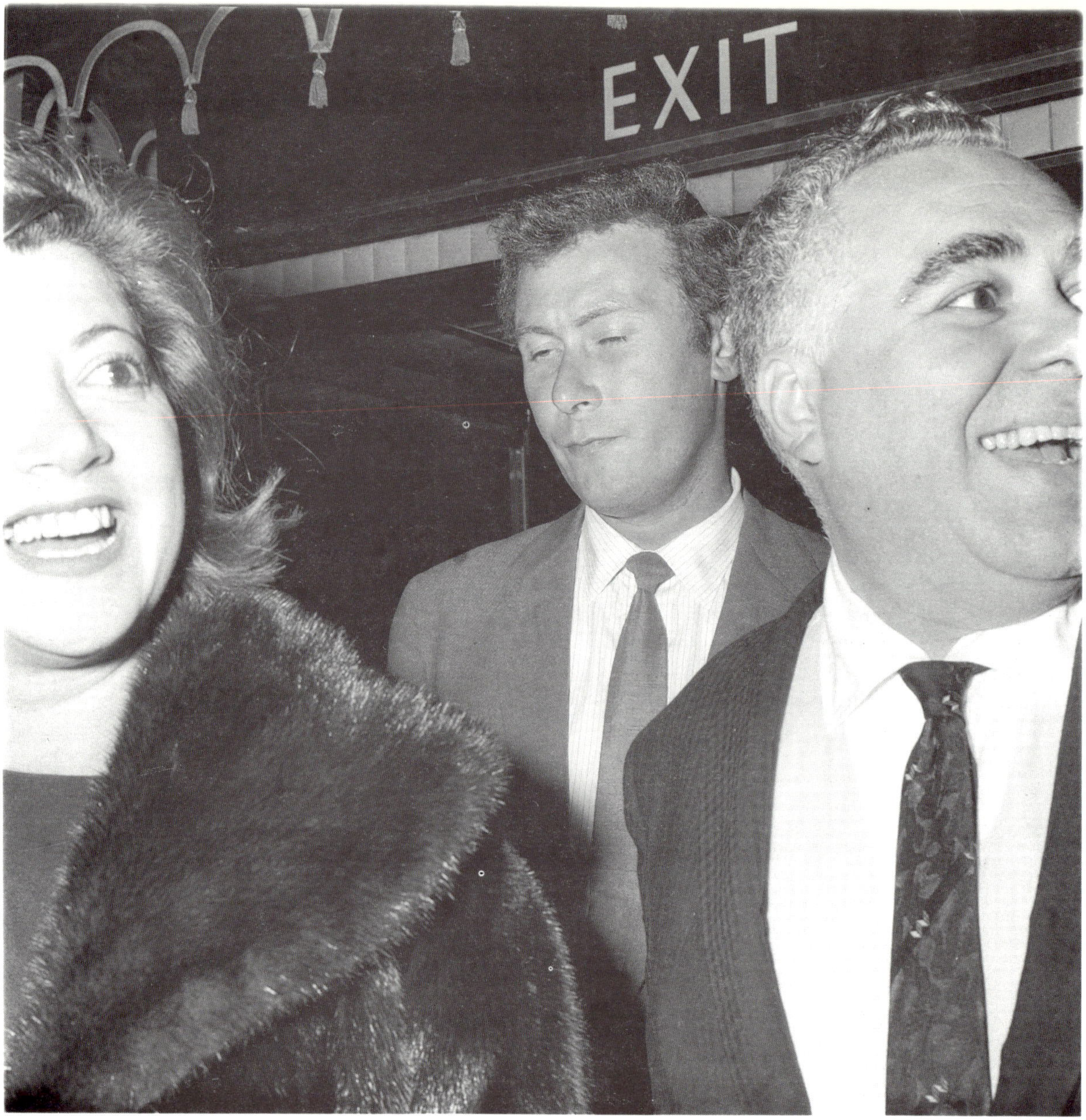

John Osborne taken for NBC in 1963. Just another press shot but I like it because of his expression framed by two smiling faces, two eyes between them.

The editor was a nice man and appeared to be overjoyed that I'd agreed to take pictures for them.

'We can offer you £45 a week, Mr Cryer, for a 38 hour week plus two Saturdays a month.' That was less than my London hourly rate and it was also £1 less than my earnings related dole. He went on, 'You'll also travel a bit, sometimes as far as Northallerton to the north and Pudsey to the south west.'

I felt for a moment he was having a joke but, having studied the newspaper, I realised that the standard was pure Mickey Mouse. Kelly, my eight year old daughter, took better pictures. They obviously took any fool on, good, bad or indifferent, if you were daft enough to sweat for about a pound an hour.

'Do you pay overtime?'

'Oh no, Mr Cryer. We expect you to work one evening a week on top of your day's work and you get time in lieu.'

Bloody hell, they were paying us with our own time! 'What about expenses?'

'We pay all genuine out of pocket expenses, plus forty five pence for your lunch if you have to work through and fifty pence for your dinner if you work through to the evening.'

He was serious. At first my reaction was to decline his offer but there is always a plus side to any situation. I weighed things up. If I took the job, what were the fringe benefits? There would be access to film, paper, chemicals and a company van. I could see North Yorkshire at their expense, make connections which could lead to private work and most important I would be taking pictures every day, all day. I said yes. One further advantage was now revealed. When I'd been there 2 years they would pay me an extra £2 a week experience money.

I stuck it for three years. They never paid the £2, although my early expectations of the fringe benefits were adequately fulfilled. An occasional kind word and a flower to the switchboard lady ensured that all commercial enquiries were passed on to me privately. I had a key to the publishers' wine store, all the film I needed and, unbelievably, complete creative freedom on what kind of picture to take, except when I was doing a shot of the Harrogate Mafia. It's safe to say that I enjoyed taking pictures for a local paper more than any job I've ever done, although the Dickensian attitude of the management did take some swallowing.

Most of my spare time was spent freaking about the Dales with the kids and working on restoring the house. In the evenings I would take to the darkroom and continue with my printing. At first, I concentrated on gum bichromates and cyanotypes and then platinum, a process which proved to be excessively expensive. Eventually I moved into none silver printing, using casein made from cheese and an obscure process using pepper and alcohol which was only partially successful.

Looking back I see that a grassroots understanding of any craft is not a waste of time. This was something I realised when I went into teaching. I was appalled at the lack of understanding by the students and tutors of the nature of photographic image. At one school the Head of Art asked me if I had twenty minutes to spare one lunchtime to show him how to print. I told him it had taken me a lifetime. He replied that he didn't want to be good at it he only wanted to teach it. Is it any surprise that the British have produced so few masters of the medium compared to the French and Americans?

◆

In 1979 an advert appeared in the Guardian Educational Supplement inviting applications from photographers for the position of Artist in Residence at a school in Huddersfield. A writer friend advised me to apply, although I hadn't the faintest idea of what the job entailed. My CV was three pages long and included a reference from the Deputy Permanent Under Secretary for Education (Arts & Science) who had lived next door to me in the south. I think I was included in the final selections out of sheer curiosity. To the surprise of some people, I got the appointment, although the Yorkshire Arts officer, who was funding the Fellowship, threatened to withdraw if I was appointed. However, the headmistress told him that I was. He took his bat home and we never saw him again.

The fee was £1000 for ten weeks work plus board and lodgings for overnight stays. It seemed reasonable so I gave seven weeks' notice to the paper in unpaid overtime and got myself over to Huddersfield.

The school was a comprehensive, quite big, slightly seedy, with 53 teachers. The head told me 50 of the staff were opposed to the whole idea so my battle would be uphill. For my part I know that the analysis was only partly correct. The real battle was with myself and at the end of the first week I was on my eyebrows. I was emotionally drained. Eight years previously I'd stopped smoking but by the end of the second week I was on 25 a day.

The school had a large darkroom with six cheap enlargers but no cameras. Some children had instamatics and the odd kid had a Pentax but that was about it, so I took to lending out my two Nikons and a Hassel. One or two teachers had warned me about leaving valuables lying around and lending out cameras but I had no trouble. I'm a believer in the theory that children know when you like and trust them and respond accordingly. It's safe to say they taught me more than I taught them. My eyes were opened by these kids. Some of the photos were nothing short of amazing. Much of the credit must go to the assistant art teacher Nick Gaunt who had laid down a good foundation in the Art Department and was himself a highly competent photographer.

For the first two weeks we had no materials as the Resource Department hadn't got its act together but thanks to the Harrogate paper we had stacks of film and developer. Unfortunately we had no paper to print the negatives.One morning I took 25 pupils for an art class. They wanted to do portraiture so I got them to shoot close up head shots of each other with strong side lighting from a window. The film was developed and dried then the negatives were projected in the enlargers on to sheets of white drawing paper. A pencil was used to draw around the image, shading the shadow areas. The dark areas were then cut out with a knife and the back of the paper painted black. Sheets of plain paper were coated with ferric ammonium citrate, dried and the template placed on the sensitized paper under a sheet of glass. This was then placed in the sunlight. After five minutes the print was washed over with Ferricyanide. A brilliant blue portrait appeared. There wasn't one in the whole class which was less than excellent and the kids were thrilled. Apart from developing the film the whole technique was achieved without a darkroom or expensive materials, using a process developed by Sir John Herschel in 1842.

By the time the Fellowship came to an end I had the full support of the teaching staff and we had a big exhibition of about 350 prints. It was nice for some young blood to have a show. Sadly no one from Yorkshire Arts came to see it. Also the £500 set aside by Kirklees to buy my work had been spent on film and paper for the schools exhibition. On the whole I think Yorkshire Arts got a bargain; the kids certainly did. After the residency I went back to freelancing.

◆

I made my final commercial trip to Moscow in 1970 for another trade fair. It wasn't the kind of photography I was fond of any more but was a quick and easy way to build up the company finances. A bit like catalogue photography in a big studio, very naff but it pays the rent while you're waiting for the plum jobs to come in.

To go on business to Russia you have to be invited. I was going as usual on a tourist visa and chancing my arm on Russian bureaucratic incompetence. I had the greatest respect for Russian courage and creativity and knew fortunately that their creativity didn't extend to their administration. Fortunate for me, that is, not for the poor sods outside the hierarchy. For over 80 years the country was run by thieves and plunderers pleading socialism and lining their own pockets, blaming incompetence on criminals and hooligans while selling the country's treasures to greedy capitalists. Some party members mouthed Marx and lived fat on good brandy and whores.

There were one or two jobs on my list for this

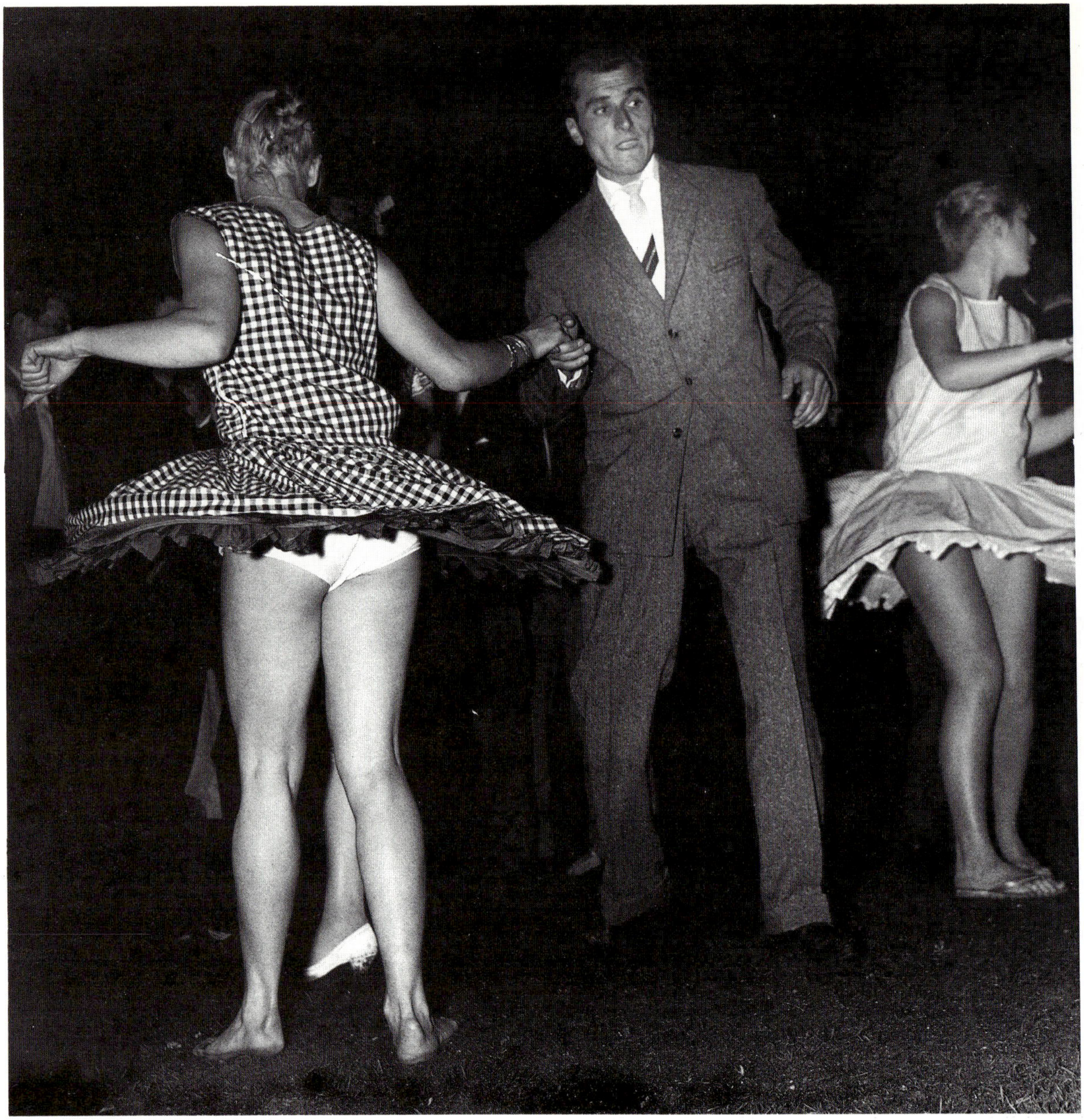

I did an exhibition of jazz photos for Bingley Library in 1983. Somebody complained that we were exhibiting photos that were in questionable taste. The library told me it was the most successful show they had ever put on. This photo was stolen from the exhibition.

assignment which were a bit iffy. Alfa Laval, a Swedish company who manufactured milking machinery, asked me if I could get pictures of a milking carousel located somewhere in Moscow. They didn't know where it was but it would be worth a considerable amount for a detailed set of pictures. Finding the location didn't prove too difficult. There was only one place it could be, the Permanent Exhibition of the Economic Achievement of the Union of Soviet Socialist Republics. This was a huge area which held exhibitions of almost everything the Soviets produced; aeroplanes, sputniks, lorries, furs, medical equipment, model farms, guns, tanks, artificial limbs, machinery of every conceivable use. None of these existed outside the park with the possible exception of tanks, aeroplanes and sputniks. The place was a staggering example of Russian engineering skill. If the Russians could only get their act together they would lead the world.

I found the carousel where I expected it to be and it was in use; a large revolving platform with stalls. I had milked cows as Ann's father had a farm in North Yorkshire and we went every holiday and helped out. One day I was leading the cows out of the byre when the last one raised its tail and started to crap. At the same time it coughed violently. This compressed its colon, brown liquid shot out in a stream and hit me all down one side. George, Ann's father, said, 'Nah then, lad, let me give thee a piece of advice. Always walk behind a shooter and in front of a shitter.' Good advice.

With the carousel, the cows came through a door, entered a stall, a man fixed suckers to each teat and the milk was drawn out. By the time that was done another cow entered and so on. At any one time there were 10 cows being milked. When the platform had completed one revolution the suckers dropped off, a spring lifted them clear of the area and the cow left through a second door. This method allowed 100 or 200 cows to be milked in a fraction of the time it could be done by hand. I made quite a few pictures without any interference from the man operating the machine and gave him a packet of Senior Service.

◆

When working away from home a speculative freelance photographer must have a clear idea of the daily revenue potential for a location. The amount must, of course, be geared to the sum invested, that is to air fares, hotel, food, taxis and bribes. Russia is very expensive and when earnings drop below £300 a day it's time to book a flight out. With an open ticket this is not easy so one must look ahead. When I saw there wasn't much left to pick up on this trip and the sky was looking very leaden, an ominous sign at the back end of the year in this part of the world, I recognised that it was time to go home. The most popular places in Moscow are hotel restaurants

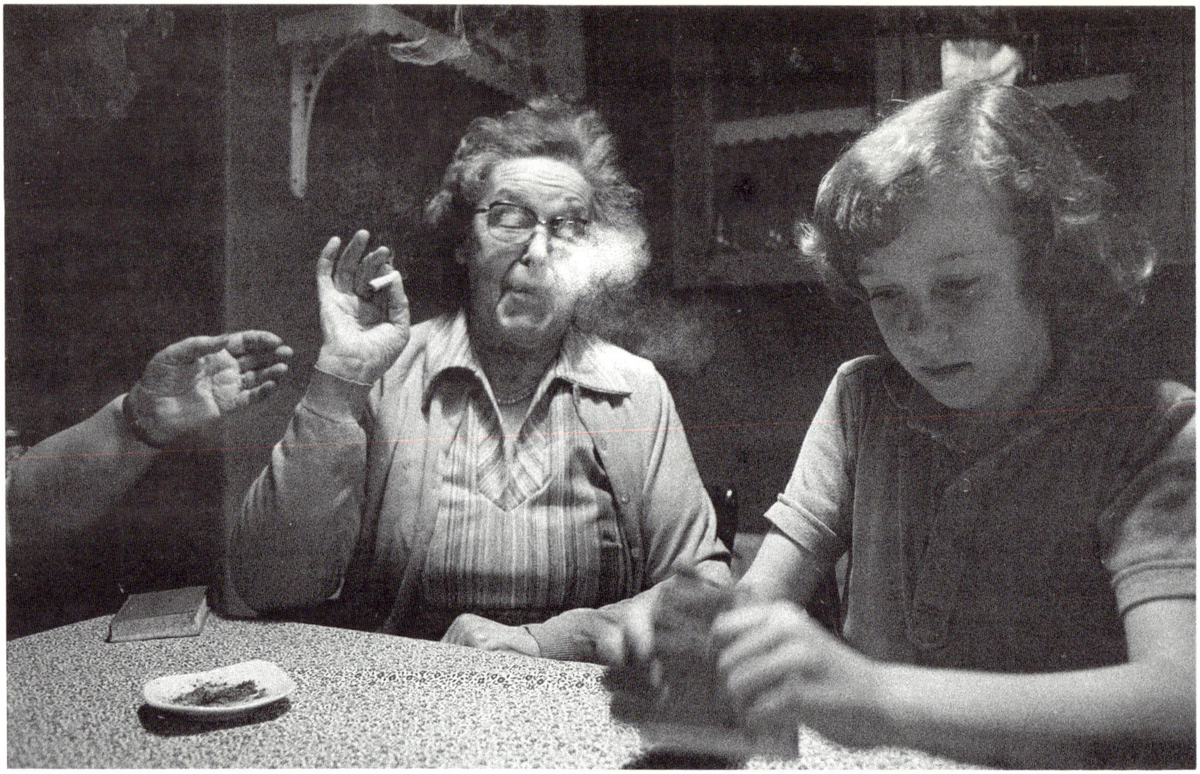

Playing cards at my house in Harrogate. Danielle, my second daughter, is on the right, Aunt Millie in the centre and Aunt Ginny's hand is coming into the picture for the joint. Aunt Millie didn't smoke but she would try anything for a laugh.

and the Bolshoi but a close third is the airline booking office. At the Intourist desk there is always a queue of people with urgent reasons for leaving. The girls on the desk are efficient and pleasant but their usual reply for a immediate flight is, 'Certainly, Sir, how about next week?'

Most Brits and all the Americans react with blustering anger which reduces their chances even further. Most offences committed by visitors to Russia are ones of bad manners and these are always met with blank incomprehension. My first act on booking into a hotel is to put myself about and smile a lot. Next is to spread a few goodies, ballpoints, tights, and Dinky toys, but for the girls on the ticket desk I always give a bunch of flowers. Flowers work magic in Russia. They can be given to men as well as women and are always received with pleasure and affection.

Since it is my firm conviction that there is no such thing as a full hotel or a full aeroplane, my faith is rewarded by the girls on the desk. It was on this occasion. I got a seat on Aeroflot for the next day.

The drive to Sheremetevo Airport takes 40 minutes. It was snowing lightly, just enough to create the right atmosphere. I was always glad to leave Moscow even though I had been having a love affair with the Red Giant for ten years. To work there as an illegal is a five ulcer risk, as photography is a very sensitive subject high up on the KGB hit list. I'd been getting away with it for years; the feeling was creeping over me that this was my last trip.

When we reached the airport the snow was falling heavily and it came as no surprise that by the time we had got through all the tedious formalities of the paranoid bureaucracy the flight was cancelled.

On my first assignment to Moscow in 1961, Sheremetevo Airport was a grotty collection of shoddy buildings and although a lot of construction had been completed it was still rough. There was little in the way of food, no coffee or tea and a surly staff. I thought of that visit as I joined a group of English people waiting for the same flight and lashed into the vodka, cursing Russian incompetence. Unfair? Maybe, as the weather was also causing problems.

The group was a mixed bag; a sales engineer from Racal Electronics, clipped moustache, regimental tie and an impediment in his reach when it came to buying his shout; a girl from a travel company who collapsed in tears after her 8th vodka; a young lad who had been fitting machinery for a Lancashire textile company; a middle aged managing director of a woollen mill and a public school type in a blue pinstriped suit. The latter took charge of the proceedings. We had nothing to eat and, although there was a buffet bar, we had handed in all our Russian Monopoly money at the exchange before we passed through Immigration. The hours dragged and the snow continued to fall in flakes as big as pigeon's eggs.

Three of the party were carrying bottles of

vodka and after six hours of waiting they were drunk. The rest of us were starving and out of booze. To move things along a deputation was raised and the airport authorities approached. After much pleading, permission to spend sterling was granted. Unfortunately all the bar could offer was salt fish, caviare, black bread, sour cream, vodka and one bar of chocolate. We bought some of everything.

At the bar stood a family of people from Bangladesh, father, mother, two teenage boys and a small thin girl of about six. They were refugees en route to the UK and like us had been grounded because of the weather. They had been at the airport much longer than we had and were obviously in some distress. They had no money and had nothing to eat. Although Aeroflot were legally obliged to feed them they hadn't and quite apparently had no intentions of doing so.

As we staggered back to the table, laden down with our appalling goodies, the public school type slipped the little girl a bar of chocolate. Her face showed no expression. She just stood, one arm wrapped round her mother's legs, the bar of chocolate clutched down by her side, and stared. Then I noticed she had a label tied to her dress, with her name on it. She was like an evacuee. I was stricken. There was no judgement in the child's face, no questions. Children of the poor and disenfranchised, the illiterate, the shabby, dirty, the shoeless, don't ask questions. That is because they can't get together enough information to realise there are questions to ask.

The appalling indifference of the authorities exploded inside me. I saw that with my 'take the money and run' conscience, I'd been kissing Russian arses for 12 years. Duck, weave, smile, yes tovarishch, certainly comrade. Pasternak, Solzhenitsyn, Katyn Forest, Hungary.

I walked across the lounge and spoke to the father. They had been stranded at the airport for sixteen hours, waiting for the same flight we were to catch. He was a refugee and his entry permit to the UK was due to expire yet he showed no signs of concern, although the lack of food distressed his wife and children. I went over to the bar to negotiate. For my Parker ballpoint I managed to get some jars of yoghurt and a couple of bottles of orange juice. The mother accepted these with quiet dignity. I crept off to the lavatory and broke down.

The hours passed and by now the snow was two or three feet thick. The table was covered with empty vodka bottles, guilt festered in me, I was sick with black rage and legless drunk. Then at about four in the morning it was announced that a flight had been laid on to take us to Leningrad where our plane was waiting. Would we please hurry? We did.

The plane was a twin prop and must have seen service in World War Two. It even had static lines for parachutists running down the interior. The flight was a nightmare, people puking, hand luggage rolling about the aisle, one bog for 60 people, no paper, no smoking. I was sober now, dehydrated and craving a cup of Earl Grey.

A red hot Russian pilot landed in the snow at Leningrad and we taxied to the far side of the airport and waited. We were kept sitting in the freezing plane for three hours with no explanations. My level of tolerance had just reached meltdown when two buses arrived and we all scrambled aboard. A young soldier with an automatic weapon stood at the door. The bus drove round the field to the arrival building and we stood to file out. 'Nyet.' We weren't allowed off. We then sat for another two hours fuming and freezing.

We could just see through the steamed up windows of the bus that the snow was packed solid. The airport staff were either locked panic stricken in their quarters or, and this is probably closer to the truth, drinking vodka and playing cards. Mercy was finally shown and we were allowed into the crowded lounge. Then an official appeared and collected our passports. The visas in them were no longer valid and by their crazy logic we shouldn't be on Russian soil. Following that we were stuck there for another three hours; no food, no explanations.

I'd had enough. I was sitting on my camera case talking to an Irish lad when a man appeared clutching a pile of passports. He started to call out names and hand over the passports to the various owners.

'Cryer, Terence Anthony.'

No answer.

'Cryer, Terence Anthony.'

No answer.

The Irish lad said 'That's you, Terry.'

'I know it's me; let the bastard sweat.'

And he did. The thought of losing an alien without a visa was beyond his experience. Eventually fingers were pointed in my direction.

'Are you Terence Cryer?'

'Yes.'

'Come and take your passport.'

I was still angry about the Asian family. 'You can keep the bloody thing. I wish to protest about the way you have treated this child,.' I pointed at the little Asian girl. The man went red in the face, very appropriate.

'Are you going to accept this passport?'

'No, stuff it,' I said. He stalked off. The Irish lad took me to one side. 'Terry, you are causing them to lose face. I strongly advise you to give up.'

The man returned with several officials and offered the passport. The English people in the crowd were now staring at me as if I was the villain. They didn't care. Embassy people, commerce was their bag, sod all else. I gave in and took the passport. The Asian father gave me a secret smile. We all filed out to the plane waiting on the runway.

Seeing as our tickets had been collected at Moscow and we didn't have boarding cards for this flight I walked straight up the stairs into first class

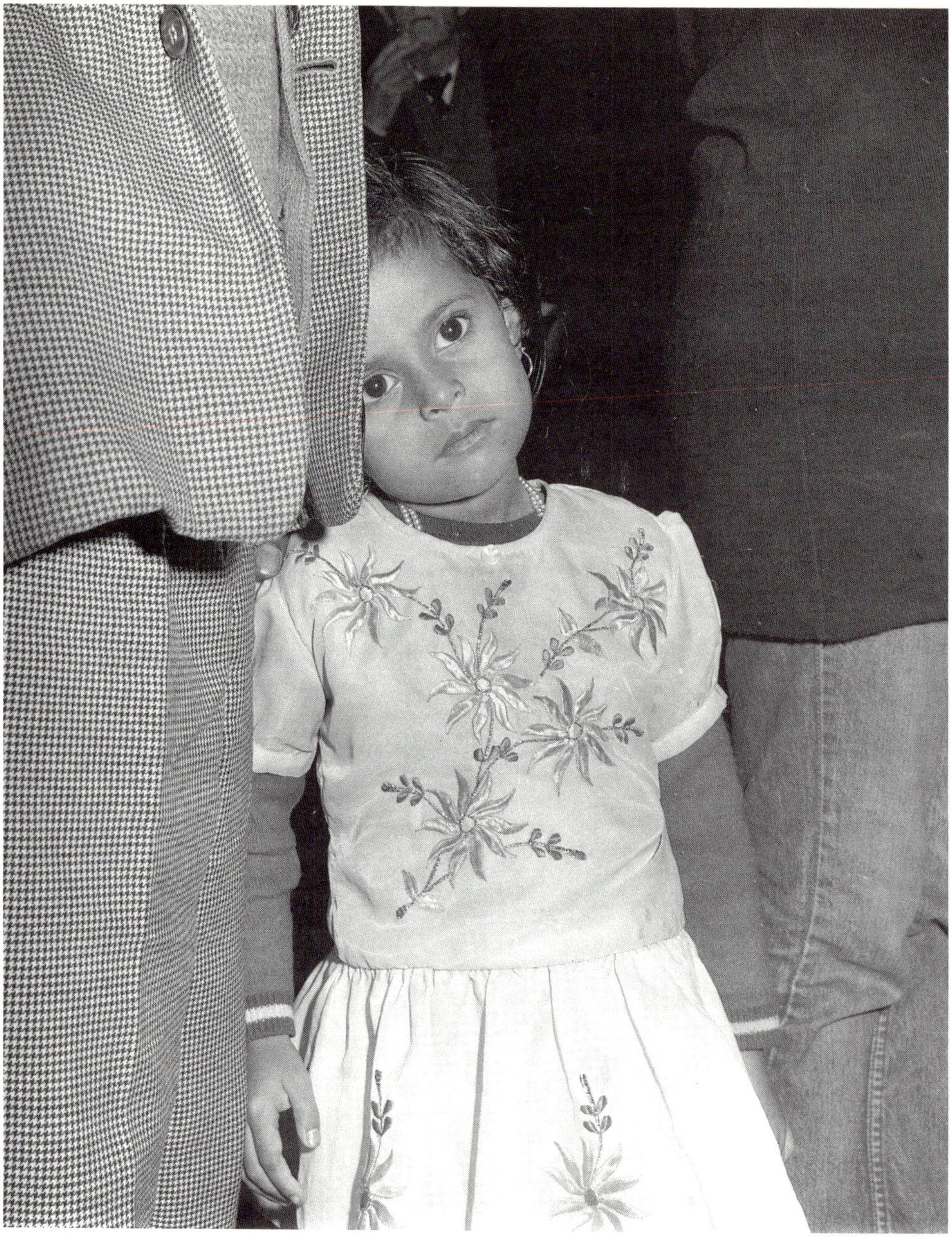

The little Bangladeshi lass taken at Sheremetevo Airport.

and had the whole compartment to myself. I say this for Russian Air Lines, their big jets are the best for comfort and service, BOAC only comes second. The stewardess brought me Beluga caviare and a perfect Chicken Kiev. After that I fell asleep and woke as we parked at London Heathrow.

On the way to Immigration I met the Asian family and helped them with their luggage. At the passport desk I stood behind them as the Immigration Jack-in-Office started to give them a bad time. It was something about the dates on their entry permit.

'Is this woman your wife? Can you prove the kids are yours?'

My gorge started to rise again. 'Bloody hell, man, we've been buggered about in Russia for the last 24 hours. The man's got a permit, stop treating him like a bloody animal.'

He looked at me with that superior sneer people who have power reserve for victims. 'You can shut up or you will be here all day.'

So I shut up. The Asian family got through. I saw them boarding a coach some time later and the little girl waved.

◆

Years ago by a paddling pool in Edlington, when I was very young, a coalminer gave me two pennies for an icecream. It was the first I'd ever seen, let alone tasted. It was a cornet, the ice was chocolate and as I was about to lick it, the ice dropped off into the dirt. It was a tragedy which made me cry. An old lady came up and put her arm on my shoulder.

'Nay, love, it's not finished. Put yer foot over it. No, not on it, over it in t'air, that's it. Now slap yer toes down on it.'

I did and the icecream like hyperactive brown worms shot up between my toes and collapsed coolly over my instep before slowly melting back into the dirt. I started to laugh.

'There you are, love. Nowt's ever so bad yer can't get a laugh out of it.'

She was right and I've pursued that philosophy ever since.

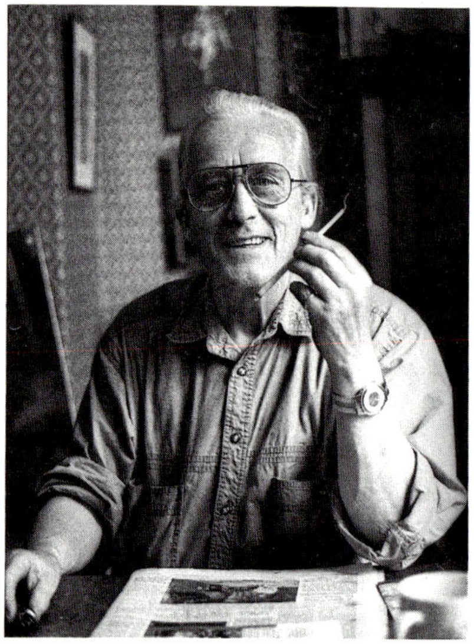

Terry Cryer 1992.

Photograph by Kevin Reynolds.